D1451821

MAGNA CARTA UNCOVERED

2015 marks the 800th anniversary of the grant at Runnymede of Magna Carta. The story of how Magna Carta came into being, and has been interpreted since, and its impact on individual rights and constitutional developments has more twists and turns than any work of historical fiction.

The authors bring their wide legal experience and forensic skills to uncover the original meaning of the liberties enshrined in Magna Carta, and to trace their development in later centuries up to the drafting of the Constitution of the United States of America. By providing that the powers of the King were not unlimited, the Charter was groundbreaking, yet it was also a conservative document, following the form of Anglo-Saxon charters and seeking to return government to the ways of the Norman kings.

This book tells the enthralling, ultimately inspirational, story of Magna Carta in a concise and readable fashion and will captivate laymen and lawyers alike.

Magna Carta Uncovered

Anthony Arlidge

and

Igor Judge

·H A R T·
PUBLISHING

OXFORD AND PORTLAND, OREGON
2014

Published in the United Kingdom by Hart Publishing Ltd
16C Worcester Place, Oxford, OX1 2JW
Telephone: +44 (0)1865 517530
Fax: +44 (0)1865 510710
E-mail: mail@hartpub.co.uk
Website: http://www.hartpub.co.uk

Published in North America (US and Canada) by
Hart Publishing
c/o International Specialized Book Services
920 NE 58th Avenue, Suite 300
Portland, OR 97213-3786
USA
Tel: +1 503 287 3093 or toll-free: (1) 800 944 6190
Fax: +1 503 280 8832
E-mail: orders@isbs.com
Website: http://www.isbs.com

Hart Publishing is an imprint of Bloomsbury Publishing plc.

British Library Cataloguing in Publication Data
Data Available

ISBN: 978-1-84946-556-4

Typeset by Hope Services Ltd, Abingdon
Printed and bound in Great Britain by
CPI Group (UK) Ltd, Croydon CR0 4YY

Acknowledgements

Our thanks are due to all those who have helped in the production of this book. Richard Hart commissioned the work; he has since sold Hart Publishing to the Bloomsbury Imprint and bears no responsibility for the eventual text, though without his enthusiasm it would never have been written. Hart Publishing continues under Bloomsbury. We thank their team for indefatigable work on the final production – Sinead Moloney (Publisher, who happened to have written a dissertation on Pope Innocent III), Mel Hamill (Managing Editor, who suffered grievously at our hands), Bill Asquith (Commissioning Editor), Rachel Turner (Assistant Editor), Jo Ledger (Sales and Publicity), Carolyn Fox (our stringent but indispensable copy editor) and Nick Clarke (who designed the jacket for the book). We thank Bloomsbury Publishing for their digital support.

Cambridge University Press have kindly given permission to reproduce the 'Translation' of 'Magna Carta 1215' that appears on pp 449–473 in JC Holt, *Magna Carta* 2nd edn (1992) © Cambridge University Press, 1992.

A special word of thanks is due to The Reverend Robin Griffiths-Jones, Master of the Temple Church. As many of the important events leading to the Charter occurred in the Church, he has carried out his own academic research on the Charter and made it available to us. He has already organised a Conference on Magna Carta, Religion and the Rule of Law.

We must also thank Gresham College and Professor Michael Mainelli for arranging a launch in the City of London Art Gallery.

We express our admiration of the work of the many historians who have trawled over this small piece of parchment. For us, writing the book has been a steep learning curve based on their scholarship.

Contents

The Authors

Anthony Arlidge has been a Queen's Counsel for over 30 years. He is author of text books on Fraud and Contempt of Court and also 'Shakespeare and the Prince of Love', the first knight of Twelfth. He was Treasurer (head) of the Middle Temple in 2003.

Igor Judge was Lord Chief Justice of England and Wales from 2008 to 2013. He is President of the Selden Society. He is Dickson Poon Distinguished Fellow and Visiting Professor at King's College, London and, for 2014, Treasurer of the Middle Temple.

Timeline

The Route to Runnymede

October 1154   Henry II ascends the throne of England; of his five legitimate sons, three die before they can succeed him. In 1173–74 Richard rebels against him and in 1188 Richard and John rebel and are in rebellion when Henry dies in 1189.

Late 1190   Richard I departs on crusade, naming Arthur of Brittany as his heir. He appoints William Longchamps as regent during his absence.

December 1192   On his way back from the Holy Land, Richard is taken prisoner in Austria. Shortly afterwards John returns to England and heads a baronial party which succeeds in forcing Longchamps to flee. John becomes regent.

February 1194   Richard is released. On his return he defeats John's baronial army at Nottingham and pardons John.

January 1198   Innocent III is elected Pope.

April 1199   Richard dies, naming John as his heir. John is crowned.

August 1202   John defeats rebellious barons in Poitou at the Battle of Mirebeau. Arthur, Duke of Brittany, the rival claimant to John's throne, is captured and disappears, probably murdered. In 1204 John is defeated in battle by Philip Augustus, King of France, leaving Aquitaine as John's only remaining possession in France.

July 1205   Hubert Walter, Archbishop of Canterbury, dies. The Chapter of the Cathedral elects one of their number to succeed him. John and the Bishops favour the Bishop of Norwich. The Pope orders the Chapter to elect a third candidate, Stephen Langton, which they do. John refuses to accept Langton as Archbishop.

August 1207   The Pope issues an interdict, banning all ecclesiastical offices in England, save for baptism and deathbed confession.

January 1209   John is excommunicated.

1212   Two barons, Eustance de Vesci and Robert Fitzwalter, are accused of plotting to murder the king. They flee the realm.

January 1213   The Pope pronounces a sentence of deposition on John and authorises Philip Augustus to wage Holy War against him.

15 May 1213   John submits to the Pope's special representative and accepts the Pope as his spiritual and feudal lord; he reaffirms his coronation oath to protect the Church and to rule according to old established law. His excommunication and later the interdict are lifted. John surrenders his kingdom to the Pope and receives it back as a fief of the Pope. He is now the Pope's vassal, and the Pope requires him to allow de Vesci and Fitzwalter to return to England.

February 1214   John departs with an army to France, intent on recovering his territories there, in alliance with Otto of Brunswick and the Count of Flanders

17 July 1214   John's allies are heavily defeated at the Battle of Bouvines. John retreats to La Rochelle, landing in England on 13 October. The treasury is empty, and his authority almost irretrievably damaged.

16–23 November 1214   John, at the Temple in London, is attended under sanctuary rules by a large number of barons, including some of those who are to rebel against him; John grants a Charter to the Church which guarantees the Church's right of election to offices in cathedral churches and monastic communities.

6 January 1215   The Epiphany meeting at the Temple between the King and a large number of bishops and barons. The disaffected barons have formed a *conjuratio* or sworn association to seek satisfaction for their grievances. They demand a return to the rights expressed in the Charter of Henry I. They refuse payment of scutage ('shield money') to fund the unsuccessful campaign in Poitou. The barons arrive fully armed. This enables John to complain of their disrespect and to refuse to respond to the threat of force. A truce is agreed until 26 April when the parties will meet at Brackley in Northamptonshire.

Early months of 1215   Unsuccessful negotiations continue between the two sides. At the same time both are sending representatives to the Pope seeking his support. John declares his intention to go on crusade. The timing is significant both as a method of ingratiation with the Pope, who was very attracted to the idea of another crusade, but also because it offered John personal immunity against violent attack.

19 March 1215   The Pope responds to the arguments put before him. His judgment is that Langton and the clergy have failed to achieve a reconciliation because they, in effect, have supported the rebel barons and that the rebels are to abandon any plots against the King and to make their demands respectfully, eschewing coercion. The letter to John has not survived, but from the contents of the letters which do, it appears that the Pope urges the King to accede to the barons' just demands; which demands are just is not spelt out. The letters are received in England in late April or early May.

30 March 1215   The Pope accepts the Charter granted to the Church the previous November. On the very next day the Pope directs the disaffected barons that they are obliged to pay the scutage for the Poitevin campaign. These letters arrived in England in early May. The message is clear enough; the Pope is supporting his vassal.

26 April 1215   The disaffected barons gather at Brackley; John does not; instead Langton and Marshal receive the barons' demands on behalf of the King. John rejects them. The barons move to besiege Northampton Castle. Although described in the Charter as 'the quarrel', this is now outright civil war, exemplified by the fact that Marshal's son and heir, also William, is a member of the rebel party.

Early May 1215   The rebel barons formally renounce fealty to John and appoint Robert Fitzwalter as the commander of their forces, burdening him with the rather overwhelming title 'Marshal of the Host of God and Holy Church'. Both sides prepare for war. Immediately after the arrival of the papal letters John proposes that each side send four representatives to Rome for the decision of the Pope. The rebel barons reject the proposal. John writes to the Pope seeking the excommunication of the rebels and an interdict over their lands. At much the same time, for domestic consumption, he states that any judgments against the barons will be by the law of the land or by judgment of their peers. He renounces the evil customs introduced by Henry II and Richard I and himself and offers reform, but subject to appeal to the Pope.

9 May 1215   John grants a Charter to London confirming its liberties and granting the City the right to elect its own Mayor. He has previously demanded £2,000 for such a Charter, but now grants it without payment.

17 May 1215   The rebel barons lift the siege of Northampton and proceed to London, entering with the apparent support of some of the citizenry. London continues to support the rebels throughout the hostilities.

27 May 1215   Negotiation for a possible settlement begin. Sometime shortly after this the rebels' demands are set out in the 'Articles of the Barons'.

8 June 1215   The king grants a safe conduct to rebel barons to come to Staines and a truce is arranged until 15 June.

10 June 1215   John seals the 'Articles of the Barons', an indication that he accepts them. There are 49 articles and they provide the first draft of the Charter.

15–19 June 1215   The Charter is granted, dated 15 June. It is not called Magna Carta or the Great Charter; it is simply a Charter. Negotiations may have continued until 19 June, when the royal seal is probably attached. Homage is renewed. In theory peace is established.

The Route from Runnymede

7 July 1215   The Pope excommunicates all those who disturb the Kingdom of England. He appoints three judges delegate, the Bishop of Winchester, the papal legate and the Abbot of Reading, to ensure that the excommunication is publicised.

16 July 1215   A Council is convened at Oxford to implement the Charter; John attends on 17 July, but it is adjourned until 20 August. In the meantime he writes to the Pope seeking an annulment of the Charter.

Mid-August 1215   The Pope's order of 7 July arrives in England. The rebels learn of it and they again renounce their fealty to John. They refuse to leave London.

24 August 1215   The Pope issues a bull, utterly repudiating the Charter and declaring it void; the King is forbidden 'to presume to observe it'.

Mid-September 1215   The bull arrives in England. Langton is suspended for failing to publicise it. He leaves for Rome to appeal but is unsuccessful. The rebels declare that John is deposed. In the meantime John starts to besiege Rochester castle.

November 1215   The rebels offer the Crown of England to Prince Louis of France. He accepts.

December 1215   Rochester castle falls to John; he marches north and takes Carlisle.

21 May 1216   Louis lands on the Isle of Thanet with a powerful army. He enters London where he is proclaimed King by the rebels. He takes Winchester in June. John cannot face him in the field.

July 1216   Innocent III dies. He is succeeded by Honorious III.

August 1216   Alexander of Scotland occupies Carlisle and then marches south to pay homage to Louis for the northern counties. Louis besieges Dover Castle, which holds out against him; John relieves Lincoln and then turns to King's Lynn. During his campaign he develops dysentery.

18 October 1216   John dies at Newark.

28 October 1216   John's infant son, Henry, is crowned King Henry III at Gloucester Cathedral.

21 November 1216   William Marshal is appointed regent. He immediately reissues a revised edition of the Charter, in the name of the young king but under his own seal and that of the papal legate.

Early Spring 1217   Louis resumes the siege of Dover Castle, but splits his forces. He sends a significant force to assist the rebel barons who are besieging Lincoln Castle.

20 May 1217   An army led by William Marshal decisively defeats the rebel forces at the Battle of Lincoln. The baronial party effectively surrenders. The siege of Dover is abandoned by Louis.

24 August 1217   In a sea battle off Sandwich, the royal forces led by Hubert de Burgh defeat a fleet bringing French reinforcements for Louis.

29 September 1217   The Treaty of Lambeth is signed; Louis abandons his claim.

Early November 1217   After a meeting of the Council, the Charter is reissued for a second time in the name of the king and sealed by Marshal and the legate. A separate Forest Charter is issued, which leads to the main charter being called Magna.

April 1219   Marshal resigns as regent and dies a month later.

1220 de Umfraville of Northumbria seeks a decision about his claim to maintain a castle at Harbottle to be made 'in the court of the lord king by the judgment of my peers'.

February 1225 Magna Carta is reissued 'in perpetuity' under the seal of Henry III, specifically in exchange for an agreement for a tax on moveables to be raised to fund his campaign to defend Gascony. Magna Carta is never reissued, but successive monarchs confirm the 1225 reissue.

1226 In the case of the 10 wapentakes of Ancaster in Lincolnshire, it is successfully argued that the actions of the sheriff are 'contrary to their liberty which they ought to have by the charter of the lord king'.

1236 In the context of legal proceedings, an adjournment is ordered until the next meeting of 'parliamentum', the first formal as opposed to colloquial reference to Parliament.

1297 Edward I confirms Magna Carta in return for a tax on moveables and enters this in the statute book.

1331–51 Statutes extend the right against arbitrary action by the Crown to 'all men of whatever condition whatsoever' and provide a guarantee for due process.

1508 Probably the first printed version of Magna Carta printed and published by Richard Pynson.

1628 Petition of Right.

1638 The Assembly in Maryland expressly adopts Magna Carta.

1687 The Charter is published in Philadelphia by William Penn.

1689 The English Bill of Rights.

1787 United States Constitution adopted.

1789 United States Bill of Rights (ratified in 1791).

Introduction

Car n'a tele gent en nule terre
Comment il dedenz Engleterre
De divers corages chascuns

There is no country anywhere like England
Where everyone has his own opinion

L'Histoire de Guillaume le Marechal, c 1225

ETWEEN 1215 AND 1225 four Magna Cartas were issued. The 1215 Charter was annulled within 10 weeks. The reissues in 1216, 1217 and the final text in 1225 were all different from each other and omitted parts of or amended the original. None of the Charters was visually impressive. They were all small pieces of parchment, covered in closely written Latin. Yet Magna Carta[1] is the most famous document in the common law and continues to be a powerful symbol of our liberties. Within its clauses are the germs of constitutional principles which resonate to this day.

The Grant of Liberties made by King John to his subjects in 1215 did not spring suddenly from a muddy field. It was grounded in medieval political thought. There had been similar earlier grants in England and on the continent of Europe, but these had withered away. Many myths have grown up about the Charter. It did not immediately give us trial by jury, although when jury trial did evolve it came to be regarded as based on the Charter's guarantee of trial by one's peers. It did not offer sweeping statements about personal freedoms or human rights or fair trials and, in fact, for the most part did not establish general rights, but rather created or recognised privileges. Nevertheless, in the promise that justice would not be delayed or denied, the right of an individual not to be kept in custody indefinitely nor subjected to penalty without trial was established. The word 'Parliament' does not appear in the Charter and the meeting at Runnymede could not conceivably be called a Parliament; the Charter did not create parliamentary sovereignty. Nevertheless, the 1215 Charter made the king subject to the law in the form of oversight by a group of his subjects, who were granted stringent enforcement powers if he failed to comply with its terms; their obligation of fealty was effectively suspended until he did so.

Beyond the Charter of 1225, as ideas and concepts were built upon the original by amendment or interpretation, the perception of what the Charter stood for became as important as the actual language of the original clauses. In this country we now take for granted that law should not be handed down by government diktat and

---

[1] For ease of reference we use the singular unless the context otherwise requires.

that the community should be involved in its creation; that those in authority are subject to the rule of law and that the rights of the citizen should be protected by the efficient administration of justice. In due course, through the influence of the Charter, these ideas spread to many other countries, including some undiscovered in 1215.

This book seeks to uncover the medieval meaning of the Charter and the process by which it evolved and expanded over succeeding centuries, being in effect updated in a series of constitutional documents, which included the Constitution of the United States of America. Only three clauses of the original Charter remain in force in England today, those which protect the freedom of the Church and the liberties of the cities, and the right to speedy trial by one's peers. On their own they have a limited direct impact on modern law. Yet the excitement that surrounds the Charter's 800th anniversary is a tribute to its continuing talismanic status.

We have personal reasons for attempting to write about the Charter. Our professional lives have been spent in close proximity to the site where many of the most important events leading up to the Charter occurred. The Knights Templar were granted land just outside the wall of the City of London in the mid-twelfth century. The Round Church which they built on the model of the Holy Sepulchre in Jerusalem still stands. It was from the Temple that in November 1214 King John issued a Charter which guaranteed the freedom of the Church in England and which was subsequently incorporated in Magna Carta. On 6 January 1215 the rebel barons brought their demands to the King while he was at the Temple. It was from here on 9 May 1215 that John, in an attempt to secure the support of the City of London, granted the City the sought-after privilege of electing its own mayor.

The Templars were disbanded in the fourteenth century and lawyers gradually moved into the Temple. It was lawyers from the Inns of Court, and the Temple in particular who challenged royal claims to absolutist authority. Members of the Middle Temple in the seventeenth century played a vital part in the export of Magna Carta to North America where, in the eighteenth century, several of its members were signatories to the Declaration of Independence and the Constitution of the United States.

We were both called to the Bar by the Middle Temple, one of the four Inns of Court where barristers qualify. We were pupil barristers at the same time in the same chambers, and when neither of us was given a permanent seat, we fantasised about writing a book together if ever we succeeded in the profession. Each of us has since become Treasurer of the Inn. In due course, when Judge had become a judge, Arlidge argued before him the meaning of the clause in the Charter which guaranteed that there would be no delay in the delivery of justice.[2] The trial of a police officer had been delayed for two years; previous cases had decided that where delay in the process of prosecution had prejudiced the defendant's position in the trial process, the trial should be stayed. This police officer, however, had made contem-

---

[2] *A G's Reference No 1 of 1990* [1992] 95 Cr App R 296.

poraneous notes of the relevant incident, and so should have had little difficulty in recalling it. Arlidge turned to Magna Carta with its guarantee of swift justice and the absence of any requirement for prejudice. Lord Lane, Chief Justice and Mr Justice Judge rejected Arlidge's argument. For the trial to be stayed the delay had to be wrongful and there had to be such prejudice that a fair trial would be impossible.

These personal connections have encouraged us to embark on this review of the Charter. We do so with temerity and humility, conscious that we are not scholars or historians, and that we do not possess their depth of knowledge. Instead, we offer an approach to Magna Carta based on our own experience as lawyers, recognising that in the process of writing, we ourselves have learned a great deal about it. We trace the route to the Charter, and scrutinise its text, considering its background and meaning, grouping its clauses into topics, each with its own fascinating back story. We consider the astonishing survival of the Charter, and the gradual accretion to it of concepts now in general legal currency such as 'due process' and the 'rule of law' and 'cruel and unusual punishment', which provided the basis for our liberties. We examine how the Charter became the foundation for the opposition to royal despotism in England in the seventeenth century and the opposition to the sovereignty of Parliament in the United States of America in the next century, and eventually produced two great democracies with different constitutions. In the process our study focuses not only on the text, but on the people who were involved in the creation of the Charter and its evolution, who made the Charter what it was, and what it continues to represent.

1

Who Made Magna Carta?

Confrontation at Runnymede

RUNNYMEDE LIES BY the river Thames near to Windsor Castle. On 15 June 1215 two groups of armed men met there, one headed by King John, supported by barons loyal to him, the other a much larger group drawn from his tenants in chief who had rebelled against his rule. In its original Anglo Saxon form, Runnymede meant 'council island', for it had been an occasional meeting place for the Saxon Witanagemot or council of advisors to the King. Runnymede lay on the south side of the river; the name Magna Carta Island is now attached to an island on the north side of the river, but the precise spot where the two groups met is not known.

Two years earlier, in May 1213, John had surrendered his kingdom to the Pope and became the Pope's vassal. Shortly afterwards John departed England for France in an attempt to recover lands he had lost 10 years earlier. He formed an alliance with rulers to the east of France. In July 1214 these allies were heavily defeated at the Battle of Bouvines and John retreated back to England. His treasury was empty and his authority irretrievably damaged. On his return on 13 October the rebel barons sought redress of their grievances, eventually meeting with the King in January 1215 in the Temple. The negotiations were unsuccessful and on 5 May 1215, wearying of delay, the rebels renounced their oaths of allegiance to the King. They resorted to arms and on 17 May they entered and held London.

This gave them a strong military advantage and forced John on 15 June to make a grant of liberties to the freemen of his kingdom. The document which recorded its terms subsequently became known as Magna Carta or the Great Charter.[1] It was sealed on 19 June when the rebel barons renewed their oaths of allegiance to the King. Both sides swore on oath to abide by the terms. Copies of the Charter were circulated to important cities and towns throughout the country. Four copies still survive, one each in the cathedrals of Lincoln and Salisbury and two in the British Library.

The rebels were practical men dealing with their own political grievances, and the King was facing the stark reality that, as things stood in June 1215, he had no alter-

---

[1] Generally see JC Holt, *Magna Carta* (Cambridge, 2001) and RV Turner, *Magna Carta* (Harlow, 2003).

native but to make concessions. When the situation changed and his military position improved, despite his oath, he would destroy the Charter.

The Rebel Barons[2]

The names that appear in the Charter are supporters of John; the names of the rebel barons do not appear. The chronicler Matthew Paris, writing around 1250, gives us the names of the principal rebels. Their families were of Norman origin. Their leaders were Eustace de Vesci, Lord of Alnwick in Northumbria and Robert Fitzwalter, Lord of Dunmow in Essex and of Baynard Castle in the City of London. In 1212 they were accused of conspiring to murder John and fled the kingdom. According to the *Histoire des Ducs de Normandie*, Fitzwalter went to Paris where he told a papal legate that he could not serve an excommunicant and also told the French King that John had tried to ravish his daughter.[3] The Pope compelled John to accept their return in 1213 and they became the focus for baronial dissatisfaction. When armed conflict began, Fitzwalter was appointed commander of the rebel forces and assumed the rather grandiose title 'Marshal of the Host of God and Holy Church'. His half brother, Saer de Quincy, Earl of Winchester, was the chief spokesman for the rebels in the subsequent negotiations.

When John repudiated the Charter, civil war broke out again and Robert Fitzwalter and Saer invited Prince Louis of France to invade England and claim the English Crown. Eustace travelled south with his troops to meet Louis, but stopped on the way to besiege Castle Barnard in Durham. He was killed during the siege. Robert and Saer continued military opposition to the last. Eventually in 1217 the armies of Louis and the rebels were defeated at Lincoln and Robert taken prisoner. Shortly after he was pardoned.

The title 'baron' was a French term, deriving initially from the Latin 'baronis'. The Anglo Saxon equivalent was 'earl'. Earls governed large tracts of land in the name of the King, but under the Normans their jurisdiction was generally confined to one shire. 'Baron' was used by William I to denote those who held land directly of the Crown. The position was complicated by two factors: a barony was a form of landholding and you did not have to be a baron to hold a barony; furthermore the Normans themselves created earls – a baron could also be an earl. King Stephen, in particular, created a large number of earldoms. From Henry II onwards, however, the Crown was concerned that too much power was devolving on the earls and fewer were created. The term 'lord' was used to denote the superior in a feudal relationship – the lord granted a fief to his vassal.

The hugely important clause 61 provides that the security of the Charter is to be guaranteed by the barons choosing 25 of their number with powers of distraint and

---

[2] See Appendix B, which details their background.
[3] F Michel (ed), *Histoire des Ducs de Normandie* (Paris, 1840) 119–125.

distress against the Crown, if the King does not observe its terms. These are the men named by Matthew Paris.[4] They provide an illustrative snapshot of the rebel party and their potted biographies are found in Appendix B. Some general comments can be made about them.[5]

Their families were, with two exceptions, of Norman origin. John fitz Robert's family dated back to pre-Conquest England, but they had married since with families of Norman origin. The other exception is the mayor of London, who was of Anglo Saxon descent. The Domesday Book reveals all too graphically how the Anglo Saxon aristocracy had been replaced by their Norman conquerors. Several of the rebels' families originated from an area just to the south of the Cotentin or Cherbourg peninsula (maybe coincidentally this was an area which had not sworn feudal loyalty to the King of France). Some retained lands in Normandy, but by 1215 they regarded themselves as Anglo Norman with their principal seats in England. Under feudal law, a vassal owed an obligation to his lord to produce knights to defend the lord – he owed the lord 'knight service'. The number of knights the vassal had to produce was defined by the number of 'knights fees' his landholding bore. This service was often performed in person, but with time came to be replaced with a money payment, which enabled the King to hire more efficient mercenaries. This tax was called 'scutage'. The initial focus of opposition to John was resistance to payment of scutage for military campaigns outside England and Normandy, particularly for the failed campaign John had recently conducted in Poitou.

The rebels were drawn largely from the north of England and East Anglia. They came from powerful families, such as the Percys in Northumberland or the Bigods or Mandevilles in East Anglia. They held strong castles and had fighting men at their disposal. Some held land in more than one place, so that although they held lands outside the north and East Anglia, they also had estates within them. Robert de Vere was Earl of Oxford, but his mother was a daughter of an Earl of Essex and through her he inherited lands in East Essex, including Castle Hedingham, which became his principal seat. William de Lanvelei held land in several counties and a hereditary claim to Colchester castle. A number of the rebels served in the Poitou campaign – John de Lacy, William Huntingfield, William Malet and William Lanvelei. Some joined the rebels late in the day after they had taken London – John de Lacy, William d'Aubigny and William de Forz. Some flip-flopped back to the royal party when the Charter was repudiated by John – William de Forz and William Marshal junior, though he was probably influenced by his father, who remained loyal to the King. John de Lacy returned to allegiance to the King, but only after his castle at Donington was seized.

---

[4] Chron. Major II 605; he named Roger de Mowbray in error as Roger de Montbegon; see also Holt (n 1) App 8.

[5] There is an illuminating analysis of the make-up of the baronage in S Painter, *The Reign of King John* (Baltimore, MD, 1949) 286–89. He concludes that though the rebel party was probably larger than that of loyalists, the bulk of the baronage tried to remain on the sidelines.

The most striking aspect of the biographies of the 25 is the extent to which they are interrelated. Like royalty, the baronage used marriage as a means of extending their landholdings and power. Without going through all the connections we point out a number. The northern rebels de Vesci and de Ros had both married illegitimate daughters of Alexander, King of Scotland. Saer de Quincy's father had served an earlier king of Scotland and been created Lord of Leuchars, a title which de Saer inherited. We have already noted that de Saer and Fitzwalter were half brothers. John fitz Robert, lord of Warkworth near Alnwick in Northumbria, was related to the de Lacys, Quincys, de Veres and Bigods. Geoffrey de Mandeville, Richard Mountfichet and Robert de Vere were linked by marriage. There was a similar connection between Richard Mountfichet, William Lanvelei and Robert fitz Walter. Huntingfield's mother was a daughter of Saer de Quincy. It is necessary to proceed with caution before ascribing rebellion to relationship as just noted; William Marshal, father and son, were initially on opposite sides. No doubt if one analysed the families of the loyal barons a similar pattern would appear. These connections, however, must have facilitated communication and cohesion.

All of the 25 sureties of the Charter were substantial landholders and their lands bore a high number of knight's fees. In 1968 Professor Cheney published details of a manuscript from Reading Abbey, which he had found in the library of Lambeth Palace.[6] This lists the sureties (with some errors) and also the number of knight's fees they held, which ranged up to 200. All of the 25 would have borne a large burden of such dues, which must have informed their opposition to the payment of scutage.

King John

John did not want to grant the Charter. Mathew Paris described John's reaction to events at Runnymede as 'gnashing his teeth, scowling with his eyes and seizing sticks from the trees, [he] began to gnaw at them and after gnawing them to break them, and with increased extraordinary gestures to show the grief and rage he felt'. Both Paris and his fellow chronicler in the Abbey of St Albans, Roger of Wendover, are heavily biased against John, but allowing for dramatic licence, this passage no doubt reflects the King's reaction. Pope Innocent III was correct to describe him as acting under duress.[7]

John was the youngest son of Henry II; later historians labelled the Norman dynasty from Henry II onwards Angevins. The label came from the fact that Henry II's father Geoffrey was Count of Anjou. Henry inherited Anjou and Maine to the south of Normandy from his father. Geoffrey has also been credited, through his marriage to Matilda of England, with founding what later became called the Plantagenet dynasty (he wore a sprig of broom or *planta genista* in his cap).

---

[6] Lambeth Palace manuscripts 229, fo 96; BJRL I 107, reproduced in Holt (n 1) 479.
[7] See section on Pope Innocent III below and Chapter 4.

John is described as 5 feet, 5 inches tall, barrel chested, with dark red hair. He is said to have enjoyed reading, music, wine and rich apparel. Roger of Wendover, writing probably between 1220 and 1235, stresses his self-indulgence.[8] He describes how in 1203 the nobles of England travelled with John to Normandy, preparing to defend his French possessions, but left him and returned to England because of his incorrigible idleness: 'He feasted with his Queen daily and prolonged his sleep in the morning until breakfast time'.[9] Later Roger recounts how in 1216, when John was travelling through the Wash near Kings Lynn, he contracted a violent fever, which was 'increased by his pernicious gluttony, for that night he surfeited on peaches and drinking new cider'.[10] The double effect caused his death.

John had a reputation for violent behaviour. He was believed to have been responsible for the 'disappearance' of his nephew, Arthur of Brittany. Arthur was born in March 1187, the posthumous son of John's elder brother Geoffrey, who died of injuries sustained in a tournament the previous year. As the son of John's elder brother, Arthur had a serious claim to the throne on grounds of primogeniture and initially, after a treaty with Philip Augustus of France, Richard I named Arthur as his successor. Immediately before his death, however, he nominated John. In 1202, in the course of John's successful campaign in Normandy, some 200 leaders of the army which supported Arthur were imprisoned in such appalling conditions that 22 of them died.[11] Arthur himself was captured at the Battle of Mirebeau. He was imprisoned, first in the Castle of the Falaise and then in Rouen Castle. His jailors were trusted followers of John. Arthur simply disappeared in 1203. It seems probable that John was concerned in his murder. He had a clear motive to kill him and John's lieutenants, whether for fear of John or to ingratiate themselves with him, had ample opportunity. Arthur was only just 16. He was not the last Plantagenet prince to die in a tower at the instigation of an ambitious uncle.

William de Braose was responsible for Arthur's custody. In due course John came to regard him as an over-mighty subject, but initially he played a large part in the subjugation of Wales and was granted substantial lands there. When he fell from favour, apparently for failing to pay a large sum of money demanded by the King, he was harried and pursued, and eventually fled to France. His wife and son were incarcerated and were killed or died in captivity. The most chilling example of John's capacity for ruthless cruelty, shocking to this day, was the execution in 1212 of 28 boy hostages, for the most part the sons of Welsh princes, who were in captivity to guarantee the good behaviour of their fathers. When they rebelled, the sons were hanged.[12] By 1215 the rebel barons must have realised that the consequences of a failed rebellion would be dire.

---

[8] See Appendix B.
[9] JG Giles (ed), *Flowers of History* II (London, 1849) 207.
[10] ibid 208.
[11] Turner (n 1).
[12] Painter (n 5) 267.

John also had a reputation for making free with the wives of his most powerful subjects. In 1204 Alice, wife of Hugh de Neville, one of the King's closest companions, offered the King 200 chickens for the right to lie with her husband for one night.[13]

Many of the sources of resentment voiced in John's reign had grown up during the reigns of his predecessors. John inherited the efficient administrative and judicial system established by his father, Henry II, and he himself appears to have been an efficient administrator, maybe at times too efficient. His constant financial needs caused him to raise monies in whatever way he could. Richard I exacted heavy taxes to fund a crusade, and later for his personal ransom; even if resented, they were difficult to oppose. John's exactions were aimed at the recovery of distant territories in France, which, notwithstanding their Norman ancestry, were of reducing interest to the English barons. By the twelfth century they had become so anglicised that English had started to replace French as their language.[14] Even his most loyal subject, William Marshal, refused to pay 'scutage' to help fund one of John's early expeditions to France. Furthermore, John's reign was distinguished from his predecessors by his presence in England for much longer periods; he took a personal interest in raising money, whether from feudal dues or the proceeds of the judicial system. After the humiliation at the Battle of Bouvines it seemed inevitable that John would have to seek to restore his finances by new exactions.

The Clergy

Pope Innocent III[15]

Having presented John as its author, the Charter recites that it was granted for the reform of the realm on the advice of certain named reverend fathers and illustrious noblemen and 'others our faithful subjects'. One of the reverend fathers is Master Pandulph, 'sub-deacon and member of the household of the Lord Pope'. Pope Innocent III is not named personally, but Pandulph had already been used as his agent in dealing with John. In fact. the Pope played an important role in English politics throughout John's reign. From the beginning of his papacy, Innocent made it clear that he intended to assert his power in the temporal as well as in the ecclesiastical sphere. Born Lothar de' Segni, he was the nephew of Pope Clement III.[16] In the twelfth century the Schools at Paris were the intellectual hub of Western Europe,

---

[13] RL Warren, *King John* (New Haven, CT, 1997) 190 and D Crouch, 'Hugh de Neville' in *Oxford Dictionary of National Biography* (Oxford, 2004).

[14] HM Thomas, *The English and the Normans, Ethnic Hostility, Assimilation and Identity* (Oxford, 2003) 144.

[15] Generally see J Sayers, *Innocent III Leader of Europe* (London, 1994).

[16] CR Cheney and WR Semple, *Selected Letters of Pope Innocent III (1198–1216) Concerning England* (London, 1953) Intro, x.

where about 200 students studied theology and liberal arts. Some time in the 1180s Lothar went to study there. During this period he also visited the shrine of Thomas a Becket at Canterbury. Back in Italy Lothar probably studied for a time at Bologna, where there was a famous law school. At the end of the 1180s he was made a Cardinal Deacon, and elected Pope in 1198. In his sermon after consecration, he took as one of his texts, Jeremiah 1: 10 'I have set thee over nations'. He later asserted:

> [O]nly St Peter was invested with the plenitude of power. See in what manner of servant this is, appointed over the household, he is indeed vicar of Jesus Christ . . . less than God but greater than man, judge of all men and judged by none.

On this basis he claimed the right to examine the credentials of an emperor elect before his consecration.[17] Throughout his pontificate, Innocent's determination to exercise his influence in the temporal sphere was unrelenting.

In 1203 Philip Augustus of France picked a quarrel with John, complaining of his treatment of the Church of St Martin of Tours and also of the way John had arbitrarily deprived some of Philip's vassals of their castles. In relation to his lands in Normandy, John was Philip's vassal. John was summoned by Philip to answer the charges. John did not attend, and Philip prepared to wage war. Innocent intervened, but Philip denied his jurisdiction to judge a feudal dispute. On 31 October 1203 Innocent wrote to Philip expressing his amazement, and asserting his authority and duty in matters of salvation. Accordingly Philip should make peace or a truce or submit to the judgment of the Archbishop of Bourges: 'We do not intend to judge concerning a fief, judgment on which belongs to him . . . but concerning sin, a judgment which unquestionably belongs to us and which we can and should exercise against anyone'.[18] Innocent's attempt to influence these events was unsuccessful, since by 1204 Philip had seized all of John's French possessions with the exception of Aquitaine.

Not content with dictating to the King of France, from 1205 Innocent became involved in a long-running conflict with John over appointments to ecclesiastical office in England.[19] In 1207 this led Innocent to place England under interdict, which limited the church offices that could be performed there, and in 1213 to excommunicate John. The Pope authorised Philip Augustus, King of France, to wage holy war against John. Shortly afterwards, faced with a threat both to his soul and his reign, John submitted to the Pope as his feudal lord as well as his spiritual leader. He reaffirmed his coronation oath to protect the Church and to rule according to established law.

The argument about Church appointments was now resolved in favour of the Church; thereafter Innocent gave his support to his vassal, John, throughout the conflict with the rebel barons. On 4 March 1215 John undertook formally to go on

---

[17] ibid, Intro xii.
[18] CR Cheney and MG Cheney, *The Letters of Pope Innocent III (1198–1216) Concerning England and Wales* (Oxford, 1967) no 506.
[19] See below Chapter 4.

a crusade to the Holy Land. Innocent's principal interest at this stage was that the rebellion should come to an end, and John go on crusade. Immediately after Runnymede, John persuaded the Pope to pronounce the Charter null and void. The papal bull announcing this arrived in England in mid-September 1215. In short, the Charter was annulled by John's feudal lord and the spiritual head of Christendom. It now contained no more than out-of-date words on a piece of parchment.

Stephen Langton[20]

The first of the reverend fathers identified in the Charter as advisors to the King is the Cardinal Archbishop Langton. He was born in Lincolnshire and studied in the Schools in Paris at the same time as Innocent III. When the future Innocent III returned to Italy, Langton remained in Paris, conducting *questiones* on theological and moral problems and carrying out biblical studies. He became a canon of Notre Dame Cathedral and later a cardinal priest.[21] On the death of Hubert Walter, Innocent named Langton as Archbishop of Canterbury, and in 1208 consecrated him, but John refused to allow Langton to take up his see. In 1213, as part of his submission, John allowed him to do so.

Langton's role in the negotiation and drafting of the Charter has been the subject of major debate among historians. John Baldwin, in an article in the *English Historical Review*, 'Langton, the Paris Schools and Magna Carta', closely analysed the writings of Langton when he was studying and teaching in the Paris Schools and demonstrated that these revealed a philosophy which in due course underpinned Magna Carta.[22] Roger of Wendover certainly gives a pivotal role to Langton. According to Wendover, on 25 August 1213 Stephen preached a sermon at St Paul's and thereafter drew aside the bishops, abbots and barons and told them that he had obliged the King to swear at Winchester that he would abolish evil laws and establish good ones. Thereupon he produced and read out a copy of Henry I's Charter of Liberties, claiming that it had been found recently. The barons swore to defend those liberties with their lives, and the archbishop promised to furnish them with aid.[23] Thereafter, a meeting of the barons took place at St Edmundsbury (Bury St Edmunds) where the barons swore on the altar that if the King did not grant the liberties in Henry I's Charter they would withdraw their allegiance.[24] No other source confirms these events, and there is a degree of dramatic licence in the text which undermines confidence in Roger's reliability. Nevertheless, Baldwin is prepared to entertain the idea that Roger's account may be truthful and concludes 'if the Archbishop's direct contributions to Magna Carta were limited to specific items,

---

[20] See FM Powicke, *Stephen Langton*, Ford Lectures (Oxford, 1927).

[21] ibid 31.

[22] J Baldwin, 'Master Stephen Langton, Future Archbishop of Canterbury: The Paris Schools and Magna Carta' (2008) CXXIII(53) *English Historical Review* 811.

[23] Giles (n 9) 342–43.

[24] ibid 303.

the prominence of his name in the Charter none the less confirms his overall respon-sibility'. Yet Langton would have had little interest in stirring up rebellion against a king who by now had submitted totally to the Pope.

In 2012 David Carpenter responded to Baldwin's views in 'Archbishop Langton and Magna Carta: his Contribution, his Doubts and his Hypocrisy'.[25] He pointed out that Langton's views at the Paris Schools were commonplace in Medieval thought. A draft grant known as the Articles of the Barons, probably completed in early June 1215, contains no reference to the freedom of the Church. This may indi-cate that Langton is unlikely to have played a part in their drafting. Clause 1 of the Charter must have been inserted later, possibly at Langton's insistence.

Those named as the King's advisors, including Langton, were committing them-selves on the face of the document to the Charter as a whole. It was, we emphasise, a far more ambitious document than any of the earlier grants of liberties in Europe. It was an attempt to bring together a body politic of King, Church and freemen, and expressly speaks of a community of the realm. It seems likely that Langton was at least influential in ensuring this approach. His difficulty was that Innocent III took the rather simplistic view that just as John should obey him, John's vassals should obey the King.

In fact Langton was dealing with a more complex situation than Innocent realised. On 19 March 1215 the Pope wrote to the archbishop[26] expressing surprise and annoyance that Langton had ignored the differences between the King and barons, wilfully shutting his eyes and not troubling to mediate a settlement. 'Some instead suspect and state that . . . you are giving help and favour to his opponents'. There are some indications that Stephen was sympathetic to the rebel cause. Roger of Wendover describes Stephen as being at the head of the rebels when they arrived in Brackley in Northamptonshire shortly after Easter, although Roger may give him a greater role than that he in fact played.[27] On 27 May 1215 the King granted Langton a safe conduct to come to Staines as he did to the representatives of the rebels.[28]

In modern terms, Langton was caught between a rock and a hard place. He would have been well aware of the strength of feeling among the rebel barons and their potential military power. He was nevertheless answerable to his spiritual leader for the way he responded to a political situation which his leader did not understand. Consequent on the annulment of the Charter, Wendover describes how the Bishop of Winchester and the papal legate required the archbishop to publish the excom-munication of the rebels.[29] Langton intended to set out for Rome and decided that the Bull of Excommunication should not be published until he had spoken to the Pope. He was immediately suspended from office by the Bishop of Winchester and the papal legate, and when Langton eventually arrived in Rome to appeal against

[25] D Carpenter, 'Archbishop Langton and Magna Carta: His Contribution, His Doubts and His Hypocrisy' (2011) CXXVI(522) *English Historical Review* 1041.
[26] Cheney and Semple (n 16) no 75, p 196.
[27] Giles (n 9) Part 1, 306.
[28] See Holt (n 1) 242.
[29] Giles (n 9) 342.

the suspension, his appeal failed. It seems likely that his reluctance to follow the orders of the Pope immediately indicates that he wanted to explain the realities on the ground in England. According to Roger of Wendover, Langton's suspension was lifted early in 1216.[30] Innocent's successor restored him to the archbishopric in 1218. By then there was an entirely different political climate.

Langton's name appears at the head of the list of witnesses to the reissue of an amended Charter in 1225. His position on the list may have reflected his position as archbishop, but he is likely to have played an important part in securing this grant. This was a Charter which was clearly intended to unite the community of the realm, for the list of witnesses included former rebels. Langton's support for such an approach would be all of a piece with his attempt in the autumn of 1215 to postpone excommunication of the rebels until the Pope knew of the reality on the ground in England. The Pope's aim at this time was to ensure that John went on crusade as soon as possible. Peace in England was a necessary precondition. The best way to achieve that was to unite the community of the realm.

The Master of the Order of the Temple

The Master of the Knighthood of the Temple in England in 1215 was Aimeric de St Maur. He is named in the Charter as one of the reverend advisors. The Knights Templar were a military order, founded in 1118, to protect pilgrims on their way to and from the Holy Land. The English Crown first granted them land in Holborn and then in an area to the west of the city wall near the Lud Gate, which became known as the New Temple.[31] The Temple still nestles, largely unseen by the general public, between Fleet Street and the Thames. It is a site of about 6.5 acres (2.63 hectares). In 1160 work commenced on the construction of a round church, on the model of the Church of the Holy Sepulchre in Jerusalem; it was consecrated in February 1185 by Heraclius, Patriarch of Jerusalem, who took the opportunity to offer Henry II the Crown of Jerusalem. This offer was declined.

The order was monastic and knights were required to take a vow of poverty. Rich men who entered would donate their wealth, and others, no doubt in the hope of spiritual benefit, made gifts. Accordingly the order flourished. In very simple terms, knights and pilgrims travelling to the Holy Land needed safe places to stay and feed. With time the order built up a network of castles and other buildings throughout Europe and the Near East and as a result, apart from the military knights, a considerable administrative organisation grew. The order created an early banking system, issuing letters of credit to pilgrims who deposited money with them in their home country. It also managed the affairs of its members and also the affairs of others who were away on pilgrimages. John borrowed money from the Templars and used them himself on diplomatic missions to the Pope and other rulers in Europe.

---

[30] Giles (n 9) II 648.
[31] See M Barber, *A New Knighthood: A History of the Order of the Temple* (Cambridge, 1994).

John often stayed in the Temple when he was in London. In 1200 Innocent III had granted immunity from local law to those staying in Templar property, so that the rebel barons would have seen the Temple as a safe place to meet. By the time John met the rebel barons at the Temple on the day of the Epiphany 1215, they had formed a conjuration or sworn association to seek satisfaction for their grievances. They demanded a return of the liberties expressed in the Charter of Henry I. They refused payment of scutage to fund John's recent unsuccessful campaign in France. As the barons had arrived fully armed, however, John was provided with an excuse to complain of their disrespect and he refused to respond to the threat of force. A truce was then agreed, until 26 April, when the parties arranged to meet in Brackley in Northamptonshire. In due course emissaries of the King attended, but not the King himself.

In May 1215, again from the Temple, John granted a Charter to London, confirming its liberties and London's right to elect its own mayor. The granting of this Charter was a concession, or perhaps a bribe. Whatever it was, it failed to secure the loyalty of London to his cause. This Charter to London continues in force, and the annual Lord Mayor's procession to the Royal Courts of Justice in the Strand, where the Lord Mayor is sworn in before the Lord Chief Justice, represents its continuing survival.

Within the original Round of the Temple Church lies the effigy of William Marshal, Earl of Pembroke.

2

William Marshal

WILLIAM MARSHAL[1] IS the unsung hero of these convoluted events. Without him Magna Carta might well have been relegated to a minor footnote in history, one more charter in an age of charters. Yet, except by professional historians of the period, he is virtually unknown today.

The characteristic at the heart of Marshal's achievement (which virtually all his contemporaries came to appreciate) was the striking depth of his commitment to his oath of allegiance. This contrasted markedly with the extraordinary level of dysfunction among the Angevin monarchs he served. Henry II imprisoned John's mother, for well over a decade. His sons warred openly with their father and he with them, and they warred with and betrayed one another. We have already touched on the likely complicity of John in the murder of his nephew Arthur. These were poisonous feuds. To serve one member of this family when he was in dispute with another was not the way to steady advancement.

Marshal was the fourth of his father's sons, and like his brothers he took his father's hereditary office, 'Mareshal', as his surname. On any view his prospects of advancement were limited, but he was fortunate that his talents were recognised at an early age by Henry II's consort, Queen Eleanor. Thereafter he was entrusted with responsibility for the King's son, Henry, who although crowned and known as the Young King never reigned, predeceasing his father. After the Young King's death, Marshal fulfilled the Prince's vow to go on crusade to the Holy Land. He returned to the service of Henry II and served him loyally to his death. Shortly before Henry died, his eldest surviving son and now heir, Richard, rebelled against his father. Marshal and Richard encountered one another in the field in Normandy; Marshal unseated Richard from his horse, but spared him; no doubt to make a point, he killed his horse. After Henry's death Marshal's public career seemed to be at an end. Nevertheless, when he offered his fealty to Richard, the new King accepted it. When Richard went on crusade he appointed Marshal first of four co-justiciars to the Chancellor, William Longchamps. Among the burdens which fell on Marshal and his co-justiciars was a siege of John at Windsor Castle. In passing, as lawyers

[1] Generally see D Crouch, *William Marshal, Court, Career and Chivalry in the Angevin Empire 1147–1219* (London, 1990); S Painter, *William Marshal, Knight Errant, Baron and Regent of England* (Baltimore, MD, 1933); D Carpenter, *The Struggle for Mastery of Britain 1066–1284* (London, 2004); and JC Holt *Magna Carta* (Cambridge, 2001).

we cannot help noticing that, although illiterate, Marshal appeared on the judicial bench at Westminster Hall as a Justice.

On Richard's return from captivity, Marshal became increasingly influential. As a public acknowledgement of Richard's increasing favour, he was allowed to marry the heiress, Isibel of Striguil (Chepstow). His standing with Richard would have been undiminished by his stupendous folly in leading the way up a scaling ladder and knocking out the constable of Beauvais Castle, when it was under siege. When Richard died in 1199, William was consulted by the Archbishop of Canterbury about the succession, and William recommended that, in accordance with Richard's last wishes, John rather than Arthur should become King. Shortly after John was crowned, William was invested as the Earl of Pembroke. His strong connection with Wales is still visible in the dominating remains of a series of castles, of which Chepstow and Pembroke are the most striking.

Marshal's fortunes during the early years of the reign were in the ascendancy. They then slumped. Importantly for the issues which culminated in the Charter a decade or so later, the most contentious area of dispute with John arose from Marshal's determined refusal to join an expedition to Poitou. William held land in France, in respect of which he swore fealty to the King of France, Philip Augustus. He argued he could not breach his oath. This may have been special pleading, but there can be little doubt that the rebel barons would later have recollected Marshal's refusal to serve abroad. As a result of Marshal swearing allegiance to Philip Augustus, John charged him with treason. William elected trial by battle, but his reputation as a warrior was widely respected and none would challenge him on behalf of the Crown.

From 1205 Marshal languished in political exile in Ireland. His wife was descended from the royal family of Leinster; when managing her lands there, Marshal learnt administrative skills. Ireland was not overlooked when the Charter later came to be reissued in 1216, and again in 1217, when Marshal ensured that both were distributed in Ireland as in England. Indeed, when the Irish version of the Charter was issued, it is recorded that Irish subjects should enjoy the same liberties which had been granted in England (a promise which, over the centuries, was not destined to be fulfilled).

The reconciliation with John took some time. By 1213, however, the King was short of allies. In May of that year, Marshal received a summons to return to England. In due course he did so, and advised John to make his peace with the Pope, which, as we have seen, John did. When, after the battle of Bouvines, an invasion of England by Philip Augustus emerged as a real threat, Marshal organised the mustering of troops in England and the preparation of defensive positions.

When, at the feast of Epiphany on 6 January 1215, a truce was agreed between the King and the rebels in the Temple, William was the only civilian (as opposed to clerical) guarantor of John's good faith. William is named in the Charter as the first of John's lay advisors. After the Charter was sealed in June, it was Marshal who was given the responsibility of informing the City of London, hostile to the King, of its terms. If there is no precise evidence of the part Marshal played in negotiations with the rebels, these events underline how close to their heart he must have been.

Civil war followed the Pope's annulment of the Charter. When the rebels invited the French Prince, Louis, to invade and claim the English Crown, Marshal was sent as an emissary to France to dissuade the Capetan French King from supporting his son's claim. William failed in his mission and some 7,000 French soldiers invaded, to be joined by the Prince on 20 May 1216. Although the Pope tried to prohibit the invasion and excommunicated the Prince, Louis entered London and took homage from the mayor. At the same time, Alexander of Scotland invaded from the north.

It is a fortunate accident of our history that John died in 1216. Marshal was at Gloucester when this happened and took urgent action to secure the Plantagenet succession, summoning the loyal barons to Gloucester Abbey. Within 10 days of John's death, they selected Marshal as Guardian of the boy King and Regent of the Kingdom (*Rector Noster et Regni Nostri*). He arranged for Prince Henry to be conveyed to Gloucester Abbey and crowned there, as Westminster Abbey was under French control. The coronation was conducted by Peter de Roches, Bishop of Winchester, John's former Chief Justiciar and one of the reverend fathers named in the Charter. William entrusted the care of Henry to Peter.

The position of the boy King and his council was perilous. Less than a month after John's death the Charter was reissued in Henry's name, but under Marshal's personal seal and that of the new papal legate. Some of the more stringent provisions restricting the power of the monarch were omitted, perhaps just because he was a boy, who should not be punished for any misconduct of the Regent. But whatever the reason, the reissue must have been intended as a gesture towards reconciliation with the rebel barons. As such it failed.

So the war continued. Next year, the rebel army, backed by Louis of France, besieged loyalist troops at Lincoln Castle. Marshal, now very close to the current age of judicial retirement, led an army to relieve the siege. Anxious to take advantage of the unfolding military situation, he charged forward into battle without a helmet. Fortunately his supporters reminded him to wear one, because during the hand-to-hand fighting which followed, the helmet was dented in more than one place. The result was a great victory. Forty-six rebel barons, including Robert Fitzwalter, were captured. Shortly afterwards the French fleet was defeated off Sandwich. The Treaty of Lambeth in September 1217 formalised the end of the civil war and the departure of the defeated French.[2] Encouraged by a generous payment, Louis abandoned any claim to the throne of England and agreed to return to France. Under the terms of the Treaty, former rebels were to be pardoned and they renewed their homage and were absolved from excommunication. Marshal and the new legate Guala undertook that the liberties demanded by the rebel barons would be restored.

---

[2] This is sometimes referred to as the Treaty of Kingston. This serves to distinguish the 1217 Treaty from an earlier Treaty of Lambeth in 1212. The sources for the 1217 Treaty contain different versions of where it was agreed, including an island in the Thames near Kingston, Surrey.

As part of what today would be described as the 'peace process', after a meeting of the council, the Charter was again reissued in November 1217 in the name of the Young King, but again under the seal of Marshal and the papal legate. Apart from the involvement of the council, the significance of this reissue was that unlike the 1215 and 1216 Charters, it was not made under the pressure of imminent defeat or the crisis of the infant succession to the throne, but in the aftermath of victory in battle. Indeed, to secure this peace, Marshal made concessions which Henry III himself later came to regard as something of a betrayal.

In early 1219 Marshal died. He was given what today would be described as a state funeral. Archbishop Langton was not alone in his praise of this 'greatest knight that ever lived'. Within a very short time the story of his life was being told in *L'Histoire de Guillaume le Mareshal* (the History of William the Marshal), the first, and with the exception of an autobiographical effort, the only known or surviving 'lay' of the story of a life of an individual who was not a monarch, or in our language, head of state.

If, on John's death on 19 October 1216, you had sought odds on the next ruling dynasty in England, they would have been shorter on the Capetans than the Plantagenets. If Prince Louis had become Louis I of England, French would have been reinforced as the official language and the British Constitution would have been absolutist – witness the eventual fate of the Estates General in France. It was Marshal who was largely responsible for securing the Plantagenet succession and the survival of the Charter. His was a remarkable life and it is time for his contribution to our history to be uncovered.

3

What Was Magna Carta?

MAGNA CARTA EVIDENCED a grant of liberties by the Crown to the Church, freemen and cities of the kingdom. It was addressed to the 'archbishops, bishops, abbots, earls, barons, justiciars, foresters, sheriffs and all royal servants and officials'. Having confirmed the liberty of the English Church, it continued: 'To all free men of our kingdom we have also granted for us and our heirs for ever all the liberties written out below to have and to keep for them and their heirs, of us and our heirs'. At the close of the document these words appear: 'Given by our hand in the meadow called Runnymede between Windsor and Staines on the fifteenth day of June in the seventeenth year of our reign'. It was a grant in traditional form, evidenced by a written Charter.

Once England had become Christian, rich men would donate land to the Church in the hope (sometimes expressed) that the Church would pray for their souls. The Church required evidence of these gifts and took to recording them in a writing called in Anglo Saxon a 'boc', or in Latin 'carta'. Thus in 672 a Charter recorded a gift by Frithuwold, who ruled over part of Surrey, to the monastery at Chertsey. Frithuwold could not write, so he authenticated the document simply by putting a cross on it.[1] With time, the Crown too used charters to evidence the gift of land to a follower, often with obligations in return.[2] Land granted by the Crown was known as 'bocland'. The grants were often witnessed in assemblies of notables, the numbers varying from 20 to 100. These assemblies carried out legislative and judicial functions.[3] The Angevin kings followed similar models. For political documents they used a variety of wordings. In some the notables 'recognised' the terms of the document, in others 'advised' (as in the 1215 Charter), in others 'witnessed' (as in the 1225 reissue of the Charter).[4] The presence of the notables was regarded as validating the gift. The wording of Magna Carta is that of a gift from the King to his Church and the freemen of England and Wales.

The document does not bear the title Magna Carta, in fact it is unnamed. The 1215 Charter contained three clauses relating to forest law. While the Norman kings granted lands to their followers, they retained large swathes themselves, which became known as the royal *demesne* (domain). Much of this was made up of forest

---

[1] D Douglas (ed), *English Historical Documents* I (London, 1973) No 54, 479.
[2] A collection of examples is found ibid I 480–62.
[3] See JR Maddicott, *The Origins of the English Parliament, 924–1327* (Oxford, 2002) 25.
[4] Below, Chapter 10

used by royalty and their guests for hunting expeditions. These royal forests were subject to their own laws with harsh penalties for those who broke them. Magna Carta 1215 sought to reduce the extent of royal forest and to curb the activities of local officials who administered it.[5] When the Charter was reissued in 1217 and again in 1225 these clauses were omitted and a separate and much more detailed Charter of the Forest granted.[6] The term 'magna' soon came to be used to differentiate the main Charter.

The Charter is sometimes said to have been signed; it was not. It was sealed with the royal seal, because that was the method used to authenticate a royal charter. Although it is expressed as a grant, it is the result of an apparent agreement between the King and his barons. Clause 63 recites that both the King and the barons have sworn an oath that its terms will be observed in good faith and without evil intent. It is not in the form of a treaty – that would have involved the exchange of counterparts. It was expressed to be 'given for the reform of the realm' on the advice of the senior clergy, certain named barons and 'others our faithful subjects'. This reflects the medieval notion that a King should rule with the advice of his magnates. The nature of government was at this time in the process of transition between assemblies of wise advisors and a representative parliament. Magna Carta was a step on the way. It was a kind of legislative act, but cannot properly be called a statute until, in 1297, it was confirmed by King Edward I to an early form of parliament and recorded in the statute book.

In practice, it was a political settlement. The introduction to clause 61 states that:

> [W]e have granted all these things to God for the better ordering of our kingdom and to allay the discord that has arisen between us and our barons and. . .we desire they shall be enjoyed in their entirety with lasting strength for ever.

Clause 62 provides that 'we have completely remitted and pardoned to all any ill will, grudge and rancour that have arisen between us and our subjects, clerk and lay, from the time of the quarrel'. The use of force as a means to an end was commonplace in medieval Europe. We have already noted the dysfunction within the royal family.[7] On two occasions (1173 and 1188) Henry II's sons, including Richard and John, rebelled against him. Richard I, before leaving on pilgrimage, extracted a promise from John not to come to England from Normandy while Richard was away, presumably because he feared his brother might attempt a coup. When Richard's Chancellor, William Longchamp, became unpopular, John broke his promise, returned and headed a party of barons who declared him regent. These family quarrels were patched up, but if the rebels of 1215 sought an example it was there in recent history.

Nevertheless, although they resorted to the threat of force, the rebels did not initially go so far as to dethrone the King. This may have been simply because they did

---

[5] Below, Chapter 13
[6] Below, Chapter 15
[7] See Chapter 2.

not have any credible alternative candidate for the throne. Whatever the motivation, however, Magna Carta was an attempt at a legal settlement, secured by the oaths of all parties. In effect, the rebels had negotiated what they saw as a compromise between themselves and the King. It was a compromise that the King was likely to reject if he could and in short time he did. The agreement also occurred at a time when custom was growing into law. The rebels were dissenting, but what they wanted was a return to the status ante quo – the good old days. They did not want so much to change the law as to return to the way they thought it had been administered from Anglo Saxon times. Like many later generations they were averse to change – something often misunderstood by politicians who are constantly promising it. William the Conqueror was more politic than this; he offered continuity, promising to uphold the laws of his predecessor, Edward the Confessor.[8] He maintained the old court system of the shire and hundred, though the word 'shire' came to be replaced by the French word 'comte', which became 'county' (maybe this makes 'county' cricket, 'French' cricket). William's successors followed his lead, repeating promises to uphold Edward's laws. Appeal to established custom dominated medieval thinking.

While the thinking behind the Charter was influenced by past custom, it also reflected the changes that flowed from the introduction after the Conquest of a strict feudal hierarchy. Most of the Norman and Angevin kings promised on their accession to rule justly; in order to gain the general support of their barons, they usually acknowledged that their predecessors had abused their position. Much of this 'abuse' related to how the Crown raised money and to how it exploited the legal system, in particular the levying of scutage in lieu of personal military service.

The introduction of feudalism inevitably produced legal innovation. Angevin government centralised power in the King's court, which was principally located in London but was also peripatetic. In turn, this resulted in the development of royal courts of justice, initially sitting where the King was and then relying on royal judges who either sat in London or travelled round the country. Crucially these royal courts developed important new procedures, particularly relating to land holding. There was also a growing recognition that some crimes were too grave to be dealt with in the old local courts. Treachery, murdrum, robbery and rape were breaches of the King's peace and punishable in his court. At least from the time of Henry II, these crimes were dealt with by royal judges travelling round the kingdom on circuits. High Court judges still visit the various Crown Courts around the country, following the ancient practice. Apart from charters, Anglo Saxon rulers had made use of less formal written orders to grant privileges.[9] The Normans found good use for these 'writs' and the royal courts soon issued them, summoning litigants to appear before them. Gradually royal judges built up a body of law that was common to all the kingdom – hence its continuing title of the common law. Several

---

[8] Below, Chapter 7
[9] F Barlow, *The Feudal Kingdom of England 1042–1261* (London, 1999) 44.

clauses of Magna Carta demonstrate that the rebels had an appetite for royal justice.

Although the Charter impresses as a practical document dealing with immediate problems, there is, however, an assumption behind its provisions that the King has broken law and established custom and must be made to observe them. The large number of provisions relating to legal procedure indicate that the rebels perceived that there were rules of law which ought to prevail over unpredictable acts of government.

Although it sought to re-establish an earlier state of affairs, there were clauses in the Charter which were on their face innovative, in the sense that other European Charters of Liberties did not have similar terms. They subjected the government to a degree of control not hitherto attempted. The argument as to whether tenants in chief were liable for scutage in respect of service outside England and Normandy was not specifically resolved. Clause 12, however, provided that 'no scutage or aid is to be levied in our realm unless by the common counsel of the realm', and clause 14 set out the mechanism for summoning the greater and lesser tenants of the King to provide that counsel. This obviously taps into the tradition in the Anglo Saxon charters that the King ruled with the advice of his magnates. They were regarded as speaking for the realm. Looking forward, the connection can be seen with the tag 'no taxation without representation'.

The Charter went even further than this. The rebel barons clearly did not trust John to keep his promises and so clause 61 provided that the barons were to choose a committee of 25 from among their number; if the King or his representatives broke the terms of the Charter, they could distress and distrain the King's property until redress was achieved. These clauses represent practical powers given to practical men to ensure that a particular agreement was honoured, rather than an attempt to establish a democratic Constitution. In any event they never took effect. When the Charter was reissued in 1216 by the regency government, clauses 12, 14 and 61 were omitted as they were in later confirmations. They were, however, powerful examples of subjects trying to control the actions of government and were not forgotten. We shall see that there was at least one example during Henry III's reign of the tenants in chief refusing to consent to a proposed tax, because they had not been summoned in accordance with clause 14 of the Charter.[10]

When the Charter was reissued in 1216, 1217 and 1225, there were other omissions apart from clauses 12, 14 and 61. Some clauses were amalgamated so that clauses 39 and 40 were now together clause 29. The Charter of 1225, which became the final form, contained 37 clauses as against 63 in the 1215 version. Later confirmations of the Charter in the thirteenth century traded taxation for liberties. In 1297 what might be regarded as a modern form of parliament agreed to supply Edward I with a fraction of the value of moveable property in return for the confirmation of the Charter. The parliament contained representatives of the 'commons'

---

[10] Below, Chapter 16

as well as the great barons, though these representatives were either knights or bur-gesses. The King recorded this confirmation as one of the earliest entries in his book of statutes.

Although the Charter of 1215 was expressed to bind the King's successors, later generations up to the fourteenth century insisted on its confirmation. Whatever its precise meaning, the aristocratic community plainly regarded it as of the first importance.

4

Religion

RELIGION AND MAGNA Carta may seem unlikely bedfellows, but the Church, at least, played a major part in the events leading to the Charter. The very first clause defines the relationship between Church and State:

[W]e have granted to God, and by this present charter have confirmed for us and our heirs in perpetuity, that the English Church shall be free, and shall have its rights undiminished, and its liberties unimpaired: we wish this to be observed as is evident from the fact that of our own free will, before the quarrel between us and our barons began, we conceded and confirmed by our charter the freedom of the Church's elections, which is thought to be of the greatest necessity and importance to the English church and obtained confirmation of this from the lord pope Innocent III, which we shall observe and wish our heirs to observe in good faith in perpetuity.

This clause had its own history, which is entwined with papal policy throughout Europe. By the death of Henry II of England in 1189, there were three important seats of temporal and one spiritual power in western Europe. The first temporal power was the Holy Roman Empire, which covered modern Germany and beyond and also the kingship of Lombardy in northern Italy. The second was the Angevin Empire, stretching from England down western France to Aquitaine in the south. Sandwiched between them was the much smaller kingdom of France, anxious to expand into its rivals' territories. The Pope in Rome was the spiritual leader, or, as he would have it ruler, of western Europe. The papacy actually had temporal power over a band of minor states stretching across middle Italy, known as the Papal States.

The origins of the Holy Roman Empire go back to the beginning of the ninth century. In 778 Pope Leo III came under serious attack in Rome, fled the city and turned to Charlemagne, King of the Franks, for help. He marched with an army to Rome, expelled Leo's enemies and was rewarded on Christmas Day 800 by being crowned Emperor of the Romans (the word Holy was added later), a title which survived until 1806. The Emperor's coronation oath came to include promises to be the faithful shield and protector of the Church. This new relationship, however, created continuing tensions, particularly with regard to clerical appointments. Eventually a compromise was reached in 1122 in the Concordat of Worms.[1] It was

---

[1] Generally on this see S Reynolds, 'Fiefs and Vassals, the Medieval Evidence Reinterpreted' (1997) 15(2) *Law and History Review*; RH Davis, *A History of Medieval Europe* (London, 1958).

agreed that throughout the Empire, after election by the canons of their houses, bishops and abbots would receive from the Pope the papal ring (the symbol of spiritual power) and receive their regalia from the Emperor with the lance (the symbol of earthly power). Within the Emperor's German territories, however, the election of bishops and abbots was to take place in the presence of the Emperor, who in case of discord could decide which of the competing parties had the right. This was a somewhat uneasy compromise, which inevitably led to trouble.

After their conquest of England, the Norman kings were determined to have bishops on whom they could rely. Hence the first two Archbishops of Canterbury were Lanfranc and Anselm, who, though both born in Italy, were Benedictine monks at the abbey of Bec in Normandy. When Henry I came to the throne in 1107 his right of succession was doubtful and he needed the support of the Church. The first clause of his Charter of Liberties declared the Church in England free. Little was said in detail. His grandson, Henry II, was more assertive. In 1164 he gathered together, at Clarendon in Wiltshire the great laymen of the kingdom and all the senior clergy, including Archbishop Thomas a Becket. He required them to inquire and recognise the customs, liberties and dignities of his predecessors, which ought to be observed in the kingdom.[2] Amongst other things, it forbade priests to leave the kingdom without the King's permission. It limited the Church's right to excommunicate in England. In clause 12 it provided that, where the office of an archbishop, bishop, abbot or prior fell vacant, the revenues of the see or monastery should fall to the Crown until a successor was appointed. The King should then summon the more important persons of the Church to his own chapel to elect a successor with his assent. Becket initially was prepared to agree them, but changed his mind. He was then summoned to the King's Council to meet charges of contempt of the King and previous malfeasance when Chancellor. He did attend, but then fled into exile. In due course Pope Alexander III sought a compromise and in 1170 Henry agreed to allow Becket back to Canterbury. He promptly excommunicated a number of Henry's supporters in the Church. Henry's equally prompt reaction led (though probably not intentionally) to Becket's murder.

Trouble brewed between King John and Pope Innocent III over the election of a new Archbishop of Canterbury. In July 1205 the incumbent, Hubert Walter, died. The monks in the chapter of the Cathedral had the right to appoint the next Archbishop, but in this case the chapter seems to have split into two camps. The chronicler, Roger of Wendover, gives an account of what happened.[3] Originally sub-prior Reginald was chosen by his fellow members of the chapter and hurriedly installed without obtaining the King's consent or following the usual ceremonies. Reginald travelled to Rome to obtain the Pope's confirmation of his office. By this time the secret installation had become common knowledge and a separate party of monks, possibly fearing for their safety, went to the King and asked him to appoint

---

[2] W Stubbs, Select Charters and other illustrations of English Constitutional History from the earliest times to the reign of Edward I (Oxford, 1870) 135.
[3] JA Giles (ed) *Flowers of History* II, 1215–238 and see Appendix A.

another. He told them that John Bishop of Norwich was a great friend of his and knew all his secrets and the rival party appointed him at the behest of the King and bishops. Both parties of monks argued their case before the Pope in Rome. Each contended that the election of the opposing candidate was null – opponents of Reginald said that his installation at night without the consent of the King or the usual ceremonies nullified it; his supporters said it was valid because the consent of the King was not required. The Pope sought to persuade the chapter collectively to elect Stephen Langton, whom Wendover describes as 'a man skilled in literary science and discrete and accomplished in his manners'. Some of the monks insisted that they did need the consent of the King, but the Pope responded that it was not 'the custom that consent of princes is to be waited for concerning elections in the apolistic see'. The Pope then ordered the chapter to elect Stephen and fearing excommunication they did.

John almost certainly regarded him as too much of an unknown quantity and a creature of the Pope.[4] What followed may be gleaned from the letters of Innocent III.[5] On 20 December 2006 the Pope threatened John with evil consequences if he did not accept the new Archbishop.[6] John did not bend and so in June 1206 Innocent wrote to the chapter at Canterbury saying he had consecrated Stephen. Stephen nevertheless remained on the continent. On 27 August 1207 the Pope wrote to the Bishops of London, Ely and Worcester ordering them to bid the King receive the Archbishop. If he refused, they were to publish a general interdict forbidding any ecclesiastical office in England, except baptism of infants and confession in dying. When John would not give way, the interdict issued. In the same year Langton himself wrote a pastoral letter to the English people:

> [W]hatever is imposed by a temporal king in prejudice of the eternal king produces, without doubt, sedition. Therefore, my beloved children, when any rebel persists in schism, the holy church has decreed that his vassals are absolved from fealty to him, through just retribution. Just as a schismatic tries to withdraw the fealty of his men from the eternal lord, their fealty is thereby withdrawn from the schismatic.[7]

In May 1208 the Pope instructed the Bishops of London, Ely and Worcester to confer the regalia if John would not do it.[8]

In January 1209 Innocent authorised Langton to go to England and negotiate with John, but also gave him power to excommunicate the King.[9] Langton arrived at Dover in October and travelled as far as Chilham near Canterbury. John would not meet him and so Langton pronounced his excommunication and left for the

---

[4] There is another account of these events in a chronicle written by Gervase of Canterbury, which suggests that John disliked Stephen because he had studied in the enemy country of France, W Stubbs (ed), *The Historical Works of Gervase of Canterbury* (London, 1879)

[5] See CR Cheney and MG Cheney, *The Letters of Pope Innocent III (1198–1216) Concerning England and Wales* (Oxford, 1967) nos 657, 699, 700, 701 and 725.

[6] ibid, no 725.

[7] K Major (ed), *Acta Stephani Langton Cantuariensis Archiepiscopi AD 1207–1228* (Oxford, 1950).

[8] Cheney and Cheney (n 5) nos 793 and 795.

[9] ibid, no 823; CR Cheney and WH Semple, *Selected Letters of Pope Innocent II (1198–1216) Concerning England* (London, 1963) no 37, p 110.

continent.[10] In January 1213 Innocent pronounced a sentence of deposition on John and authorised Philip Augustus of France to wage Holy War against England.[11] On 7 March Innocent wrote to Langton, saying that, as John was violating the peace between him and the English Church, none of his successors should be anointed king.[12]

These spiritual penalties were severe. An interdict suspended ecclesiastical rites within a particular territory. Excommunication meant exclusion from the communion of the Church – the excommunicant remained a member of the Church and could attend mass, but not take the eucharist (holy communion) or participate in any church liturgy. Deposition was undoubtedly the most controversial of these powers. The other sanctions depended on the regulation by a religious society of its members. Deposition sought to control those (albeit members of the Church) who had achieved power in the civil sphere. About 1075 Pope Gregory VII claimed the power to depose emperors in his *Dictatus Papae* and he deposed Emperor Henry IV, absolving all Christians from their oaths of loyalty to him. It was the penalty of deposition which made John finally succumb to papal authority.

It is remarkable that John held out against the Pope for six years. He could hardly have done this without support from his barons. Perhaps crucial was the support of the military orders. When in March 1208 the interdict was imposed on England, John immediately responded by seizing church property, including that of the military orders.[13] Both the Hospitallers and Templars, however, had their property swiftly restored to them. Almost certainly John saw the need for their support. When he decided to make his peace with the Pope in 1213, it was the Templars who negotiated on his behalf. John sent six envoys to Rome, two of whom were Templars. They, together with the Abbot of Beaulieu, reached Rome. The remaining three were taken captive on their way there and John passed money to the Templars to secure their release.

It was obviously not religious fervour but political realism that led John to succumb. By 1212 there were the first signs of baronial opposition, when rumours reached the King that De Vesci and Fitzwalter intended to murder him. Philip Augustus was making preparations to invade. John had already lost most of his territories in France to Philip and he could not risk losing England. He conducted a complete volte-face. He had sent negotiators to Rome in November 1212 and now he agreed not only to admit Stephen as Archbishop, but to surrender his kingdom to the Pope as his feudal lord and do fealty to him.[14] On 15 May 1213 the papal nuncio, Pandulph, arrived at Dover and, at the house of the Templars there, John surrendered the kingdom to him and issued a guarantee of the liberty of the Church in

---

[10] FM Powicke, *Stephen Langton*, Ford Lectures (Oxford, 1927) 77.
[11] ibid 78.
[12] Cheney and Cheney (n 5) no 910; Cheney and Semple (n 9) no 49, p 142.
[13] P Webster, 'Military Orders at the Court of King John' in PW Edbury (ed), *The Military Orders. Volume 5: Politics and Power* (Farnham, 2012).
[14] See JC Holt, *Magna Carta* (Cambridge, 2001) 216.

England.[15] He later repeated his submission at the high altar of St Paul's. Langton himself arrived in July and, according to Roger of Wendover, met John at the door of Winchester Cathedral. John, having sworn to love, defend and maintain the Church, was absolved from excommunication. Pending reparation by John for damage suffered by the Church, the interdict was not raised.

It is possible at this stage to see the beginning of the conflict between the new Archbishop and the Pope, which developed later. As soon as Stephen had arrived in England, the Pope despatched a papal legate, Nicholas de Tusculum, with supreme powers. In the short term the two men disagreed about Church appointments and the amount of restitution John should pay to the Church. Nicholas remained until the autumn.[16] Stephen may well have resented the fact that, having at last gained his see, the Pope should appoint someone, even temporarily, over him.

On 4 November 1213 Innocent accepted John's submission.[17] On 21 November 1214 John issued a Charter from the Temple guaranteeing the liberty of the Church. It was reissued and sealed on 15 January 1215[18] and the Pope incorporated its text in a letter to the English clergy on 30 March 1215.[19] This Charter is expressed to be a voluntary act carried out with the consent of the barons. It decrees that for the future in all and each of the churches, monasteries and cathedrals of England there will be free elections of whatever grade of prelate, great or small. 'After an election let our assent be sought, which . . . we will not refuse unless we have offered and lawfully proved some reasonable cause'.[20] On 4 March 1215 John took the Cross,[21] that is undertook to go on crusade. Those who undertook crusades received special protection from the Church. In 1146 Pope Eugenius granted absolution and remission of sins to those who undertook a crusade to free the Holy Land.[22] He added that until the crusader's return or proven death, no lawsuit should be instituted in regard to any property in his peaceful possession when he took the Cross. Moreover, he was freed from paying interest on any debt for the period of the crusade. The Fourth Crusade, earlier in Innocent's papacy between 1202 and 1204, had been diverted from its purpose of freeing the Holy Land by the attack and conquest of Constantinople. After John's undertaking, Innocent's main purpose was to ensure that the King did set out on crusade; any domestic conflict which distracted from this was to be stifled. At the Lateran Council in November 1215 Innocent organised a fifth crusade.

---

[15] Stubbs (n 2) 283–84; Cheney and Cheney (n 5) no 941.

[16] Powicke (n 10) 104.

[17] Cheney and Cheney (n 5) no 941.

[18] FM Powicke and CR Cheney, *Councils and Synods With Other Documents Relating to the English Church I* (Oxford, 1964) 2.

[19] Cheney and Semple (n 9) no 76, p 198.

[20] 'Post celebratum electionem noster requiratur assensus, quem similiter non denegabimus, nisi aliquid rationabile proposuerimus et legitime probaverimus propter quod non debeamus consentire'.

[21] Holt (n 14) 230.

[22] His predecessor, Urban, had granted a more limited concession: see DC Munro, *Urban and the Crusaders I*, (Philadelphia, 1894) 2, cited in Fordham University On Line Sourcebook.

On the 19 March 1215 the Pope wrote three letters to the King, magnates and Archbishop.[23] In the letter to the magnates he recited that he had heard news of dissensions between the King and some of the barons. He declared all sworn conspiracies formed against the King null and condemned any attempt to enforce claims by force of arms. He told the barons and knights to provide customary services humbly. He criticised the Archbishop for not mediating a settlement.

The obligations of the barons were more specifically stated in a further letter of 1 April from the Pope to the barons and knights ordering them to pay scutage for the Poitevin campaign and not delay the King's crusade.[24] This was followed by a letter later in the same month exhorting John to commence his crusade.[25] The time it took for letters to reach Rome and a reply to reach London meant that when the Pope wrote in July he was unaware of what had occurred at Runnymede. On 7 July he wrote to the Bishop of Winchester, the Abbot of Reading and the papal legate complaining that the rebels were worse than Saracens, since they were trying to drive from the kingdom the man on whom hope chiefly rested of aid for the Holy Land. Any disturbers of the King and kingdom were to be excommunicated and their lands placed under interdict. Their sentence was to be published and enforced.[26]

By 24 August the Pope did know of the Charter, for he issued a bull annulling it. It recited how John's sinfulness had led him to submit to the Pope as his vassal. It condemned the Charter,

> forbidding under ban of our anathema, the foresaid King to presume to observe it, and the barons and their accomplices to exact its performance, declaring it void and entirely abolishing both the Charter itself and the obligations and safeguards made either for its enforcements or in accordance with it, so that they are of no validity at any time whatsoever.

On the same date he wrote to the parties in England explaining his position and reciting the progress of the dispute up to Runnymede.[27] His account demonstrates his attachment to proper legal procedure and to judgment – a concern which mirrors that of the Charter itself. He opens by reciting his letter of 19 March to the rebels instructing them to render customary services 'since the king ought not to lose these services without a judicial decision'. He also states that he enjoined the King to treat his magnates kindly and hear their just petitions graciously. The rebels ought not to have thrown over their oaths of fealty: 'even if the king had wrongfully oppressed them, they should not have proceeded against him by constituting themselves both judges and executors of the judgement in their own suit'. The Pope then recited that when the envoys arrived in England with his letters of 19 March, the King offered to grant the rebels justice 'before us to whom the decision of this suit

[23] See Cheney and Cheney (n 5) no 1001; Cheney and Semple (n 9) no 74, p 194.
[24] Cheney and Cheney (n 5) no 1005; Cheney and Semple (n 9) no 77, p 203.
[25] Cheney and Semple (n 9) no 78, p 203.
[26] Cheney and Cheney (n 5) no 80.
[27] ibid, no 82.

belonged by reason or our lordship'. The rebels rejected the offer. The Pope wrote that the agreement at Runnymede was forced, illegal and unjust.

The letter of 24 August ordered the barons to renounce the settlement.[28] The civil war that ensued demonstrates that they ignored his demands.[29]As a result of his failure to publish the excommunication of the rebels, Langton was formally suspended from office.[30] Langton thereafter remained on the continent.[31] The Bishop of Winchester, the Abbot of Reading and the legate now excommunicated the rebels.[32]

Clause 1 of the Charter remains on the statute book. Ironically, since the Reformation in the sixteenth century the Head of State and Church are one. In practice those who nominate archbishops and bishops are the Church Appointments Commission, consisting of clergy and lay members of the Church. The Prime Minister, however, does nominate a chairman. By custom the Commission nominates two choices, indicating their preferred candidate, which the Prime Minister passes to the Queen for her consent. In 1987 the Commission recommended James Lawton Thompson for the office of Bishop of Birmingham. The Prime Minister, Margaret Thatcher, refused to put his name forward (it was suggested because of his left wing views) and instead put forward their second nomination, who was appointed. We wonder what Innocent III would have made of Margaret Thatcher or she of him.

---

[28] ibid, no 1019.
[29] Below, Chapter 5
[30] See Cheney and Semple (n 9) no 83, p 207.
[31] Powicke (n 10) 128 and 134.
[32] Cheney and Semple (n 9) no 85, p 221.

5

Rebellion

THE REBEL BARONS had all sworn an oath of fealty to King John. They were his vassals. On its face a vassal's oath to a lord had no limitation; it offered no mechanism for an oppressed vassal to break the bond. Oaths were central to legal and political organisation, for breaking one would damn the immortal soul of the oath taker. There are two legal treatises, one before and one after the grant of 1215, which throw an important light on the legal concepts and practices of the period. They are both entitled *A Treatise Concerning the Laws and Customs of England (Tractatus de legibus et consuetudinibus Angliae)*. The first, written around 1190, is ascribed to a royal judge, Ranulph de Glanvill. The other, which is partly modelled on Glanvill, is ascribed to Henry de Bracton, another royal judge. He wrote about 1250, but relied on a collection of cases going back to 1220.[1] Glanvill described the effect of a vassal swearing homage to his lord:

> Homage should be done in the following form: he who is to do homage shall become the man of his lord, swearing to bear faith of the tenement for which he does his homage and to preserve his earthly honour in all things, saving the faith owed to the lord King and his heirs. It is evident from this that a vassal may not attack his lord without faith of his homage, except perhaps in self defence or where he goes by royal command with the king's army against his lord.[2]

He does not define self-defence, yet from classical times there had been a recognition that a lord's conduct could become tyrannical. Aristotle in his *Politics* distinguished between those who seized power illegitimately and those who held power legitimately, but abused it. He defined a tyrant thus: 'one who rules without law, looks to his own advantage rather than that of his subjects and uses extreme and cruel tactics against his own people as well as others'. This tradition descended into medieval European thought. John of Salisbury was a priest who served Thomas a Becket and went into exile around the same time as his master. He wrote numerous letters to fellow clergy and in one of them, written in 1168, he defined a tyrant as one who oppresses the whole people by force, breaks the law or reduces people to slavery.[3] He described the Emperor Frederick Barbarossa's armed attack on the papacy as the crime of schism, which made him a tyrant. In a similar way, in 1207

---

[1] For both see Appendix A below.

[2] CDG Hall (ed), *The Treatise on the Laws and Customs of England, commonly called Glanvill* (Oxford, 1993)l IX, 103.

[3] WJ Millor and CN Brooke (eds), *Letters of John of Salisbury*, II, 272.

Archbishop Stephen Langton, in his letter to the English people, stated that if a lord persisted in schism his men were absolved from their fealty.[4] By 1213, however, John was no longer schismatic. He had submitted to the Pope's spiritual jurisdiction. Nevertheless these pronouncements by the Church must have encouraged the view that there were circumstances where a lay vassal could reject his fealty to his lord. About 1250 Bracton describes the role of a king: 'he is called rex not from reigning, but from ruling well, since he is a king as long as he rules well . . . but a tyrant when he oppresses by violent domination the people entrusted to his care'.[5]

None of these definitions deals with what is to be done if a lord becomes a tyrant. In fact, feudal practice did provide a mechanism for renouncing fealty. A formal act was required. It was known as the *diffidatio* (literally defiance), which could be performed by either lord or liege.[6] It is still used in Italian football when a player is sent off. The Magna Carta rebels are said to have performed this on 5 May 1215.[7] Some of the rebels also took the precaution of receiving absolution from a canon of Durham Cathedral, but this did not prevent their subsequent excommunication.[8]

Although John stretched his rights against his barons as far as they would go, his conduct hardly came within any of the definitions of tyranny. Yet there was a gradual groundswell against his government from 1212 onwards. There was a fault line in feudal organisation. The ruler initially needed the support of his vassals to assemble an army. Hence the right to maintain military knights was devolved. Yet this in itself resulted in over-mighty subjects, who had the ability to challenge the ruler with military force. What happened in 1215 was the result of realpolitik.

This fault line was exacerbated by John's attempt to bypass his Norman barons, appointing men from Touraine to important offices. Touraine lies south of Normandy in the Loire valley; its capital is Tours. In 1205 John was instrumental in the appointment of Peter de Roches, archdeacon of the Cathedral at Tours, as Bishop of Winchester, one of the most senior posts in the English Church.[9] Peter remained a loyal supporter of the King during the period the latter was excommunicated and in 1213 was made John's Chief Justiciar. It was Peter who swiftly performed the coronation of Henry III after John's death. During John's reign, probably under Peter's patronage, a number of men from Touraine were appointed to positions of importance. These were men probably of low social standing, who had made their names as mercenaries.[10] They are named in clause 50 of the Charter. No doubt the Anglo-Norman barons saw them as aliens; clause 51 undertook to remove all alien soldiers. Clause 50 is very specific:

---

[4]   FM Powicke, *Stephen Langton*, Ford Lectures (Oxford, 1927) 97.
[5]   SE Thorne (ed), *The Laws and Customs of England* II (Cambridge, MA, 1977) f 305.
[6]   See G Althoff, J Fried and P Geary, *Medieval Concepts of the Past* (German Historical Institute, 2008).
[7]   See WS McKechnie, Magna Carta Commemoration Essays ed Malden (London, 1917) 5.
[8]   ibid.
[9]   See Nicholas Vincent, *Peter Roches: An Alien in English Politics* (Cambridge, 1996).
[10]   ibid 18; and cf below, Chapter 13

We will dismiss completely from their offices the relations of Girard D'Athee that henceforth they shall have no office in England, Engelard de Cigogne, Peter and Andrew and Guy de Chanceaux, Guy de Cigogne, Geoffrey de Martigny, with his brothers, Philip Mark with his brothers and nephew Geoffrey and all their followers.[11]

Girard d'Athee was made sheriff of Herefordshire and Gloucestershire to counter the power of William de Braose. He was dead by 1215, but had been replaced in those offices by a relative of his, Engelard de Cigogne.[12] Mark had a special significance since he was sheriff of Nottinghamshire.[13]

It is not easy to identify a single issue that bound all the rebels together. Various resentments had grown up during John's reign and indeed before under his Angevin forbears. By his marriage to Eleanor of Aquitaine, Henry II had acquired Poitou which lay between her major lands in Aquitaine and his in Maine. The lords of Poitou proved difficult to subdue. John's treatment of his prisoners after the Battle of Mirebeau (including Arthur) lost him support in France and by 1204 he had lost all but Aquitaine to Philip Augustus, King of France.[14]

In 1214 John saw an opportunity to defeat Philip. John formed an alliance with the Holy Roman Emperor, his nephew Otto Duke of Brunswick, and the Count of Flanders. He mounted an expedition to Poitou with the intention of luring Philip there, leaving Otto and the Count to advance on Paris. Unfortunately for John, his allies were slow in assembling and Otto's army was defeated at the Battle of Bouvines in Flanders in July 1214. Some of John's local supporters withdrew and he retreated to La Rochelle and eventually England. Philip Augustus forced John into a disadvantageous truce. John was now extremely vulnerable at home. He returned to England a failure; he was heavily in debt from an expensive campaign and now had to pay 40,000 marks to Philip, as the price of the truce. The English nicknamed him Softsword or Lackland. In October 1214 he sought to enforce the liabilities of his barons for scutage in respect of his Poitevin campaign. Some barons had refused to pay for this before he left England, on the ground that they were not obliged to pay scutage in respect of wars outside England and Normandy. This became a focus for claims for redress of other grievances.

In modern times, when a great deal of military service is foreign, it seems strange that objection to overseas service should have seemed so important. The argument was that an undertaking in the oath of fealty to protect the sovereign did not extend to supporting him when he was attempting foreign conquest. The definition of what could be required of a 'man' by his lord, however, was never exact and in any event in 1214 John was seeking to regain lands that had once been his. For the Poitevin campaign John levied scutage at three marks per fee, the highest amount ever demanded.[15] Some barons in the north of England refused to pay this, as did Robert

---

[11] For their background see Vincent (n 9) 33.
[12] See S Painter, *The Reign of King John* (Baltimore, MD, 1949) 206.
[13] Below, Chapter 13.
[14] Above, Chapter 1.
[15] JC Holt, *Magna Carta* (Cambridge, 2001) 190.

Fitzwalter, one of the leaders of the southern rebels. Many of those from the south of the kingdom, however, who became rebels, did go to and fight in Poitou. Some no doubt did so in performance of their fealty; others, such as William Malet, who had heavy debts to the Crown, may well have gone in the hope that later they could compromise their indebtedness. There was far from a united front on this issue. When the rebels refused to pay scutage, John mounted a punitive expedition to the north of England, but Archbishop Langton pursued him and, overtaking his force at Nottingham, persuaded the King to submit the dispute about payment of scutage to legal judgment.[16] This never happened. When the rebels first crystallised their demands around January 1215 they included limitation on the obligation to perform knight service to war in England and Normandy and Brittany and set a fixed amount for scutage.[17] When they came to finalise their demands in early June 1215, however, there was no clause limiting the geographical liability for the tax and no set amount. Instead there was provision for the King's Council to set the amount.[18] The Charter itself follows the same pattern. The change may have been the result of negotiation with the King's representatives; it may owe something to the fact that by June there were several among the rebels who had fought in the campaign in Poitou. While opposition to the payment of scutage can be seen as the trigger for rebellion, it is difficult to see it as the sole or even overwhelming cause.

Perhaps a more compelling factor for the rebels was the increasing amounts claimed by John from heirs of tenants in chief to take up inheritances or to obtain permission to marry. The grant of land by a lord to a vassal theoretically ended with the death of either. In practice an heir was allowed usually to enter his inheritance on payment of a fine. Similarly a tenant in chief or his children required the King's consent to marry and would also pay a fine to achieve this. A fine was not a punishment, but a payment proffered to finish the matter. Like scutage, these fines were an accepted practice, but many of the rebels were young or had only recently inherited and had had to pay large sums to do so. Some examples will suffice: Roger Bigod paid 1,000 marks in 1189 to inherit and 2,000 marks in 1211 to compound his debts to the Crown. In 1213 John de Lacy paid 7,000 marks to inherit. Geoffrey de Mandeville, who inherited the earldom of Essex in 1213, sought consent in 1214 to marry Isabella, John's former Queen, whose marriage to the King had been annulled for consanguinity. Geoffrey agreed to pay the enormous sum of 20,000 marks to obtain it. The fine was to be paid in four instalments, the first payable before John departed for Poitou, but Geoffrey was unable to pay.[19]

As John became increasingly distrustful of his barons, he took to destroying their castles and demanding and taking members of their families as hostages. He obeyed the Pope's condition that De Vesci and Fitzwalter should be readmitted to the king-

---

[16] Powicke (n 4) 118.
[17] Below, Chapter 9.
[18] Below, Chapter 9.
[19] For these examples and others see Holt (n 14) 190–91 and Appendix B.

dom, but before they arrived he destroyed their castles.[20] He also forced others to offer their castles as a pledge of their fealty. Among them were the castles of Pontefract and Donington held by John de Lacy, who became a rebel. In 1216 the King seized the castle at Donington and de Lacy then reverted to the royal cause.[21] Requiring property or hostages as security for fealty had occurred both before and after John's reign. For instance, William Marshal had been given by his father as a hostage to King Stephen in 1159. When William's father sided with Queen Matilda, Stephen threatened to execute the boy. William's father defied Stephen, who spared the boy because he had come to like him. In his turn John took William's children as hostages.[22] In a variation on this theme, when John de Lacy agreed to pay 7,000 marks for his inheritance, 20 of his tenants were required to guarantee his fidelity, undertaking to remain loyal to the Crown in the event of his defection.[23]

Some of the rebels had personal grievances. Thus Robert Fitzwalter complained to the King of France that John had tried to ravish his daughter.[24] He also resented the fact that the King had not taken his side in various legal disputes. Saer de Quincy considered that he had been unlawfully deprived of his castle at Montsorrel in Leicestershire. William de Montfichet had been deprived of custody of the Royal Forests in Essex. There was a good deal of opportunism. Some of the rebels joined after the fall of London, some returned later to the royal cause.

John may have exploited feudal dues more rigorously than his forbears, but they were all part of an accepted mechanism for the Crown obtaining income and securing loyalty. If it is difficult to identify a single issue as the principal cause of rebellion, there was undoubtedly a sense among the rebels that John had gone too far, but that hardly made him a tyrant in the classic sense. There were barons who remained loyal to him. Moreover the rebels did not initially seek to depose him. Contemporary documents indicate a readiness on the part of the rebels to negotiate. It was only after the Pope had annulled the Charter at John's request, that they invited Prince Louis of France to take the English Crown. His claim to the throne was based on the fact that his wife was a daughter of Henry II.

We have already noted many of the principal events which led up to Runnymede, but now we look at the course of negotiations in more detail, including contemporary documents which throw light on it. On 1 November 2014 John met with some of the rebels at Wallingford and offered to restore their ancient liberties, though these do not seem to have been defined.[25] A variety of sources indicate that the King met with representatives of the rebels in London on 6 January 1215.[26] Roger of Wendover describes the King spending Christmas at Winchester 'after which he

[20] HWC Davis (ed), *Essays in History, Presented to R L Poole* (Oxford, 1927) 274–79.

[21] See Holt (n 14) 193–94.

[22] See *L'Histoire de Guillaume le Marechal*.

[23] See Holt (n 14) 195 and references there given.

[24] F Michel (ed), *Histoire des Ducs de Normandie* (Paris, 1840) 119–25.

[25] J Stevenson (ed), *Ralph de Coggeshall, Chronicum Anglicanum*, Rolls Series (London, 1875) 167; Holt (n 14) 221.

[26] Holt (n 14) reviews these at 222 and 225.

hurried to London and took up his abode in the New Temple'.[27] There the nobles 'came to him in gay military array and demanded the King confirm the liberties and laws of King Edward and those contained in Henry I's Charter of liberties'.[28] This chimes with a document which historians have called the Unknown Charter. It was first publicised on a significant scale by Professor JH Round in 1893.[29] Both its authenticity and date have been the subject of considerable academic dispute.[30] The best view seems to be that it was genuine and dates from around the time of the January meeting. It initially recites the whole of Henry's Charter and then adds 12 additional clauses. It is limited in scope and rather crudely drafted. It is in the form of concessions that the King says he makes, so it seems to be a draft grant. Most of its clauses are concerned with feudal incidents. In clause 7 of the additional clauses there is a concession that the King will not exact military services outside England except in Normandy and Brittany. Clause 8 limits the amount of scutage to one mark per knight's fee; if more is required that must be approved by the council of barons.

At the January meeting further consideration of the demands of the rebels was deferred; they were given safe conduct until 26 April, when the King said he would answer their demands at Northampton. Before the London meeting, John had already sent royal agents to Rome to argue his cause; after the London meeting the rebels sent agents to Rome to argue theirs.[31] The Pope's letters of 19 March and 1 April, quoted in the last Chapter 4, make it clear that the Pope accepted the royal case. The rebels nevertheless intended to keep the meeting at Northampton. Their first muster was in Easter week at Stamford. Roger of Wendover[32] describes how by this time the original rebels had 'induced all the nobility of the whole kingdom to join them and constituted a very large army . . . computed at two thousand knights, besides horse soldiers, attendants and foot soldiers'.[33] The muster did not include all the nobility because some certainly joined after the fall of London and others remained loyal to John. The muster was followed by a march south, in the course of which the principal rebels from East Anglia joined them.[34] The King did not keep the appointment at Northampton, although he sent representatives. According to Roger of Wendover by the end of the week after Easter[35] the rebels were at Brackley in south Northamptonshire and the King at Oxford. He sent to enquire of them which laws they wished confirmed. When he saw their written response, John cried: 'Why amongst these unjust demands did not the barons ask for my kingdom also?

---

[27]   This is a reference to the headquarters of the Knights Templar just south of Fleet Street on the edge of the City.

[28]   JA Giles (ed), *Flowers of History* , II (London, 1849) Part 1, 304.

[29]   JH Round, 'An Unknown Charter of Liberties' (1893) viii *English Historical Review* 288.

[30]   See Appendix A and Holt (n 14) App IV.

[31]   CR Cheney and MG Cheney, *The Letters of Pope Innocent III (1198–1216) Concerning England and Wales* (Oxford, 1967).

[32]   See Appendix A.

[33]   Giles (n 27) II, Part 1, 305.

[34]   W Stubbs (ed), *Memoriale fratris Walteri de Coventria*, Rolls Series 2nd edn (London, 1872) ii 219.

[35]   Easter Day appears to have been 19 April.

Their demands are vain and visionary and are unsupported by any degree of reason'.[36]

The rebels must have concluded shortly after that they could not take their case further by negotiation, because on 5 May they renounced their fealty. It is not clear when the King learnt of this, but on 9 May he issued a Charter offering to submit the differences between himself and the rebel barons to the papal curia.[37] The Charter grants that four barons selected by the King and four selected by the barons, who are hostile to him, are to appear in Rome

> so that the Lord Pope may preside over them concerning all the questions and articles which they seek from us and which they themselves shall propose, and to which we shall respond that we shall wait during their consideration[38] and we shall do that which they themselves shall resolve.

The next day the King issued a further Charter undertaking to the rebel barons that none of them would be taken or disseised nor would he go against them by force or arms except according to the law of the kingdom or by judgment of their peers in 'curia nostra' (our court), until the papal court had considered the 'facta'.[39] These are the offers to which the Pope appears to refer in his letter of 24 August 1215.[40] By the time these Charters had been issued, however, the Pope's letters of 19 March and 1 April would have reached England and they demonstrated that any hearing in the papal curia would be unlikely to result in victory for the rebels.[41]

The rebels' march south apparently prompted John to offer a truce until 21 May, if Archbishop Langton announced it. Whether it was announced or, if so, whether it reached the rebels, is not clear. What is clear is that the balance of power shifted dramatically when on 17 May London admitted the rebels. Roger of Wendover describes how the rebels arrived outside the walls early on the Sunday morning and 'entered the city without any tumult while the inhabitants were performing divine service . . . the rich citizens were favourable to the rebels and the poor ones were afraid to murmur against them'.[42] It appears that there was at least a pro-rebel party in the City, because the doors of the City were opened to let them in. Some of the powerful East Anglian rebels had strong links with the City.[43]

Since the Conquest there had been three castles there – the Tower, and Baynard and Montfichet castles. The Mandeville family had in the past been Constables of the Tower. Robert Fitzwalter not only held the barony of Dunmow in Essex, but also that of Castle Baynard (near the modern Queen Victoria Street). With this

---

[36] Giles (n 27) II, Part 1, 306.

[37] The text is to be found in Holt (n 14) no 3 in App 11.

[38] The Latin word *considerationem* bore a more decisive meaning than the modern 'consider'. It might be preferable to translate it as 'arbitration'.

[39] Cheney and Cheney (n 30) no 4.

[40] Above, Chapter 4.

[41] See Chapter 4.

[42] Giles (n 27) II, Part 1, 307; he puts the date as 24 May though scholars now put it as the 17th – see Holt (n 14) 241.

[43] This is dealt with in more detail below Chapter 11.

barony went the right to carry the standard of the City and to command its militia. Although John had razed Baynard Castle to the ground in 1213, the barony still retained its rights. Richard Montfichet was one of the rebels. London was not only the capital and commercial heart of England, but it also effectively blocked the way of foreign mercenaries entering the country at Dover. Before London fell John obviously felt able to resist the barons' demands virtually totally. Now he was forced to the negotiating table. Over the period 18 May to 15 June he issued various safe conducts to enable the rebels to travel to Staines.[44]

Somewhere about this time the document that later historians have named the Articles of the Barons was drawn up.[45] It commenced with the words 'these are the articles which the Barons seek and the King concedes'. This description is reinforced by clause 48, which states 'so these are all the customs and liberties which the king has conceded'. In form, therefore, it appears to be another draft charter awaiting grant by the Crown. It apparently bore the King's seal, which suggests it was at least some form of preliminary agreement.[46] All of its clauses have an equivalent in the final Charter, though the wording is sometimes amended. It has 12 fewer clauses than the final Charter, but the additional ones relate to clauses which do appear in the Articles. It launches straight into regulation of feudal incidents – there is no clause guaranteeing the freedom of the Church. Its first clause is the second in Magna Carta.

It is quite clear that the Articles constitute a much more sophisticated document than the earlier Unknown Charter. Whereas the former relied on additions to Henry I's Charter of Liberties, the Articles do attempt comprehensive regulation of feudal society. James Holt in his *Magna Carta* suggests that it may have been drawn up by a Chancery ie government clerk. Saer de Quincy received a safe passage on 25 May to come and speak with the King and Langton and the barons received one on the 27th of that month; there was a period in which negotiation must have taken place and the Articles may very well belong to this period. Whether the barons had the services of lawyers sympathetic to their cause or whether the royal draftsmen were made available to them cannot be established with certainty.

There was considerable amendment to the Articles in the Charter. Thus comparison can be made of clause 1 of the Articles and Clause 2 of the Charter.

> *Articles Clause 1*: after the decease of an ancestor heirs of full age shall have their inheritance at the ancient relief expressed in a charter
>
> *Magna Carta Clause 2*: If any of our barons, or others holding of us in chief by knight service shall die, and at his death his heir be of full age and owe relief, he shall have his inheritance on payment of the ancient relief, namely the heir or heirs of an earl £100 for a whole earl's barony, the heir or heirs of a baron £100 for a whole barony, the heir or heirs of a knight 100 shillings at most for a whole knight's fee; and anyone who owes less shall give less according to the ancient usage of fiefs.

---

[44] See Holt (n 14) 242.
[45] See Appendix A and Holt (n 14) App V, which has the Latin text.
[46] Holt (n 14) 256.

There is surely the hand of a lawyer at work. Fixing the amounts of relief would have been something that the rebels wanted, not the King. The amendments between the Articles and the Charter do not appear to be mere legal tidying up, but the outcome of further demands and concessions.

There has been considerable academic debate about the date when the Articles came into existence.[47] For negotiation and drafting to take place in the detail evidenced above would have taken at least some days. For our purposes the exact date is not important; the Articles are principally of significance for the light they and the earlier Unknown Charter throw on the Great Charter itself. Moreover, the Articles of the Barons would not have been forgotten after the original Charter was annulled; when the Charter was reissued in 1225 former rebels were among those who witnessed it.[48] They would have been well aware that the Articles contained clauses equivalent to 12 and 61 of the 1215 Charter, exemplifying conciliar control of the Crown. In 1225 that control was created by bargaining reissue of the Charter for taxation.

What happened at Runnymede can be gleaned from a document entitled Electio Hugonis.[49] Hugo had been elected the Abbot of St Edmondsbury. He went to Windsor to receive the King's consent to his appointment, arriving on 9 June. He found both the King and Simon Langton there and was told to attend at a meadow in Staines the next day. He did so and after a long delay the consent was given. The coincidence of time and place strongly suggests that the barons or their representatives met there with the King on the 10th. The eventual grant was not until 15 June. It seems likely that some form of final agreement was reached on the 10th, leaving the intervening days for redrafting. It may even be that the Articles of the Barons were produced on the 10th. Roger of Wendover describes the meeting thus:

> [T]he king and the nobles came to the appointed conference and, when each party had stationed themselves apart from the other, they began a long discussion about the terms of peace . . . at length after various points on both sides had been discussed, King John saw that he was inferior in strength to the barons and without raising any difficulty granted the underwritten laws and liberties.[50]

Some of the rebels' demands were clearly watered down between the Unknown Charter in January and the final draft, for instance provisions on the levying of scutage were weakened in the King's favour.[51] On the 19th all parties swore to observe the terms of the Charter and it is probable that a sealed version was produced at this date. Although John had little intention of abiding by its terms, the fact that negotiation occurred does indicate that he, or at least his advisors, thought that he might be held to its provisions.

---

[47] See Appendix A and Holt (n 14) 429.
[48] Below, Chapter 15.
[49] 168ff.
[50] Giles (n 27) II, 309.
[51] Below, Chapter 9.

6

Freemen

WE HAVE SEEN that clause 1 of Magna Carta (apart from granting the freedom of the Church in England) grants the liberties it sets out in the succeeding clauses to all freemen of the kingdom. In addition, freemen are specifically referred to in clauses 15, 20, 27, 30 and 39. The English language, deriving from its Anglo Saxon and Latin roots, sometimes has two words which mean more or less the same. Thus the Germanic *freidom* and the Latin *libertas* appear equivalent. They both distinguish between someone who has a master and one who does not. Magna Carta, being in Latin, uses the latter, so that a freeman is *liber homo*. This apparent similarity, however, should not mask a critical difference between the medieval use of the words and their modern usage. Liberty was a privilege. The fact that the grant in the Charter was confined to a limited class of men who were free, by itself demonstrates this. The liberties of the Cities were privileges that only their citizens could call upon. In fact in a feudal society no one, apart from the King, was truly free and even he owed duties to others. The theory of feudal organisation was that the King owned the whole kingdom; he transferred possession of parcels of land to his tenants in chief, but they owed him service in return. They gave possession of lesser parcels to men who became their vassals, that is they owed service to their immediate lord, which could be of different kinds. Freedom came to be defined in terms of the kind of service owed.

'Feudal' and 'feudalism' were not terms which were used in the Middle Ages. The word feudal is not found until the seventeenth century and feudalism not until the nineteenth. Some modern medievalists reach for their crossbows when these terms are applied over generously.[1] When later historians began to use the word 'feudal' they derived it from the 'feodum' (German 'fief' or 'feof'), which was the medieval term for the land passed by a lord to a vassal, subject to the duty to provide services to the lord. In 842 the former possessions of Charlemagne the Great were divided into three, one of them being the foundation of modern France – a name derived from Charlemagne's Frankish kingdom. The divided possessions lacked the power of the old Empire and the succeeding monarchs of the divisions found it difficult to raise sufficient armed forces. As a result they took to passing control of parts of their lands to local aristocracy in return for an obligation to supply troops in time of war.

---

[1] E Brown, 'The Tyranny of a Construct' (1974) 79(4) *American Historical Review* 1063; S Reynolds, 'Fiefs and Vassals: The Medieval Evidence Reinterpreted' (1997) 15(2) *Law and History Review*.

This system of landholding eventually became established in Normandy. The Normans were Vikings who had gone native in France.[2] Viking literally means 'men of the fjords'. In the eleventh century they were the most skilful boat builders and warriors in northern Europe. Pressure on resources caused them to travel abroad, at first to plunder and then settle. From 830 they began to settle in eastern England. Other Vikings raided and settled in northern France.[3] In 885 Hrolf, from what is now Norway, led a Viking band which sailed up the Seine as far as Paris and besieged it. The siege failed, but they retreated to an area around modern Rouen and settled there. About 911 the French King Charles III (or Simple) granted a feof to Hrolf of an area along the Seine and gave him the high title of Duke, in return for which Hrolf swore fealty to the French Crown. To validate his oath Hrolf converted to Christianity. Chroniclers changed his name into the Latin form of Rollo. Rollo sub-enfeoffed the land to his followers and some 5,000 warriors became Christian. Many of them married local women and soon adopted the Frankish language. Their assimilation was remarkably rapid. Eventually William the Bastard succeeded to the dukedom, though his accession was marked by rebellion and violence.[4]

There were already Norman influences in England before William conquered it; the mother of Edward the Confessor, his predecessor as King of England, was the daughter of a Duke of Normandy. Edward was brought up in Normandy and once King of England used Norman advisors. Nevertheless there was not such a clearly defined feudal organisation in England as in Normandy. That all changed with the conquest. The country was now controlled by Norman aristocracy from their rapidly erected castles. Land was the principal source of wealth, but agricultural methods remained relatively primitive. Agricultural production was limited and this led on the one hand to a lord's insatiable hunger for service and lesser men's willingness to trade their services for land.[5] This was an economic driver until the devastation of the population by the Black Death effectively freed the labour market.

Bracton describes the military relationship between the King and his barons and knights thus:

> There are other powerful persons under the king, who are called barons, that is belli robur, the strength of war. . . others are called vavasours, men of great dignity . . . vessels selected for strength . . . also under the king are knights, that is persons chosen for exercising military duties, that they may fight with the king and those mentioned above.[6]

He defines homage as the

> legal bond by which one is constrained to warrant, defend and acquit his tenant in his seisin against all persons for a service certain, described and expressed in the gift, and also,

---

[2] Generally on this section see N Davies, *The Isles* (Oxford, 1990) 240–80.
[3] See F McLynn, *1066: The Year of the Three Battles* (London, 1998) 21.
[4] ibid.
[5] See R Faith, *The English Peasantry and the Growth of Lordship* (Leicester, 1997) 201.
[6] S Thorne (ed), *Bracton, The Laws and Customs of England* (Cambridge, MA, 1977) f 32.

conversely, whereby the tenant is bound and constrained in return to keep faith to his lord and perform the service due.[7]

Seisin meant possession of land.

By 1215 the pattern of feudal relationships had become complicated. There were freemen and free tenements. Both carried obligations to a lord. A freeman might hold land on a servile tenure without affecting his free status and on occasion a person of servile status was granted a free tenement.[8] Land was held rather than owned and it was always held of another.[9] There was a great deal of sub-infeudation, land being divided into parcels let to different people down a chain of varying obligations. There were a variety of servile tenures, the principal being villeinage (the largest by a long way), but there were also bordars, cottars and slaves.

How many free tenements were there? The Hundred Rolls for 1279 for the shires of Bedford, Buckingham, Oxford, Huntingdon, Warwick and Cambridge reveal that about 30 per cent of land holdings were free.[10] How many freemen were there? Although the Domesday Book was drawn up more than a century earlier, it does provide some guide. HC Darby has analysed the classes of men catalogued in the Book throughout the kingdom.[11] Note that it analyses men, not women or children, so that it is in effect looking at heads of households. Freemen represented about one-seventh of the total population. This figure was much greater than the number of earls, barons and knights, but much less than the bulk of the population who were in some form of bondage. There were about twice as many slaves as freemen. Slavery was a recognised state from classical times. Anselm, when Archbishop of Canterbury, persuaded a Council of the English Church in 1100 to pass a resolution condemning the sale of men like cattle and this may have served to reduce the number of slaves. If this evidence throws only limited light on the position a century or more later, it is at least sufficient to state that the number of freemen was a not insubstantial section of the population. It included men who were not great landowners. In Suffolk and Norfolk, where the greatest number of freemen were to be found, there were many peasants who held land on a personal basis, rather than a servile one.[12]

Free status was of great importance. The common law courts developed procedures to protect freemen. The writ *de libertate probanda* was taken out before the royal courts to protect free status. If it were proved, any action relating to the freeman had to be heard in the royal courts.[13] Proof was usually by relatives or neighbours swearing an oath that the claimant was free.[14] By Bracton's time the decision might be made by a jury. Thus he states:

[7]   ibid, f 228.

[8]   See A Harding, *England in the Thirteenth Century* (Cambridge, 1993) 109.

[9]   ibid.

[10] EA Kominsky, *Studies in the Agrarian History of England*, trans R Kisch (London, 1966) 198–206.

[11] HC Darby, *Domesday England* (London, 1977) App 3.

[12] T Williamson, *The Origins of Norfolk* (Manchester, 1992).

[13] See Harding (n 8) 96 and 164.

[14] ibid 173.

if one raises the exception of villeinage let him have his proof at once . . . by proof of kindred . . . and according as the tenant proves his exception, the assize will remain or proceed unless both the plaintiff and tenant freely or of necessity, without the production of
kindred, put themselves on the assize in the manner of a jury, whereupon the matter will
be determined by the jury.[15]

By the same token a lord could claim back a villein who had left his land by issuing
the writ *de nativo habendo* (literally for having the bondman). The writ ordered the
sheriff to return the claimant's villein to him.

The definition of a freeman was not simple. Bracton divides persons into men,
women and hermaphrodites.[16] The last were classed as men or women according to
the closest resemblance of sexual organs. 'Women differ from men in many respects
as their position is inferior to men'.[17] They were subject to the rod.[18] Although they
were in effect their husband's chattel, married women could be classified as free as
appears from some of the examples given below. Bracton deals with illegitimate
offspring and the disabled thus:

> Those born of unlawful intercourse, as out of adultery or the like, are not reckoned among
> children, nor those procreated perversely against the way of human kind, as where a
> woman brings forth a monster or a prodigy. But an offspring who has a larger number of
> members as one who has six fingers, or it has but four, will be included among
> children.[19]

Bracton divides all men into bond and free.[20] He uses the Latin word *servi*, literally
slaves, which his modern editor Thorne translates as 'bond', probably because there
were various kinds of bond in English law apart from slavery and even the effect of
slavery was not exactly the same in the two systems of law. 'Freedom is the natural
power of every man to do what he pleases unless forbidden by law or force'.[21]
Bracton offers a justification for servitude as

> an institution of the jus gentium (law of the peoples, universal to all) by which contrary to
> nature one person is subjected to the dominion of another . . . from ancient times it was
> the practice of princes to sell captives and thus preserve rather than destroy them.[22]

Free status was decided by birth. There were complicated rules which decided a
man's status where he had one free and one bond parent. According to Bracton, the
basic rule appears to have been that a child born out of wedlock followed the mother's condition, in wedlock the father's. There were, however, more detailed rules in
which the nature of the tenement where birth occurred could be decisive. Thus a
man could be called freeborn 'if he is born of an unfree mother and a free father,

---

[15] Thorne (n 6) vol III f 106.
[16] ibid, f 29.
[17] ibid, f 31.
[18] ibid, f 36.
[19] ibid, f 31.
[20] ibid, f 29.
[21] ibid, f 29.
[22] ibid, f 30.

provided he was born outside the villein tenement and in a free bed and provided he was born in wedlock'.[23] Conversely 'if a villein has connexion with a free woman in a free tenement, their offspring will be free if they are married or if it is a villein tenement bond'.[24]

By 1215 a number of privileges and obligations attached to free status, such as the right to bear arms. These came to be regarded almost as definition of the status. The Assize of Arms in 1187 provided as follows:

> Whoever holds a single knight's fee shall have a breast plate and helmet, shield and lance and every knight shall have as many breastplates, helmets, shields and lances as he has knight's fees in his domain.
>
> Every free layman who has chattels or rent in the value of 16 marks shall have breast-plate, helmet shield and lance and every freeman who has in chattels and rent ten marks shall have hauberk, iron handpiece and lance.[25]

The obligation to provide arms appears to fall on the freeman.

Freemen could also provide agricultural services. Villeins habitually did and distinction was made between various kinds of service. Some, for example ploughing, were regarded as more servile than others. The ultimate test appears to have been whether the services were set or at the will of the lord.[26] Bracton describes villein service thus: 'pure villeinage is one for which uncertain and indeterminate service is furnished, where one cannot know in the evening the service to be rendered in the morning'.[27] The freeman while providing his fixed service was supplied with food while he worked for the lord and also had the right to eat at his table at Christmas.[28]

As Magna Carta itself demonstrates a freeman had access to the royal courts on proof of his free status. By Henry II's reign it was established that no man should have to answer for his free tenement without a royal writ. This effectively limited proceedings relating to land in the royal courts to that held freely.[29] It also became recognised that a freeman's heir could inherit. A freeman could marry off the lord's land or into a different legal category, but lords came to exact fines if the free tenant did either of these.[30] A villein by contradistinction could not leave his lord's land or marry without his lord's consent. He could not alienate his land and the land could be sold with his services attached.[31] He was his lord's chattel.[32] He could be given reasonable chastisement by his lord, though the common law courts would protect him from over-harsh treatment.[33]

---

[23] ibid, f 31.

[24] ibid, f 30.

[25] W Stubbs, *Select Charters and other illustrations of English Constitutional History from the earliest times to the Reign of Edward I* (Oxford, 1913) 147.

[26] Faith (n 5) 261.

[27] Thorne (n 6) II f 26.

[28] Faith (n 5) 259.

[29] ibid 245.

[30] ibid 252–54.

[31] ibid 255 and Harding (n 8) 3–16 and 38.

[32] Harding (n 8) 3–16 and 38.

[33] See Thorne (n 6) f 34 and Harding (n 8) 127.

The status of a man was therefore decisive in determining the life he led. Earlier instances of concessions by rulers on the continent of Europe were limited to a much narrower class than freemen, so that their inclusion in the Charter was a significant step forward. Why did the Charter include them? It is impossible at this distance of time to know for sure. The rebels probably wanted a wide support base. One possibility is that freemen were regarded as part of the community of the realm. Their right to bear arms made them part of the military establishment. Their access to the royal courts made them part of a legal community.

There is a problem of construction between the various versions of the Charter. The original versions of 1215, 1216 and 1217 confine the grant of liberties to freemen. The preamble to the Charter of the Forest of 1225[34] specifically states that the liberties contained in that Charter are granted to everybody in the kingdom. Magna Carta of 1225 seems to adopt both approaches. Its preamble adopts the same form as that of the Forest Charter, granting liberties which follow to everyone in the kingdom. Clause 1, however, follows the 1215 Charter in granting the liberties which it sets out below[35] to all freemen. There are, therefore, within the same document conflicting provisions. The text is likely to take precedence over the preamble, but in any event this problem was solved about 150 years later when statute enlarged[36] the protection to all men.

---

[34] Below, Chapter 15.
[35] See Chapter 15.
[36] Below, Chapter 16.

7

Law and Order

THE BARONS' REBELLION occurred at a time when the boundary between exercise of the King's will and the customary requirements of good government, was not clearly resolved. As we have seen,[1] the Anglo Saxons had a tradition of good government, which involved the King ruling with the advice of his Council. The Normans promised to continue this tradition, but in practice tried to rule absolutely. The Charter must be seen in the light of the Anglo Saxon tradition.

In fact in Normandy there were few, if any, written laws. By contradistinction, the Anglo Saxons had a long history of written law. When St Augustine landed in Kent in 597, the local King, Ethelbert, gave permission for Augustine to seek to convert his subjects. Writing early in the eighth century, the Venerable Bede stated that Ethelbert had established judicial decrees after the example of the Romans, which 'written in the English language, are preserved to this day and observed by the people'.[2] The West Saxons under Ine and the Mercians under Offa had their own recorded laws. King Alfred compiled laws of the West Saxons between 871 and 899.[3] Relying on the book of Exodus he enjoined: 'Judge thou very fairly. Do not judge one judgement for the rich and another for the poor; not one for the one more dear and another for the one more hateful'. He explained that he had collected various compensations which should be paid for human misdeed, which his forefathers had observed.

> I dared not presume to set in writing at all many of my own, because it was unknown to me what would please those who should come after us. But those which I found anywhere, which seemed to me most just, either of the time of my kinsman King Ine, or of Offa, King of the Mercians, or of Ethelbert, who first among the English received baptism, I collected herein and omitted others.[4]

These collections in the main fixed the compensation (*wergild*) which a transgressor had to pay to his victim or the victim's family. They were an attempt to restrain the blood feud. For example, about 940 the law code of Alfred's grandson, King Edmund, provided that 'If henceforth anyone slay a man, he is himself to bear the feud, unless he can with the aid of his friends within twelve months pay compensation at the full

---

[1] Above, Chapter 3.
[2] D Douglas (ed), *English Historical Documents* (London, 1973) I, no 151, p 664.
[3] ibid, I no 33, p 396.
[4] ibid 409.

wergild'.[5] The wrongs to be compensated included killing, robbery, burglary and adultery. 'If a freeman lies with the wife of a freeman he is to atone with his wergild and to obtain another wife with his own money and bring her to the other's home'.[6] Edmund's laws also contain the germ of an idea which was to prove of vital importance in the twelfth and thirteenth centuries – the King's peace: 'If anyone kills a man in the King's estate he is to pay fifty shillings compensation'.

The Danes brought the Danelaw, but two centuries before Magna Carta they and the Anglo Saxons agreed to follow the laws of Alfred's great-grandson Edgar.[7] In 1020 King Cnut wrote a letter to his subjects in which he undertook to be a

> kind lord and unfailing to God's rights and to right secular law . . . I will that all people, clerk and lay, hold fast Edgar's law, which all men have chosen and sworn to at Oxford, for that all the bishops say it right deeply offends God, that a man break oaths or pledges; and likewise they teach us that we should with all might and main . . . eschew all unrighteousness; that is slaying of kinsmen and murder and perjury and witchcraft and enchantment and adultery and incest.[8]

These various collections of laws were generally stated to have been made with the advice of the King's counsellors. They usually started by guaranteeing the rights of the Church. Primitive as these laws may seem, they did establish a tradition of following custom, of written law and of the importance of judgment rather than arbitrary self-help.

The Norman Conquest did not cause a break in this tradition. In 1066 William I offered to uphold the laws of Edward the Confessor and at his coronation swore to maintain just law, much as Cnut had done. Shortly after he confirmed to London the laws it had enjoyed under Edward the Confessor. According to one compilation, he later confirmed to the whole kingdom that all men should have and hold the laws of King Edward as to lands and all other things, together with those additions William had made for the good of the English people.[9] Sometime around 1122 a compilation of his 'laws' was published in the *Textus Roffensis*.[10] They did contain some innovation, introducing trial by battle as an alternative to trial by hot iron. They also abolished the death penalty, substituting castration and blinding (by the time of Henry I capital punishment had returned, because it was referred to in the *Leges Henrici Primi*). Otherwise William confirmed existing customs. His son, William Rufus, who succeeded him in 1087, became universally unpopular. The Anglo Saxon Chronicle described him as 'hateful to almost all his people and odious to God'. When Rufus died in 1100, his younger brother was crowned Henry I. His

---

   [5] Douglas (n 2) I, no 38, p 437.
   [6] ibid.
   [7] For the laws of Edgar see Douglas (n 2) I, no 40, p 431 and no 41, p 434.
   [8] W Stubbs, *Select Charters and other Illustrations of the English Constitutional History from the earliest times to the reign of Edward I* (Oxford, 1913) 98.
   [9] See F Barlow, *The Feudal Kingdom of England 1042–1261*, The Penguin History of England (London, 1999).
   [10] T Hearne (ed), *Textus Roffensis* (Oxford, 1720); see Douglas (n 2) vol II, no 18, p 431; a copy of this is now held in the archives of Rochester Cathedral and can be accessed on URL; we take the date from the Cathedral archivist.

Charter of Liberties, issued on his coronation, acknowledged that under his predecessor the kingdom had been oppressed and there had been unjust exactions. He
undertook to restore the laws of Edward the Confessor together with amendments
made by his father.[11] Once Henry had been accepted as King, he largely ignored his
undertakings. His Charter reads almost like an election manifesto, whose terms
were never to be fulfilled. Nevertheless the first negotiating stance of the rebel
barons in 1215 was to seek confirmation of Henry I's Charter of Liberties.[12]

These promises to return to established law contained an element of myth. During
his reign, Edward the Confessor is not known to have made any new laws and no
collection of laws was made. A collection of his 'laws' (*Leges Edwardi Confessoris*)
was published well after the Conquest in 1140.[13] Although it purports to be an
ancient compilation, it in fact reflected legal thought at the date of writing. Its
importance is the appeal to established custom.

By the end of the twelfth century the approach of the Angevins had become more
absolutist. For instance, about 1180 the *Dialogue of the Exchequer* stated that

> the wealth of kings is not invariably theirs by strict process of law, but proceeds some-
> times from the laws of their countries, sometimes from the secret devices of their own
> hearts and sometimes even from their mere arbitrary will; their subjects have no right to
> question or condemn their actions. For those whose hearts are in the hand of God, and to
> whom God himself has committed the sole care of their subjects stand or fall by God's
> judgment and not man's.[14]

No doubt King John would have endorsed this view heartily. The Angevin kings
had all acted arbitrarily. They seized land without judgment, seized castles and
razed them to the ground, demanded hostages for good behaviour and amerced
their subjects for substantial sums.[15] If a vassal offended against his lord he was in
his mercy, that is he could be penalised entirely at the lord's discretion; the vassal
could be amerced, that is required to pay a financial penalty. The Charter tried to
deal with these abuses and the method was to insist on judgment – the King, like his
subjects, could not seize land or chattels without judgment.

That John had acted previously without judgment is apparent from some specific
wrongs he promised to right. Thus clause 52 of the Charter promised that 'if anyone
has been disseised or deprived by us without lawful judgment of his peers of lands,
castles, liberties or his rights we will restore them to him at once'. Those similarly
deprived under Henry II or Richard I were to wait until John returned from his pro-
jected crusade before obtaining restitution. Clause 55 undertook that 'all fines that
were made with us and all amercements imposed unjustly and contrary to the law
shall be completely remitted'. Clause 49 undertook to restore at once all hostages

---

[11] Clause 13.
[12] See above, Chapter 5
[13] BR O'Brien, *God's Peace and King's Peace: The Laws of Edward the Confessor* (Philadelphia, 1979).
[14] C Johnson (ed), *Dialogus de Scarario* (Oxford, 1950) Preface, 1.
[15] J Jolliffe, 'Magna Carta' () X 88 103 *Schweizer Beiträge zur Allgemeinen Geschichte* (Switzerland,
1961) 50–136; FW Maitland (ed), *Bracton's Notebook* (Cambridge, 1887) case nos 49, 769, 994, 1593.

and charters delivered to the King as sureties for peace or faithful service. Clause 62 remitted and pardoned all rancour or ill will or offences against the Crown during 'the quarrel'.

Despite the stress on continuity and the need to return to the good government of the past, in fact the law of the land had certainly changed since the Conquest. The Angevin kings had established a system of royal courts to cement their control of the country, but which their subjects had come to use for their own ends. It covered both criminal and civil law. To understand how it operated it is necessary first to describe both the old and the new courts. The old administrative unit, dating back to Anglo Saxon times, was the hundred, roughly based on 100 households. Local men met frequently in the hundred courts to decide local disputes and offences. Periodically the sheriff would summon the shire court, where local magnates would determine disputes and where crimes were determined by ordeal. These meetings became the Quarter Sessions, because in due course they sat quarterly. They lasted until Lord Beeching recommended they be replaced by a new system of Crown Courts, which was put into effect in the Courts Act 1971.

Justice in the most important cases, however, was administered in the King's court. The King himself could decide cases, but he came to appoint a Chief Justiciar, who combined the roles of chief administrator and judge. With time the King despatched his judges around the country to dispense justice in the shires on assize. Bracton about 1250 describes the judicial system as it then existed and almost certainly did in 1215:

> [S]ome justices are major . . . general, permanent, of greater importance who remain at the side of the king and whose duty is to correct the wrongs and errors of all others. There are other permanent judges sitting in a place certain, that is the bench, who determine all pleas for which they have the warrant . . . there are other justices, travelling from place to place, as from county to county, sometimes for all pleas, sometimes for certain special pleas, such as assises only and general gaol delivery.[16]

They would hear important civil disputes and try the most serious criminal charges. The system of assize courts also lasted until 1971, when they were subsumed in the Crown Court.

The Assizes of Clarendon in 1166 provided for royal judges to summon the sheriffs to appear before the justices with 'their counties'.[17] The word 'assize' was used with a number of meanings. It derived from the Latin *assissa*, which is the form used in Latin texts in contemporary documents, meaning literally a 'sitting' – an assembly at which decisions were made. So it could mean, as in the Assize of Clarendon, a sitting of the King's Council performing what was in effect a legislative function. It was also used, however, to describe the sittings of the judges who travelled round the country, or the sittings of local men chosen to enquire into the disputed facts of a case.

---

[16]   SE Thorne (ed), *The Laws and Customs of England* (Cambridge, MA, 1977) II 307.
[17]   Cl 19.

These royal courts produced innovatory civil proceedings. Principal among these were the assizes of novel disseisin, darrein presentment and mort d'ancestor. The first protected recent possession, the second presentation to a church benefice and the third succession. These were fast-track procedures for determining who was entitled to possess land. Possession was at least nine-tenths of the law. There was a writ of right to determine ownership, but that was cumbersome and expensive, so the use of the so-called petty assizes became popular. Seisin meant possession – he who was seised of possession. Disseisin meant dispossession. He who could prove recent possession could hold the land. If there were doubt about the correct position, local men of sufficient standing were appointed to hold an inquest, ie enquire as to who held recent possession. They would swear an oath as to the truth of their finding, hence they were called jurors. They were not, however, jurors in the modern sense, receiving evidence in court. They went away from court, made their own enquiries and reported back. They were as much investigators as judges. The Assize of Northampton in 1176 required the royal judges to investigate all disseissins since 1176 and also the custody of castles.[18]

We have already seen that Magna Carta was very much concerned with feudal property rights.[19] The importance of these novel legal procedures was demonstrated by clause 4 of the Assize of Northampton:

> [I]f any freeholder dies, his heirs shall remain in such seisin as their father had of his fee on the day that he was alive and dead; and they shall have his chattels, with which to carry out the testament of the deceased. And afterwards they shall go to their lord and perform to him their obligation for relief and others things owed from their fee. And if the heir is under age, the lord of the fee shall receive his homage and have wardship over him as long as is right . . . And if the lord of the fee denies to the heirs of the deceased the seisin of the said deceased's property which they demand, the justices of the lord King shall have recognition made in the matter by twelve lawful men, as to what seisin in this respect the deceased had on the day that he was alive and dead. And according to the recognition thus made, the justices shall make restitution to the heirs. And if anyone acts contrary to this command and is convicted of doing so, let him remain in the king's mercy.[20]

Criminal proceedings were often started by 'jurors' of a locality reporting whom they suspected of crime. The Assizes of Clarendon and Northampton formalised this procedure. Clarendon was a royal hunting lodge in Wiltshire and it was here that the Constitutions of Clarendon (defining the relationship of Church and State) were promulgated in 1164 and the Assizes in 1166. The Assizes required 12 of the more lawful men in each hundred (or four in each township) to report anyone who had been charged or published as a robber, murderer or thief or someone who had harboured them. Those reported were to be put to the ordeal of the water. The Assize of Northampton added the offences of falsification (probably counterfeiting and forgery). The representatives of the hundred were now to be knights, or if they

---

[18] Cl 5.
[19] Above, Chapter 3
[20] C Johnson (ed), *Dialogus de Scarario* (London 1950) 120.

were not present 12 lawful freemen. The truth of the allegation, however, was still to be determined by ordeal. We shall consider the implications of this when analysing clause 39, which guaranteed trial by peers.[21]

The administration of justice was profitable to the Crown. In some clauses the Charter sought to limit the financial burden on litigants. A litigant in the royal courts had to pay fees. Clause 36 made an amendment to this: 'henceforth nothing shall be given or taken for the writ of inquisition of life or limb, but it shall be given freely and not refused'. This is a reference to what we still call an inquest. Sums required as amercement were seen to be arbitrary and excessive. There are specific provisions in the Charter as to the manner in which amercements are imposed. Clause 21 provided that 'earls and barons shall not be amerced except by their peers and only in accordance with the nature of the offence'. Clause 20 provided that 'a freeman shall not be amerced for a trivial offence, except in accordance with the degree of the offence; and for a serious offence he shall be amerced according to its gravity, saving his livelihood'. Similar provision was made in respect of merchants and villeins. None of these amercements could be imposed without the oaths of reputable men of the neighbourhood. Under clause 22, clerks in orders who fell into the King's mercy in respect of a lay tenement would be dealt with in a similar way, without reference to the value of any benefice they held.

The rebel barons sought to regulate royal justice. The first necessity of regular justice is the appointment of properly qualified judges. Clause 45 of the Charter provides that 'we will not make justices, constables, sheriffs or bailiffs who do not know the law of the land and mean to observe it well'. Under clause 24, no sheriff, constable, coroners or other bailiffs were to hear pleas of the Crown. The Angevins were generally fortunate in the quality of their judges. When William I established his court in England, he and his successors insisted that proceedings should be in French. With time there developed a formal language called law French, where basically the speaker or writer used French if he knew it and, if he did not, substituted an English word. One celebrated example is the case of the 'prisonier que puis son condemnation ject un brickbat a le dit juge que narrowly mist'.[22] Although Latin was used in formal documents, the use of French in the English judicial system effectively prevented the introduction of Roman law into court proceedings. Case by case royal judges developed a system of law, unique to England, but common to all the kingdom and records of their decisions were kept. From 1130 the proceedings in the Exchequer were recorded (in what became called the Pipe Rolls, because the records were rolled up). Records of decisions in the royal court and on assize were kept in the reigns of Richard I and John. From 1189 a roll of Charters granted by the King was kept. About 1190 and 1250 the first English legal textbooks appeared,[23] which attested the quality of the judges.

---

[21] Below, Chapter 8
[22] Dyer's Reports 1586.
[23] See below App A Sources, Glanvill and Bracton.

Once properly qualified judges were appointed, people wanted access to them. Initially justice was administered literally in the King's court (curia regis). Actions between subject and subject were tried in the Court of Common Pleas, which was held wherever the King established his court for the time being. Clause 17 of Magna Carta provided that 'common pleas shall not follow our court but shall be held in some fixed place'. Clause 18 granted that the assizes of novel disseisin, mort d'ancestor or darrein presentment should only be tried in the county where the relevant property was situated and undertook to send two justices four times a year to each county, who with four knights of the county chosen by the county, would hold the assize in the county court. Clause 19 appears to envisage that the hearing would last a day, for it provided that if business were left over it could be decided on the next day by the knights and freeholders of the county.

Other provisions curbed the activities of sheriffs or constables.[24] Under Clause 38 no bailiff shall put anyone on trial by his own unsupported allegation, without bringing credible witnesses to the charge. Clauses 28–31 prevented them taking any man's corn or chattels without paying cash or his timber for castles without his agreement; if he was a free man his horse and carts could not be taken for carting; no knight could be compelled to give money for castle guard if he was willing to perform the guard himself. Under clause 26, if a sheriff tried to enforce a debt to the Crown against the chattels of a deceased, his chattels had to be listed by a view of lawful men and under clause 27 the chattels of an intestate had to be distributed by the Church to his relatives.

Whilst the barons saw the advantages of justice administered in the royal court, they were not abandoning their own justice in their own courts. A lord had jurisdiction over his vassal, but he was obliged to do justice to him. Lords from sub-infeudation had their own courts, whose jurisdiction they wanted to protect, just as the King did his. The Assize of Clarendon protected royal justice by providing that in the case of those whom the 12 lawful men of the hundred had sworn were suspected of committing serious crime, 'no one shall have court or justice or [his] chattels save the king himself in his own court, before his own Justices and the lord king shall have all their chattels'.[25] The exercise of justice in the lords' courts could equally be profitable to them. Clause 34 of the Charter provided that the writ called praecipe 'shall not in future be issued to anyone in respect of any holding whereby a free man may lose his court'. The writ praecipe was used to transfer a suit from a lord's court to the King's court. Glanvill about 1190 gave examples of various writs praecipe. The first writ he describes thus:

> King to the Sheriff greeting. Command N to render to R justly and without delay one hide of land in such and such a vill, which the said R complains that the aforesaid N is withholding from him. If he does not do so summon him by good summoners to be before me

---

[24] Constables were either officials of the hundred or deputies in charge of castles.
[25] Cl 5.

or my justices on the day after the octave of Easter, to show why he has not done so. And have there the summoners and this writ.[26]

Note that the writ simply required N to justify his actions; it did not determine the result. One plea that N could advance would be that he held land by decision of his lord's court. He would have to demonstrate that the lord's court was properly constituted and had granted him possession, hence the provision that no freeman should be deprived of his court, ie his jurisdiction.

The barons plainly had a selfish interest in maintaining legal regularity; they wanted to use the law of the land to protect their persons and property. Nevertheless, this underlying insistence on legal proceedings leading to lawful judgment is probably the greatest contribution of the Charter to the development of the English Constitution and liberty of the subject. The two most famous clauses in the Charter which guarantee trial by peers and swift and fair justice, though an essential part of the law and order provisions in the Charter, deserve separate treatment.

---

[26] CDG Hall (ed), *The Treatise on the Laws and Customs of England Commonly Called Glanvill* (Oxford 1993) 5.

8

Trial by Peers – Clauses 39 and 40

Clauses 39 and 40 read as follows:

> 39 No free man shall be seized or imprisoned or stripped of his rights or possessions, or outlawed or exiled or deprived of his standing in any other way, nor will we proceed with force against him or send others to do so except by the lawful judgment of his peers or by the law of the land.
>
> 40 To no one will we sell, to no one deny or delay right or justice.

In the Charter of 1225 they were amalgamated into one clause now numbered 29 and in this form they remain on the statute book. The Latin word was *pares*, literally 'equals'.

Clause 39 offers no definitions: it does not say how your peers will judge you nor what the law of the land is. It is this vagueness which has made it a perfect vehicle to support the arguments of later generations, seizing upon it as justification for their policies. Its ambiguities have given field days to academics. On the 700th anniversary of the grant a volume of *Magna Carta Commemoration Essays* was published. Paul Vinogradoff, Professor of Jurisprudence at Oxford University, and Frederick Powicke, Professor of Modern History at the University of Belfast, locked horns on the use of the Latin *vel* between 'peers' and 'law of the land'. Powicke contended this should be translated 'or',[1] but Vinogradoff asserted that it was quite clearly conjunctive and not disjunctive.[2] Later in this chapter we will see that the difference in translation may be crucial.

It may be the drafters of clause 39 were not entirely clear what its detailed meaning was. Professor Powicke in the *Magna Carta Commemoration Essays* concluded that it is enough to view clause 39 as laying stress on the necessity for protection against arbitrary acts.[3] The majority of the clauses in the Charter are aimed at specific 'abuses'. It would seem clear by analogy that clauses 39 and 40 were an attempt to restrict arbitrary government.

The reference in clause 39 to trial by peers and judgment according to the law of the land was not original. In 1037 the Archbishop of Milan, who was also feudal lord of the city, summarily deprived a knight of the city of his fief. As a result armed conflict broke out between the knights and the greater magnates (equivalent of

---

[1] HE Malden (ed), *Magna Carta Commemoration Essays* (London, 1917) 99.
[2] ibid 78.
[3] ibid 103.

barons). Emperor Conrad II, who was also King of Lombardy, went to Pavia to settle the conflict and issued the *Constitutio Feudis*. This provided that:

> [N]o knight (not only our greater vavasours, but their knights) or a prelate, magnate or anyone else who holds a benefice of our public lands or ecclesiastical property, or held one or unjustly lost one, shall lose his benefice without certain and convicted fault, except in accordance with the custom or constitution of our ancestors and the judgment of his peers.[4]

This was clearly a very limited privilege relating to fiefs granted to tenants in chief and their knights. Over a century later in 1183, when the Emperor Frederick Barbarossa entered into the Peace of Constance with the Lombard League, the members of the League agreed to swear fealty to the Emperor, but they were granted various liberties in return. These included a clause which provided that any cases concerning fiefs between any member of the League should be settled by peers of the city (civitas) in which the case arose and in the Emperor's presence, if he were in Italy and wished to hear the case. This was still a privilege and limited in its ambit. Sometime around 1200 the Very Ancient Customs of Normandy (*Tres Ancien Coutumier de Normandie*) were published. They provided that Assizes should be held by barons and 'legal men'. 'Equal ought to be judged by equal'.[5]

It is not fanciful to conclude that these ideas had penetrated English thought. There was a good deal of contact between England and the continent of Europe. There were obvious links with Normandy. Around the mid-twelfth century the study of Roman law texts revived in Italy, particularly in the work of the Glossators (who glossed the originals) at Bologna University. In 1149 one of them, Roger Vacarius, was brought to England to give counsel to Thomas a Becket. Vacarius produced a version of the Emperor Justinian's codes and probably lectured at Oxford University. John of Salisbury, who had been secretary to Thomas a Becket, wrote frequently from 1163 from Rheims to England about continental politics. Archbishop Stephen Langton had an academic past in the Schools of Paris, where both theology and the liberal arts were practised.

There are indications from beginning of the twelfth century that these ideas had been received in England. The Laws of Henry I (*Leges Henrici Primi*) are a collection of laws made by an unknown hand early in that century. The copies that survive were made about 1200 and have interpolations, so the document cannot be seen as completely true to the original. They do provide, however, that 'each man is to be judged by his equals and by men of the same area'. The Assizes of Clarendon and Northampton, during Henry II's reign, demonstrate the importance attached to legal process. In 1174 Henry crushed a rebellion and ordered that the rebels should be tried following 'judgment and the customs of the land' (*judicium et consuetudinem terrae*).[6]

---

[4] B Keeney, *Judgment by Peers* (Harvard Historical Monographs XX, 1940) 7.
[5] ibid 8.
[6] Gesta Henrici II, i. p 79.

There is another tantalising reference to trial by peers in England prior to the signing of the Charter. In 1190 Richard I and in 1201 John confirmed in Charters the liberties granted to the Jews in England and Normandy by their grandfather Henry I.[7] There was a substantial Jewish diaspora in Normandy and William I brought Jews to England, presumably to provide the finances that Christians could not. The Catholic Church forbade usury, that is charging interest on loans; the Jewish faith had no such restriction and so Christians borrowed from Jews and paid them interest. The Crown borrowed from them and so did many powerful men in the kingdom and merchants in the cities. The Jewish community paid substantial sums for the confirmations of their liberties, in John's case 4,000 marks. What is tantalising is that the original of Henry's Charter is not extant.[8] The Charters of Richard and John, however, follow exactly the same pattern and the likelihood is that they followed that of Henry. Henry I reigned from 1100 to 1135 and no date is given in the later Charters for his. It does mean, however, that his Charter must have been granted nearly a hundred years before Magna Carta. The Charters give the Jews considerable privileges, including safe passage through the kingdom, exempt from customs and tolls. Richard's Charter provides (and John's has similar wording) that if a Christian has a quarrel with a Jew let it be decided by peers of the Jew. The Treaty of Lambeth in 1217 provided for the return of various documents, which had fallen into French hands during the invasion by Prince Louis, including Charters granted to the Jews.[9] In the decades after the Charter, hostility to the Jewish community mounted, culminating in their expulsion in 1290.

The demand for the right of freemen to trial by peers first appears in the negotiations leading to the Charter in clause 29 of the Unknown Charter (which probably represented the demands of the barons in early 1215).[10] This provided that 'the body of a free man shall not be taken, imprisoned, disseised, outlawed, nor by any other means destroyed, nor will the king go against him by force, unless by judgement of his equals or by the law of the land'.[11] We have already noted that on 9 May 1215 the King offered to have questions between himself decided in the papal curia by four barons chosen by each side and the Pope who is superior to all.[12] On 10 May 1215 the King, no doubt in an attempt to pacify the rebels, issued letters patent (open letters) stating that he had conceded to the barons, who were against him, that he would not take them or their men, nor take possession of their lands, nor use force against them except by the law of the kingdom or by the judgment of their peers in our court (*per judicium parium suorum in curia nostra*). This was a privilege confined to the barons and their men. By this time the curia regis could mean

---

[7] For the texts see J Jacobs (ed), *The Jews of Angevin England: Documents and Records from Latin and Hebrew Sources, Printed and Manuscript, for the First Time Collected and Translated (1854–1916)* (London, 1893) 134–36 and 215, and T Rymer, *Foedera* 1 (London, 1704–13) 51; they can also be found on the Fordham University Medieval Sourcebook.

[8] C Roth, *A History of the Jews in England* (Oxford, 1978) 1.

[9] See JC Holt, *Magna Carta* (Cambridge, 2001) 443.

[10] See Appendix B.

[11] See Holt (n 9) 436.

[12] The text is to be found in ibid App 11, no 3.

the actual court of the King or one of his justices on assize. The curia nostra to which John refers in his letter patent was almost certainly a hearing before him and his principal advisors.

The Articles of the Barons of June 1215 has a similar clause to number 39 in the Charter, but with a subtle difference. Previous formulae spoke of the law of the kingdom. Now the draft demand speaks of the law of the land and this form is adopted in the eventual Charter. This implies that all freemen in the land, including the barons, are protected by clause 39. In 1997 Ralph Turner, in an Essay on 'King John and Justice',[13] developed the view that the true purpose of the clause was to make it clear that the barons had the same judicial rights as other freemen. He acknowledged that others had advanced the idea before him, but he examined it in more detail. He pointed out that clauses 52 and 56 appear to concede that John had acted arbitrarily, seizing property and imposing unreasonable penalties on his subjects. According to Turner, examination of proceedings before the royal courts shows that they were concerned with disputes relating to knights and other freemen; they did not appear to deal with proceedings to which barons were party. According to Glanvill, writing about 1190, the will of the Prince was law.[14] John regarded extra-judicial seizure of land from tenants in chief as a routine administrative way of dealing with their failure to provide the services to which he felt he was entitled. Undoubtedly the barons felt the King's conduct was oppressive. Their subtenants could challenge their conduct in the royal courts, but, since the King was the fountain of all justice, the legality of his actions could not be subject to challenge by his direct tenants in his own court – he could not issue a writ against himself. The importance of peers was that John had increasingly gathered a court not of the great magnates of the land, but of his intimates led by Peter de Roches. If a baron was heard in curia regis he was unlikely to obtain a favourable result. His peers would now be there as a bulwark against royal injustice. It is possible to argue until kingdom come about the true intent of clause 39, but this view is certainly persuasive.

What did the Charter mean by judgment of peers? From its wording it is clear that the clause deals both with civil proceedings, such as for seisin, and criminal proceedings, where life and limb might be lost. The meaning of the clause may have been different in relation to the two different kinds of process.

An inquest of jurors (that is men swearing to the truth of facts) was used by the Carolingians and Normans as a method of fact finding. In 829 Emperor Louis the Pious, ordered that royal rights should be determined by the sworn statement of the best and most credible people of the district.[15] This practice appears to have been carried over to Normandy to establish ducal rights, though occasionally the right to an inquest to settle a dispute was bought by individuals. Most notably the inquest was used in England shortly after the Conquest when the Domesday book was compiled. Royal officers were ordered to enquire, by the oaths of local people,

---

[13] SD Church (ed), *King John, New Interpretations* (Woodbridge, 1999) 237.

[14] Below, Chapoter 10.

[15] T Plucknett, *A Concise History of the Common Law* (Indianapolis, IN, 2010) 104.

how many men including villeins there were in every vill and how much it was worth. It is important to notice that the information was to be gathered on oath. It was the oath to God which was the form of proof. Post 1066 jurors were on occasion sworn in civil proceedings, such as trespass, as recognitors – if there was a dispute they were to recognise the facts. They were local men who were required to discover the facts from local knowledge or enquiry.[16] The Year Books containing reports of cases show that if the facts were not in dispute the court would make a ruling, but if they were disputed then local knowledge was used to establish the truth.

Clauses in the Charter make specific requirements for the use of inquests. For instance, all 'evil customs' relating to forests or river banks are at once to be investigated in every county by 12 sworn knights of the county (clause 48). Where an inquest by local men of standing was ordered in civil proceedings, clause 39 may mean that these men had to be of equal standing with the parties, so that if a baron complained he had been unlawfully disseised, the 'jurors' carrying out the inquest into the facts had to be barons.

With regard to criminal trials, clause 39 was later interpreted to mean trial by a jury which decided the facts on evidence presented to them in court; it cannot have been intended to mean that at the time. Criminal proceedings could be commenced in two ways. The first was an appeal by a victim to the court to try the accused. The Charter intended this procedure should continue, because clause 53 provides 'no one shall be taken or imprisoned upon the appeal of a woman for the death of anyone except her husband'. The second was by a presenting jury. These were merely ways of bringing an accusation before a court. The truth was established by other means, such as battle or ordeal.

The presenting jury had its origins in Anglo Saxon England. Local people swore an oath that they believed a defendant was guilty of a crime. The truth or otherwise of the belief was then tested by ordeal. To these tests the Normans added trial by battle. This procedure was formalised in England under Henry II in the Assize of Clarendon in 1166:

Cap I

First the aforesaid King Henry established by his counsel of his barons for the maintenance of peace and justice that enquiry shall be made in every country and every hundred by the twelve most lawful men of the hundred and by the four most lawful men of every vill upon oath that they shall speak the truth, whether in their hundred or vill there by any man who is accused or believed to be a robber, murderer, thief or receiver of robbers or thiefs since the King's succession. And this the justices and sheriffs shall enquire before themselves.

Cap II

Those thus identified shall be put to the ordeal of water and made to swear they are not a robber or murderer . . . [etc] or ordered to make their law before the justices.

---

[16] JH Baker, *An Introduction to English Legal History* (London, 1990) 72–73.

The phrase 'make their law' appears to refer to compurgation.[17] In this the party would swear as to the truth of facts and would produce 12 men to swear they believed his oath was true. In other words, they did not swear to the truth of the facts, but merely to the credibility of the oath. This obviously gave opportunity for connivance and largely fell into disuse from the eleventh century onwards. It was also used in civil proceedings.

The ordeal could take various forms, for instance by fire or water, cold or hot. In trial by fire or hot water the accused was burnt. His innocence was established if his wound healed swiftly. Ordeal by cold water involved putting him in water with a millstone round his neck. If he floated to the surface he was innocent. The efficacy of these tests was based on the belief that God would intervene to protect the innocent. A priest had to be present to bless the ordeal.

We can get a picture of a criminal trial 25 years before the Charter by turning to Book XIV of Glanvill's *Treatise on the Laws and Customs of England*. He draws a distinction between cases where there is a specific accuser and ones where the accusation is based on general notoriety. If a specific accuser appears he must give security in the form of sureties. If he cannot find sureties he must state his accusation on oath. The accused must then find sureties for his appearance. If he cannot, he is imprisoned until trial. On the day of the trial the accuser makes his detailed accusation. If the accused denies it, the issue is decided by ordeal or battle. Where there is no specific accuser

> the truth of the matter shall be investigated by enquiries (inquisitions) and interrogations before the justices and arrived at by considering the probable facts and possible conjectures, both for and against the accused. He must be either absolved entirely or made to purge himself by ordeal.'

It seems therefore that the fact-finding procedures of an inquisition are beginning to be utilised in criminal proceedings at least to establish a prima facie case. The courts are not yet willing to dispense altogether with the more primitive procedure of ordeal. The jury adopted by the Assize of Clarendon was destined to develop into the Grand Jury, which considered the evidence and in effect decided whether there was a prima facie case. It no longer exists in England, though it is still used in the United States.

The basis of this system was destroyed when Innocent III initiated reforms which forbade clerics to take part. His aim was to separate civil and ecclesiastical jurisdiction and so clerics were forbidden from taking part in civil proceedings. In Canon 18 of the Fourth Lateran Council it was stated: 'Neither shall anyone in judicial tests by hot or cold water or hot iron bestow any blessing'. This canon, however, was not promulgated until 30 November 1215 and so was not extant at the time of Magna Carta.

Of course, the barons were seeking to protect their own interests by requiring judgment by peers. Once the House of Lords was established as a separate entity, its

---

[17] See ibid.

members had the right to claim trial by the House on charges of treason or felony, a right which survived until after the Second World War. Hence in this context the meaning of the word 'peers' has been corrupted to 'lords'. The rebels must have had in mind that a presenting or accusing jury should be made up of their equals and probably any inquest as to their rights would be determined by their equals.

What was intended by the requirement that any judgment had to be according to the laws of the land? We have already noted that the phrase 'by the laws of the kingdom', which appears in Pope Innocent's letters and John's patent, is changed in the Articles of the Barons and the Charter itself to 'the law of the land'. This appears to have occurred at the instance of the barons and stresses that the laws in question are not simply the King's laws. Central to perceptions of the Charter in later centuries was the question whether the King was above the law or subject to it. The protection in clause 39 was undoubtedly to prevent the Crown from taking arbitrary action.

All of which brings us to the vexed question of the use of *vel*. Both *et*, meaning 'and', and *vel*, meaning 'or', appear elsewhere in the Charter. *Vel* is usually used in a disjunctive sense. Thus clause 18 provides for the Crown to send two justices through each county. 'We, or [*vel*] if we are out of the realm our chief justice, shall send two justices . . .'. In clause 39 itself three kinds of disjunctive are used: the latin text reads '*nullus liber homo capiatur, vel imprisonetur, aut disseisiatur, aut utlagetur, aut exuletur, aut aliquot modo destruatur, nec super eum ibimus, nec super eum mittemus nisi per legate judicium parium suorum vel per legem terre.*' 'Aut . . . aut' is translated as 'either . . . or' and 'nec . . . nec' as 'neither . . . nor'. The variations may be merely stylistic. Holt in the appendix to his *Magna Carta* simply translates them all as 'or' except for one 'nor'. They are all used disjunctively, all of which points to a disjunctive use in the final *vel*.

Does it matter which is used? Well no more, but it might have done in 1215 and succeeding centuries. If its use is conjunctive then none of the prohibited acts can occur without judgment of peers. If it is disjunctive, other lawful procedures may be used. The judgment of peers has itself to be legal (*legale judicium*), which suggests that 'law of the land' does offer other alternatives. One obvious one would be trial by battle, which an accused might wish to opt for, as William Marshal did in 1205. Similarly, his case indicates that the barons may have had in mind that judgment against them could only be pronounced by other barons in the King's court. What the clause does appear to ensure is first, that none of the prohibited acts can occur without legal process, and secondly, if an inquest or presenting jury is used it must be peopled by the equals of the accused. Care should be taken in visiting the words of the Charter with modern canons of interpretation. On the other hand the clerks from the royal chancery and possibly the Church had experience of drafting legal documents and were careful. The use of the disjunctive 'or' could also leave it open to the Crown to argue that the law of the land embraced prerogative powers – trial by peers was a common law right, but the prerogative might offer alternative trial procedures in its own courts. It was here that the battleground was set in later centuries. Could the 1215 draftsmen have seen this possibility?

If clause 39 was to some extent vague, clause 40 (now amalgamated with 39 in clause 29 of the 1225 Charter and 1297 statute) was more specific. It undertook not to sell, deny or delay right or justice to any man. We have already noted that royal justice was an important source of income. About 1180 the *Dialogue of the Exchequer* put it thus:

> Offerings are said to be made in hope, or for future advantage, when a man offers a sum to the King to obtain justice about some farm or rent; not, of course, to ensure that justice is done – so you must not lose your temper with us and say the King sells justice – but to have it done without delay. Note also that the King does not accept all such offers even though you may think him to overstep his limit. To some he does full justice for nothing, in consideration of their past services or out of mere goodness of heart; but to others (and it is only human nature) he will not give way either for love or money, sometimes owing to the deserts of those who hold what is sought, sometimes because the petitioners have done nothing to deserve, being censured for offending against the realm or the King himself.[18]

The writer is obviously keen to protest that payments made in respect of justice would not determine the outcome of proceedings. Clause 40 at least implies that this was too rosy a view of royal justice. Whether it was or not, the objective of this clause is clear – justice must be done, untainted by corruption or delay. Without expressly saying so, the clause underlines the requirement for a court process in which justice will be truly administered.

---

[18] ibid 1.

9

Taxes

INCOME OR VALUE added tax are terms which would be as foreign to the barons of Magna Carta as the terms scutage, aids and reliefs are to modern ears, indeed the word 'tax' did not come into general use in England until the fourteenth century. Nevertheless, the contest between the revenue a government wants and the amount its subjects are willing to pay remains the same now as then. Overwhelmingly constitutional development has been stimulated by this continuing conflict. Resistance to taxation in a general sense was at the heart of the rebels' demands. In the end the 1215 Charter was not successful in restraining the King's powers of taxation. What it did achieve was to demonstrate a mechanism by which this could be achieved. In the course of the thirteenth century, confirmation of the terms of the Charter was required on more than one occasion as the price of money supply. This in its turn led directly to the establishment of parliamentary government. The development of taxation in the thirteenth century is comprehensively dealt with by GL Harriss in his *King, Parliament and Public Finance in Medieval England*.

Since the Conquest the Crown had funded its activities by income from its royal demesne, by the profits of justice and by the exaction of dues from its tenants in chief as part of the feudal relationship. The largest part of the Charter is concerned with regulating the relationship between vassal and lord, in particular between the Crown and tenants in chief. The nearly contemporary legal treatises attributed to Glanvill (about 1190) and Bracton (about 1250), throw light on the manner in which the Crown taxed its subjects. Bracton attempted to encapsulate the essence of feudal society:

> To rule well a king requires two things, arms and laws, that by them both times of war and peace may be rightly ordered. For each stands in need of the other, that the achievement of arms be conserved and the laws themselves preserved by the support of arms. If arms fail against hostile and unsubdued enemies, then will the realm be without defence; if laws fail justice will be extirpated; nor will there be any man to render just judgment.[1]

---

[1] SE Thorne (ed), *The Laws and Customs of England* (Cambridge, MA, 1977) II, 115 and see Appendix A.

This passage closely follows a similar one in Glanvill.[2] To maintain arms and the law requires finance, which the King sought from his subjects; they naturally wanted to keep this to a minimum.

There was a precedent for a king's magnates restricting his powers to tax. Following the defeat of the Anglo Saxons at the battle of Maldon, King Aethelred the Unready (strictly uncounselled, 'unraed') paid geld to the Danes. Tiring of this, he ordered that all Danes within the kingdom should be killed. This led to a continuing conflict between King Sweyn of Denmark and Aethelred, culminating in a large-scale invasion by the Danes and the rout of the Anglo Saxons. Aethelred fled to Normandy. When Sweyn died in 1016 a bargain was struck between the Anglo Saxon nobility and Aethelred. He had previously levied unpopularly high taxes (geld and heriot) from his nobles for his wars; the nobles now agreed to swear allegiance, but in return Aethelred promised to be a gracious lord and to reform what they all hated.[3] In future he would have to take counsel.

In the early thirteenth century, the authority for raising the various kinds of levies was not legislative, but customary. The rebels did not seek to invalidate these customary demands for financial support, but rather to restrict their ambit. The Crown had sought to stretch established forms of taxation as far as it could. Some taxes were levied as of right and others were granted of grace by the realm. Bracton described the distinction thus:

> There are some customs which are appendages to certain services as to royal and military services and also homage and need not be set forth in charters for if homage has been done and it is royal service it follows therefrom . . . There are other customs which are called neither services nor the concomitant of services, as reasonable aids for the making the lord's eldest son a knight, or marrying his eldest daughter, aids that are furnished of favour, not of right, because of the need and indigence of the chief lord. These aids are personal for they look to persons not fees . . . And since these aids depend on the favour of tenants and not the will of lords and are not feudal, but personal, regard ought to be had to the person of each . . . that the lord's need, whether great or small be relieved and the tenant suffer no hardship.[4]

The Crown was entitled to levy scutage as a matter of right not grace. The vassal's obligation flowed from his homage for knight's fees. The vassal was bound to protect his lord from attack. We have already seen that one of the early arguments put forward by the rebels was that they were not bound to defend the King's interest in all of his overseas territories.[5] Clause 16 of the Charter provided that 'no man shall be compelled to perform more service for a knight's fee or any other free tenement than is due therefrom', a rather vague formula. Scutage was dealt with separately. The nature of scutage was described about 1180 in the *Dialogus de Scaccario*[6]

---

[2] CDG Hall (ed), *The Treatise on the Laws and Customs of England Commonly Called Glanvill* (Oxford, 1993), and see Appendix A.

[3] On this see JR Maddicott, *The Origins of the English Parliament 924–1327* (Oxford, 2002).

[4] Thorne (n 1) II, 115.

[5] Above, Chapter 5

[6] See Appendix A.

(Dialogue of the Exchequer). The Exchequer was the government office where taxes were collected. The dialogue appears to have been written by a Crown servant who had worked there. He says:

> It sometimes happens that when a design of enemies is at hand or breaks out in the realm, the king decrees that a sum be paid from each fee, a mark, to wit or a pound, when he may have to pay grants to soldiers. For the prince prefers to set against the risks of wars hired soldiers to his subject. So this money, because paid in the name of shields, is called scutage.[7]

In January 1215 in the so-called Unknown Charter,[8] the rebels sought to fix the level of scutage at one mark per fee.[9] In June of that year, in the Articles of the Barons,[10] no specific limit was fixed; instead they demanded that no scutage or aid should be levied without the consent of the common council of the realm.[11] Both this provision and clause 12 of the eventual Charter confined demands for aid to meet the expense of knighting the eldest son, marrying the eldest daughter or ransoming the King, this last being an extension of customary rights presumably accepted because of the fate of Richard I. In these instances the amount levied had to be reasonable. Clause 15 imposed similar limitations on tenants in chief levying an aid from their subtenants. The requirement that scutage should also require the consent of the council of the realm was novel. The distinction between right and grace was destroyed.

As the Dialogue of the Exchequer indicated, the Crown preferred to commute knight service to scutage in order to employ mercenaries. This obviously caused resentment because it gave the Crown a means to control not only threats from without, but also opposition from within. Clause 51 of the Charter provided that 'immediately after concluding the peace we will remove from the kingdom all alien knights, crossbowmen, sergeants and mercenary soldiers who have come with horses and arms to the hurt of the realm'.

Another tax levied as of right was tallage.[12] This was a tax on property which William I introduced from Normandy to England. Its name derived from the French *tallies* or tally sticks used to calculate tax. Tallage was used to describe various kinds of imposition, including a tax levied by the Crown on subtenants of land within the royal demesne – which included chartered cities. Clause 32 of the Articles of the Barons demanded that tallage and aids should only be imposed on London and other boroughs in the same manner as scutage and aids generally, that is with the general consent of the council. This once again cut across the distinction between right and grace. The Charter made no reference to tallage; instead, in clause 12, it added to the general provisions on scutage and aids, that aids from the city of

---

[7] C Johnson (ed), *Dialogus de Scaccario* (London, 1950) Bk I IX.
[8] Above, Chapter 5.
[9] Cl 8.
[10] Above, Chapter 5.
[11] Cl 32.
[12] Compare below, Chapter 11.

London are to be dealt with similarly. No mention was made of other boroughs, though it may have been thought that the provision in the succeeding clause that all other cities, boroughs and towns should have their liberties was sufficient to cover them. Clause 12 was omitted from the reissues and the Crown continued to impose tallage.[13]

There were other rights relating to the feudal relationship from which a lord could profit. The act of homage was personal, ending with the death of either party. When a vassal died possession of his lands reverted to the Crown (was escheated to the royal demesne). In practice the heir to the vassal was recognised, but had to undertake his own homage and pay a relief to enter his inheritance. Glanvill described the position:

> Heirs of full age may immediately after the death of their ancestors remain in their inheritance; for although lords may take into their hands both fee and heir, it ought to be done gently that they do not dispossess the heirs. Heirs may even resist the violence of their lords if need be, provided they are ready to pay them relief and do other lawful services.[14]

There had been several recent examples of heirs of tenants in chief being required to pay large sums for their inheritance.[15] Clause 2 of the Charter of Henry I undertook only to take legitimate and just relief. The Articles of the Barons demanded the ancient relief. Now the Charter set out express sums – for a barony or earldom 100 pounds, for a knight's fee 100 shillings and for lesser fiefs whatever had been anciently paid. Glanvill had given the same price for a knight's fee. Clause 43 of the Charter contains further provisions limiting the amounts payable in relation to land held in escheat.

If the heir was a minor, different rules applied. Glanvill again:

> When, however the heirs are clearly minors, then, if they are heirs of a military fee, they are kept in wardship of their lords until they are of full age, that is until twenty one . . . the Lords have full custody of the sons and heirs and may freely dispose of them . . . but they may not alienate any of the inheritance permanently.[16]

Clause 3 of the Charter provided that an heir who was a minor should have his inheritance without relief on attaining his majority. Clause 4 ensured that the guardian of the land of an heir who was a minor should not take from the land more than the reasonable revenues or customary services 'and that without waste or destruction of men or goods'. Clause 5 required the lord to maintain the value of the land and its revenues.

There was also a profitable marriage market under royal control. The lord's consent was required for the marriage of an heir who was a minor or the widow of the tenant. In practice this meant he could arrange the marriage. We have already seen the high degree to which the rebel barons were interrelated by marriage.[17] Marriage

---

[13]   JC Holt, *Magna Carta* (Cambridge, 2001) 321.
[14]   Hall (n 2) VII, 82.
[15]   Above, Chapter 5 and see Holt (n 13) 54–55.
[16]   Hall (n 2) VII, 82.
[17]   Above, Chapter 1.

was an institution used to preserve or augment property or cement political alliances. Clause 6 of the Charter provided that heirs should be given in marriage without disparagement (that is to someone of lower social status). Clauses 7 and 8 provided protection to widows. The Pipe Rolls, which recorded government business in the period leading up to the Charter, show many examples of widows or their families proffering money to the Crown for the right either to remain single or to marry at their choice.[18] For instance, in 1199 the widow of William de Rouse offered 100 pounds that she should not be forced to marry. It was accepted on the basis that if she did decide to marry she would take the King's advice. The widow of Ralph of Cornhill paid 200 marks that she should not have to marry Godfrey of Louvain, but be free to marry the man of her choice and to have seisin of her lands.[19] Clause 8 now provided that

> no widow shall be compelled to marry so long as she wishes to live without a husband, provided she gives security that she will not marry without our consent if she holds of us or without the consent of the lord from whom she holds if she holds of another.

Clause 7 protected a widow's right to her dower and inheritance and gave her the right to stay in her husband's house for 40 days after his death. Bracton clearly treats these rights of wardship or marriage as feudal: 'if homage has been done and it is royal service, it follows therefrom that relief of wardship and marriage will belong to the King'.[20]

Clauses 10, 11 and 12 deal with debts owed by the estate of a vassal to a Jew. The Jewish community had spread throughout the land and became so prosperous there was a separate Exchequer to tax them. Aaron of Lincoln became so rich the Crown had an Exchequer just to tax him. In feudal terms the Jew ranked as a serf of the Crown; in theory at least, anything a Jew acquired was not for himself but for the King.[21] When a man died owing money to a Jew, the Crown could take the repayment. Hence clause 10:

> [I]f anyone who has borrowed from the Jews ... dies before the debt is repaid, it shall not carry interest as long as the heir is underage ... and if that debt fall into our hands we will take nothing except the principal specified in the bond.

Clause 11 similarly protected the dower of a widow from being taken by a Jewish creditor.

The taxes we have considered so far were imposed as the result of the feudal relationship between the King and his vassals. In turn his tenants in chief would extract taxes from their vassals. In general these feudal incidents did not enable the King to tax subvassals directly. When the Charter was reissued in 1225 the regency government agreed to this course in return for a tax approved by the council on the

---

[18] Holt (n 13) 32–33.
[19] Both these are cited with reference to the Pipe Rolls in ibid.
[20] Thorne (n 1) II, 115.
[21] F Pollock and FW Maitland, *The History of English Law to the Time of Edward I* (Cambridge, 1895) 451ff.

moveable property of all men in the kingdom. This was a development of great significance not only for the Crown's right to tax, but also for constitutional development. The connection to 'no taxation without representation' is clear.[22]

22 Below, Chapter 25.

10

The King Under the Law

MAGNA CARTA WAS granted on the cusp of assemblies of notables growing into something recognisably related to a modern parliament. For several centuries previously the King had granted laws to his kingdom on the advice of his wise councillors.[1] The importance of Magna Carta in the developments leading to modern government is twofold. Firstly it was an initial and powerful example of subjects forcing a king to subject himself to freshly defined laws. The only comparable example was that of the Lombard League forcing the Treaty of Constance on the Emperor.[2] Secondly, though the rebel barons were not named amongst those who advised the King to make the grant, the 1215 Charter contained clauses giving them stringent powers to enforce it provisions. For the first time there was a specific mechanism to restrain the power of a king. When the Charter was reissued under the regency government during Henry III's minority, these enforcement clauses were omitted and nothing strictly comparable appears in later English constitutional history. When the Charter was reissued in 1225 they were also omitted, but in their place we can see the beginnings of conciliar control of the Crown.[3]

Late Roman law had been absolutist. In the second century AD, Ulpian wrote in his Digest 'what pleases the Prince has the force of law'.[4] In the first part of the sixth century AD, the Codex that bears the Emperor Justinian's name stated that the Emperor was the sole legislator.[5] The Anglo Saxon tradition, however, was that the King should take the advice of his wise men or magnates, sometimes called notables. Glanvill, writing before Magna Carta, reflects both views:

> Although the laws of England are not written, it does not seem absurd to call them laws
> – those that is that are known to have been promulgated about problems settled in council
> on the advice of the magnates and with the supporting authority of the prince, for also it
> is the law that what pleases the prince has force of law.[6]

Bracton, writing after Magna Carta, borrows this passage, but with some amendment. He too accepts established custom as law, but goes on to say 'whatever has

---

[1] Above, Chapter 3.
[2] Above, Chapter 8.
[3] Below, Chapter 15.
[4] Digest, I 4 1.
[5] Codex, I 14 12.
[6] CDG Hall (ed), *The Treatise on the Laws and Customs of England Commonly Called Glanvill* (Oxford, 1993) 2l.

been rightly decided and approved with counsel and consent of the magnates and general agreement of the community, with the authority of the king or prince first added thereto, has the force of law'.[7] The passage about the will of the prince having the force of law is omitted and to the consent of the magnates is added 'the general agreement of the community'. This obviously reflects attitudes changed by the Charter.[8] The tradition of laws being granted by the king before assemblies of notables went back to Anglo Saxon times.

We have already noted that Anglo Saxon England had a much greater tradition of written legal codes and general assemblies than Normandy.[9] Between 899 and 1022 there were 22 different codes for various parts of England.[10] These were generally recorded as being granted on the advice of notables. There were local assemblies of hundreds and shires. In the century leading up to the death of Edward the Confessor, however, central assemblies played a greater part in the administration of the various Anglo Saxon kingdoms. For much of this time there was more than one kingdom in the land, each with a separate assembly and law code. The assembly which advised a king was sometimes called a *witanagemot* – literally a meeting of the wise: the king ruled with the advice of his wise men, though not necessarily on their advice.

These assemblies carried out multiple functions. Sometimes they would choose a new king, for instance on Alfred's death his son Edward was chosen by the chief men of the kingdom (*a primatis electus*).[11] We have already seen how the Dane, Swein, forced Aethelred into exile.[12] When Swein died in 1014 the invitation to Aethelred to return was described as being made by the full council (*pa witan aelle*). It was on condition that he ruled more justly than before – he had become unpopular particularly because of the level of taxation. He accepted the offer.[13] A similar bargain may have been struck by the council who chose Cnut as King of England.[14] After Aethelred's death a witan in London chose his son Edmund Ironside as King, but the chronicler John of Worcester states that thereafter a larger witan chose Cnut as King. He for his part promised to be a faithful master (*fidelis dominus*) and subsequently issued with the advice of his witan a law code confining his ability to tax, much as Aethelred had had to do. These events could have been regarded as a precedent by the rebels in 1215, since they represented a pact between ruler and ruled, but there is no evidence they knew of them. In any event, there is an obvious distinction between Aethelred and Cnut, who plainly wanted the kingship and were willing to make concessions to obtain it, and John, who was forced by arms to agree to the Charter.

---

[7] SE Thorne (ed), *The Laws and Customs of England* (Cambridge, MA, 1977) II, 19.
[8] And compare below, Chapter 16.
[9] See JR Maddicott, *Origins of the English Parliament, 924–1327* (Oxford, 2002) 49–51 and 65.
[10] ibid 28.
[11] ibid 33.
[12] Above, Chapter 9.
[13] Maddicott (n 9) 37.
[14] ibid.

The feudal system was grafted on to this traditional organisation. A vassal was bound to give his lord *consilium et auxilium* (advice and aid). Under the Normans the King's tenants in chief were bound to attend on him in what became called a *consilium* to give him advice.[15] 'Counsel' was turning into 'the Council' where it was given. William the Conqueror consciously continued this Anglo Saxon tradition.[16] There were assemblies of his tenants in chief (now Norman) on the great Christian festivals. They were occasions of some pomp for he would wear his Crown before the assembly. He, of course, had previously been duke to these same men and now needed to reinforce his changed role. His claim to the English Crown could be doubted, so he was anxious to impress the English people with his legitimacy and power. Under the Angevins the habit of Crown wearing on these occasions declined. These assemblies carried out what we would regard as both legislative and judicial functions. They were no doubt also occasions for obtaining patronage and networking. Taxation was not generally dealt with, but in 1188 Henry II backed his decision to impose the Saladin tithe of one-tenth the value of moveable property for a crusade by asserting it was levied with the advice of his magnates.[17] Sometimes the King genuinely sought advice, for instance when Henry II consulted his council in relation to the marriage of his daughter to a Sicilian prince.[18] On many occasions, however, the council was expected to do the King's bidding. When Thomas a Becket was summoned to Northampton in 1164 to answer why he would not support the King's ecclesiastical reforms, Henry is said to have required a speedy judgment 'on him who is my liege man and refuses to stand trial in my court'.

Anointing a King was seen as giving him divine authority – hence the rush in 1216 to crown Henry III. Without theorising about the divine right of kings, the Angevins would have agreed with Glanvill that their will was law. The King was still expected to rule justly. There is an interpolation in a collection of the laws of Edward the Confessor made in 1140 which states:

> [T]he king ought to do everything in the realm and by judgment of the great men of the realm. For right and justice ought to rule in the realm, rather than perverse will. Law is always what does right; will and violence and force are indeed not right. The king, indeed, ought to fear and love God above everything and preserve his commands throughout his realm.[19]

This implies that the King must be trusted to act correctly. No indication is given as to what should happen if he does not. Bracton stated that the King has no equal in the land, but added that

> the king must not be under man, but under god and under the law because law makes the king. Let him therefore bestow upon the law what the law bestows on him, namely, rule and power, for there is no *rex* (king) where will rules rather than law.[20]

---

[15] ibid 75–77.
[16] ibid 57.
[17] ibid 100.
[18] ibid 90.
[19] JC Holt, *Magna Carta* (Cambridge, 2001) 92–95 and 121.
[20] Thorne (n 7) II, 33.

This was the authority advanced by Sir Edward Coke to refute James I's claim to divine right.

It is possible to see a subtle change in the wording of royal charters from the time of Henry I. Henry I's Charter of Liberties in 1100 was addressed to some senior clergy and all his barons, both French and English. It recited that by the mercy of God and the advice of his barons of the kingdom he had been crowned King of England. He goes on to *make* the Church free and to take away all bad customs which the kingdom has suffered. It is in the form of a decree. The Constitutions of Clarendon[21] in 1164 (regulating relations between Church and State) recite that the senior clergy, barons, earls and great men of the kingdom, in the presence of King Henry II, have *recognised* the customs, liberties and dignities that ought to be observed in the kingdom and they should be held and observed. The manner in which the King dealt with the reluctance of Thomas a Becket to accept the Constitutions indicates that Henry did not consider the assembly had any alternative but to accept his view. The Assizes of Clarendon in 1166[22] (regulating criminal procedure) stated that King Henry II 'by the counsel of his barons for the preservation of peace and the observing of justice has *decreed*'. Wording changes with Magna Carta. Now the phrase used is *granting or conceding*. The formula is that we have granted (*concessimus*) on the advice of senior clergy and of noble men (*per consilium venerabilium partum nostrorum . . . et vir nobelium virorum*).

Among those named as advisors to the King in the 1215 Charter were clerics who were his supporters, notably Peter de Roches, Bishop of Winchester and John's Chief Justiciar. The laymen named, such as William Marshal, appear to be at the heart of John's court, those he trusted.[23] Only three have the title earl, which probably reflects the strength of the rebel party, which had a great many more. One of the King's advisors, Hubert de Burgh, did become an earl after John's death. He was a member of a small land-holding family, but rose rapidly in John's service after 1210. He served with valour in France, defending Chinon castle against Philip Augustus for over a year. He was appointed seneschal of Poitou (the title he is given in the Charter), and witnessed the truce between Philip Augustus of France and John. Within 10 days of the grant he replaced Peter de Roches as Chief Justiciar. William Longespee, Earl of Salisbury, was the illegitimate son of Henry II and was brought up with Hubert de Burgh. He was a considerable military commander, who fought with distinction against Philip Augustus of France and also had a significant command at the Battle of Bouvines. He and de Burgh were sent to London in the early part of 1215 to try and ensure the city's loyalty. Roger of Wendover named Longespee as one of John's evil counsellors. William D'Aubigny, Earl of Arundel, was a favourite of John's and was a witness to the King's submission to the Pope in 1213. William, Earl of Warenne was an illegitimate son of Geoffrey of Anjou and so

[21] Above, Chapter 4.
[22] Above, Chapter 7.
[23] The information in this section is taken chiefly from the *Oxford Dictionary of National Biography* (Oxford University Press, 2004–14); see also N Vincent, 'King John's Evil Counsellors' therein.

half brother to Henry II. He fought alongside John in France and went on the campaign to Poitou in 1214. According to Mathew Paris, Hugh de Neville was brought up at the court of Henry II with Prince Richard. Richard made him Chief Justice of the Forest and he continued in this office under John. He was one of those who witnessed John's submission to the Pope. Warin Fitzgerald was royal chamberlain. Robert Fitzpeter became Baron of Barnstable on receiving lands formerly de Braose's, when the latter fell into disfavour. These men all had powerful links to John. Given this, it may be that the formula that the grant was made on their advice may not be entirely fiction. They could have advised John to accept the rebels' terms as there was no realistic alternative. Whatever precise part they played, they were on the face of the document fulfilling the same role as the Anglo Saxon wise men.

The rebel barons did not trust John to carry out his word and so provided independent determination and enforcement procedures. We have seen that clause 12 provided that 'no scutage or aid is to be levied in our realm except by the common counsel of our realm' (*per commune consilio regni nostrl*). Clause 14 provides in detail how that counsel shall be obtained:

> To have the common counsel of the realm for the assessment of an aid or scutage, we will have archbishops, bishops, abbots, earls, and greater barons summoned individually by our letters and we shall also have summoned generally, through our sheriffs and bailiffs, all those who hold of us in chief, for a fixed date with at least forty days notice and at a fixed place; and in all letters of summons we will state the reasons for the summons. And when the summons has thus been made, the business shall go forward on the day arranged according to the counsel of those present, even if not all those summoned have come.

The clause effectively draws a distinction between greater and lesser tenants in chief. Various estimates of the number of tenants in chief have been given.[24] Painter computes about 500 of them in John's time.[25] The lesser tenants in chief became known by the collective name of 'knights'. The rebel army certainly included a good many knights, who would have been encamped at Staines near Runnymede. There is no evidence they took part in any of the negotiations between the King and the rebel leaders. It was not until after the Charter that the knights began to appear in some councils that became known as parliaments. Nevertheless their recognition in the Charter is of significance. They were to be summoned, along with the greater tenants, to give counsel common to the realm. Those attending are seen, in effect, as representing the realm. Moreover, since the liberties are granted to all the freemen of the realm, presumably they too would be regarded as part of the community of the realm. The effect would be to bind all of status in the realm to whatever action was agreed. The realm would include the whole of England and Wales This kingdom was protected by the sea and just about small enough to control from London. It had relatively clear geographical boundaries.

This notion of representing the realm is reinforced by the security clause, number 61. It is the longest in the whole Charter:

---

[24] Maddicott (n 9) 79.
[25] S Painter, *Studies in the History of the English Feudal Barony* (Baltimore, MD, 1943) 48.

[T]he barons shall choose any twenty five barons of the realm they wish, who with all their might are to observe, maintain and cause to be observed the peace and liberties we have granted and confirmed to them by the present Charter, so that if we, or our Justiciar, or our bailiffs or any of our servants offend against any one in any way or transgress any of the articles of peace or security and the offence is indicated to four of the aforesaid twenty five barons, those four barons shall come to us or our Justiciar, should we be out of the kingdom, and shall bring it to our notice and ask that we have it redressed without delay and if we . . . do not redress the offence within forty days from the time when it brought to our notice . . . the aforesaid four barons shall refer the case to the rest of the twenty five barons and those twenty five barons *with the community of the whole land* shall distrain and distress us in every way, they can by seizing castles, lands and possessions and such other ways as they can . . . until in their judgement amends have been made.(emphasis added)

The clause goes on to allow anyone in the land to take an oath to obey the orders of the barons in this regard and to promise to compel those who will not take such an oath to do so. It also provides that, in the event of one of the 25 dying, the others can choose a substitute. If the 25 disagree as to the appropriate course of action, what is to happen shall be determined by a majority of them and that decision shall bind all of them. Clause 55 provides that all fines or amercements, which have been unjustly and unlawfully made shall be remitted or else they are to be settled by a majority of the 25. Thus clause 61 establishes representative action and majority voting.

Membership of the community of the realm had benefits but also conferred responsibilities. The Charter itself provided, in clauses 18, 26 and 48, for knights or lawful men to carry out legal duties. Clause 60 aims to spread the liberties in the Charter down the feudal hierarchy:

[A]ll these aforesaid customs and liberties which we have granted to be held in our realm as far as it pertains to us and our men, shall be observed by all men of our realm, clerk and lay, as far it pertains to them, towards their own men.

The barons need not have entertained such a provision unless they wanted the settlement to affect the whole community. It specifically includes priests. John had already granted a Charter guaranteeing the freedom of the Church and it may seem strange that this was repeated in the Great Charter. The medieval mind seems to have craved constant confirmation of legal rights. On the other hand, it may be that Magna Carta was seen in effect as a constitutional document. It embraced not just the barons, but all freemen and the cities of the realm, so that it was fitting that the Church, which occupied a central role in the affairs of the realm, should also be included.

In this notion of the community of the realm it may be possible to see the germ of representative government. The Council that agreed the reissue of the Charter in 1225 had even greater implications for the English Constitution.

11

London and Other Cities

CLAUSE 13 OF the Charter protects the liberties of London and other cities. The mayor of London was one of those listed as advising John to grant the Charter. Its importance to the City is underlined by the fact that a copy of the 1297 Charter is kept in the City archives. The power of the City to govern its own activities, however, had developed only slowly.

In 1086, when the Domesday Book compiled the wealth of the nation, London received no mention. Nor did Winchester. Some towns, such as Lincoln and Norwich, were recorded, though the tax due from Norwich was very low.[1] Feudal organisation was based on the value of land. Wealth from trade grew in towns, but their inhabitants did not fit easily into the feudal hierarchy. In 1086 tax was assessed on the *hide* – a measure of the amount of land needed to support a household. This was not easily applicable to towns. HC Darby in his study of the Domesday Book suggests that the level of trade in England increased greatly in the period after the Book was compiled. Burghs or boroughs had become established in Anglo Saxon times. They were essentially market centres. In the course of the twelfth century many of them received Charters licensing them to hold fairs. Between 1150 and 1250 a hundred new towns grew up in England, though by modern standards they were very small. They bought Charters from the Crown licensing them to hold fairs and eventually allowing them a measure of self-government. Their ambition increased as they sought a degree of autonomy from central government, which they did by buying a royal Charter. For the Anglo Saxons, largely excluded from the feudal hierarchy, wealth from commerce was a method of self-advancement. Lists of leading citizens show names of Anglo Saxon origin.

From 1150 onwards towns all over Europe tried to establish municipal autonomy. Those on the plain of Lombardy in northern Italy had largely survived the fall of the Roman Empire and become prosperous, because of their position at a focal point between the Mediterranean and northern Europe. The Holy Roman Emperors claimed to be feudal lords and kings of Italy, but they were often absent and relied on feudal agents, who, like sheriffs in England, became unpopular.[2] The cities began to form themselves into societies (*societates*) and to elect consuls (*consultores*) from among their number to make decisions on behalf of the community. Given the need

---

[1] See G Astill, *The Cambridge Urban History of England* (Cambridge, 2000)

[2] G Raccagni, *The Lombard League* (Oxford, 2010) 12; see also C Brooke and G Keir, *London 800–1216, The Shaping of a City* (London, 1975) 72, 187, 237.

for security, these were largely chosen from the ranks of the *milites* or military aristocracy. In due course emperors began to appoint *podestas* (the name deriving from *potestas* or power) to govern the cities in their name, but gradually the cities asserted the right to chose their own *podestas*. They began to exert powers the emperors considered theirs.

This led to an ongoing conflict between the cities and Frederick Barbarossa, who became Emperor in 1154, as to who had the right to *regalia* in the cities – not simply the ornaments of power, but the right to administer and collect taxes from the inhabitants. In due course, in April 1167, 16 cities formed themselves into a league called the *Societas Lombardie*. Their oath of association (called a *pactum* or *sacramentum*[3]) sought by its terms to preserve the rights and good customs (*salvi rationibus et bonis usibus*) which were recognised before Frederick's accession.

By the mid-1170s representatives of the member cities were meeting in assemblies. The records of their decisions were described as *carta concordia* or *conventiones*. They agreed that they would not declare war or make peace without the consent of the League. They arranged for judicial hearings to deal with the situation where a citizen of one city had committed a criminal offence against the citizen of another city in the League. The struggle between the Emperor and the League continued until finally the former was decisively beaten at the Battle of Legnano in 1176. In the resulting Peace of Constance in 1183[4] Frederick granted the cities of the League the *regalia* and other rights within and without the cities, as they had been accustomed to hold them of old. This comprised not only a right to raise their own taxes and exercise criminal and civil jurisdiction, but also all other rights which concerned the welfare of the city.

The parallels with the later actions of the barons in England are obvious. The royal court in England certainly knew of the conflict for Henry II offered money for the reconstruction of Milan. The cleric John of Salisbury, who went into exile on the continent after Becket fled there, wrote regularly to associates in England. He called Frederick the tyrant and schismatic. He complained 'who made the Germans the judges of the nations?'[5] Modern Eurosceptics might make the same point, though John of Salisbury would have supported the European community of the Church.

The cities of France also sought to establish their autonomy. By the early thirteenth century, Toulouse, Soissons, Dijon, Bordeaux, Beauvais and Compiegne were all administered by consuls chosen by a city council and in some instances led by a *maior*.[6] Like their counterparts in Italy, the principal citizens of these cities bonded with a communal oath. Those who did so were known as the *communitas*, often translated as 'commune'. Henry II of England resisted such developments – the chronicler Richard of Devizes stated that on no terms whatsoever would Henry

---

[3] ibid 3, 56.

[4] Sometimes known as the second treaty of Constance, the first having been agreed in 1153. For the text see the Online Library of Liberty; http://oll.libertyfund.org.

[5] T Reuter in Wilks (ed), *The World of John of Salisbury* (Oxford, 1984).

[6] Brooke and Keir (n 3) 190 and 243.

or Richard I have assented to a commune of London.[7] Henry in fact suppressed communes in Gloucester and York[8] and in his documents he was careful not to recognise any government in terms of a commune. He did grant Charters to Carlisle and Lincoln in 1157 and Norwich in 1158, though these, while guaranteeing their ancient liberties and in some instances freeing their citizens from payment for tolls and the like, did not address matters of government. Richard I, no doubt to raise money for his crusade, gave similar Charters to Worcester and Hereford in 1189.

There is evidence of civic activity in London in 1127 when the first full list of aldermen was produced.[9] The organisation of the Anglo Saxon kingdom survived the Conquest; ealdormen became aldermen. They were roughly but not the complete equivalent of the consuls of the continent. The 1127 list shows that their names are almost all of Anglo Saxon origin. One of the principal aims of the cities was to achieve the right to elect their own sheriff. This was important for two reasons. In the first place he collected taxes for the Crown[10] and was often thought to do so oppressively or for his own benefit – several clauses of Magna Carta seek to curb the activities of sheriffs.[11] Secondly, the sheriff presided in the county court and attended the assizes.[12] The Pipe Roll of 1129–30 shows the citizens of London offering the King 100 marks to have the right to elect their own sheriff.[13] About 1131 Henry I is said to have granted London its first Charter, though there has been dispute as to its authenticity.[14] The original does not exist and the first known copy dates from the early thirteenth century. Its existence, however, is corroborated by a reference in the Pipe Rolls for 1130 saying that the King had reduced the tax farm and granted the citizens of London the right to elect their own sheriffs.[15] The problem is that the first version of it is attached to demands by the City drawn up in 1206 in response to taxation by the Crown,[16] so there is at least the possibility that it was embellished to support the City's position. What it purports to do is to grant the shrievalty of London and Middlesex to the citizens for a tax farm of 300 pounds. They may choose 'whomsoever they will from among themselves' to be sheriff. He has jurisdiction to try pleas of the Crown and no one else is to have that jurisdiction. He is also to supervise the conduct of the citizens in the husting (the local name for the county court), which may be held once a week on Monday. The citizens are exempt from the fine for murdrum and trial by battle. They are free of tolls and similar taxes throughout the kingdom. They are to have their hunting rights in the Chilterns

[7] Cited in JH Round, *The Commune of London and Other Studies* (London, 1899) 223.

[8] ibid 218.

[9] ibid 31 and 373.

[10] See F Stenton, *Anglo Saxon England* (Oxford, 1962) 540.

[11] 4, 9.26, 30, 38 and 48.

[12] See Stenton (n 11) 540ff.

[13] Brooke and Keir (n 3) 207.

[14] See W Birch, *The Historical Charters and Constitutional Documents of the City of London* (London, 1887) 5.

[15] ibid 33; the text is transcribed by C Brooke, G Keir and S Reynolds, 'Henry I's Charter for the City of London' (1973) 4 *Journal of the Society of Archivists* 575–76.

[16] See n 15 above.

and Middlesex. If all of these were granted, they are considerable concessions. At one point this Charter draws a distinction between barons and citizens of London, which indicates there were different classes even within the citizenry as there were in the European cities. In 1250 some of the citizens were describing themselves as barons.

Henry II came to the throne in 1154 and early in his reign issued a Charter similar in terms to his father's, granting to London the liberties and free customs they had in the time of Henry I.[17] He did increase, however, the farm, for the Pipe Roll for 1173–74 shows it as over 500 pounds. By 1178 William Fitzstephen, a monk at Canterbury, claimed that London was older than Rome, having been founded by Brutus before he founded Rome![18] He went on, 'London like Rome is divided into wards, has sheriffs appointed for consuls; has a senatorial order and lesser magistracies; sewers and aqueducts in its streets; deliberative assemblies; demonstrative judicial cases have their distinct places, their individual courts'. In the seventeenth century equally extravagant claims for historical continuity were to be deployed.

A vital period for the organisation of the City of London occurred in the 1190s. From 1191 the leaders of the City are named. They are not specifically called mayors, but that is in effect the office they carried out. The first named is Henry Fitzailwin, who remained as leader until his death in 1212. His family went back to the Saxon era.[19] From 1212–14 he was succeeded by his nephew Roger Fitzalan[20] and he by Serlo the Mercer.[21]

In the spring of 1193 the leaders of London swore a communal oath. It was described as *sacramentum commune tempore regis quando detentus est Alemanium* (a communal oath sworn when the King was detained in Germany).[22] The use of the word *sacramentum* mirrors its usage in Lombardy. They swore fealty to King Richard, but also that they would keep the commune and be obedient to the *mayor* of the City of London and to the *echevins* of the same and other good men who will be with them, saving at all points the liberties of the City of London.[23] This appears to be the first mention of the office of mayor of London. A seal was struck to authorise City documents.[24] *Echevin* was the name given to some of those sitting on the council of Rouen and previously may have been unique to that city.

When the quarrel between John and Longchamps arose in 1191, King Richard despatched Walter of Coutances, Archbishop of Rouen, to mediate.[25] This resulted in Longchamps being stripped of his offices and fleeing the kingdom in September of 1191. Walter was installed in his place and remained in England until some time in

---

[17] Brooke and Keir (n 3) 40.
[18] Cited ibid 93.
[19] G Williams, *Medieval London: From Commune to Capital* (London, 1970) 4.
[20] ibid.
[21] Brooke and Keir (n 3) 373 and see Appendix B below under Mayor of London.
[22] Round (n 8) 235.
[23] See ibid and Brooke and Keir (n 3) 236 where it is translated.
[24] Williams (n 20) 3.
[25] See *Oxford Dictionary of National Biography*.

1193. The city of Rouen was governed by a council of 24. The oath they swore on taking office revealed that it consisted of 12 *echevins* and 12 *consultores*.[26] In 1205, 24 citizens of London swore an oath which bore a number of similarities to the oath of the *echevins* of Rouen.[27] The proper translation of *echevins* is not easy. They are sometimes called simply aldermen, but they may have been the forerunners of the Common Council.[28] The City must have been following the precedent of Rouen.

When John became King, he granted the City three Charters:[29] one repeated Henry II's Charter, granting specific liberties similar to those set out in the Charter of Henry I; another abolished fish weirs on the Thames and Medway; the third allowed the citizens of London to choose their own sheriffs. The City paid 3,000 marks for this last. There was no specific mention of the community or the office of mayor. In 1202 John granted another Charter to the mayor and citizens, that the guild of weavers should not henceforth operate in the City.[30] In 1206 he demanded that the barons of the City look into the collection of tallage and required the City to grant him an aid.[31] A chartered borough was part of the royal *demesne* and liable to tallage, which could be levied arbitrarily.[32] An aid on the other hand was supposedly a voluntary payment. In response the City drew up a list of their demands. It contains the first surviving version of Henry I's Charter as evidence of the liberties of the City. Its declared aims included that all evil taxes be abolished and no tallage taken without the agreement of the Kingdom and City. This would appear to be the first occasion in Norman and Angevin England when an attempt was made to require consent to a tax previously levied arbitrarily. The City also urged that a mayor be elected annually and that foreign merchants could come and go freely.[33] Early in May 1215, shortly before the rebels took London, King John granted the City a fresh Charter providing that 'they may choose to themselves every year a mayor, who to us may be faithful, discreet and to have all the liberties they have hitherto had'.[34] It was a sign of John's weakness at this time that he asked no money payment for this. This Charter remains in force today.

As can be seen, those addressed in the Charters were called citizens or in some instances barons. No definition is given or found. The liberties granted, however, must have been for the few. This was a pattern established in Lombardy. Whether you were part of the *societas* depended on whether you belonged to a guild or did certain kinds of work; those who did the least prestigious work were not members of the *societas*. Thus vegetable vendors, tavern keepers, sellers of fruit and herbs

---

[26] M Giry, 'Etablissements de Rouen' cited Round (n 8) 239.
[27] See Round (n 8) 237.
[28] See ibid.
[29] See Birch (n 15), 11, 134, 18.
[30] ibid 19.
[31] Compare above, Chapter 9.
[32] For definition of tallage see *Oxford English Dictionary*.
[33] Brooke and Keir (n 3) 51.
[34] See JC Holt, *Magna Carta* (Cambridge, 2001) 321n and Birch (n 15) 3.

and chickens were not citizens.[35] In London the aldermen who came to govern the City were drawn from a narrow class. Trade guilds were developing – the Pipe Roll of 1179–80 records taxation on 19 of them. They did not, however, hold the status they did in other cities. When Henry II granted a Charter to Oxford around 1155, it recognised the liberties of its citizens and then named the first as a merchant guild.[36] Trade in merchandise in the city of Oxford or its suburbs was restricted to members of the guild. No similar clause appears in London's Charters. In fact merchants of London had banded together in 'misteries' and it was from these that the aldermen were selected. The guilds actually came under attack from the aldermanic council.[37] A handful of trades dominated the council – drapers, pepperers, goldsmiths, mercers and vintners. They were wholesale merchants. London was in effect governed by a patrician oligarchy of tradesmen. The term baron was probably used loosely to describe these.[38]

London did not institute the rebellion, but effectively joined it on 17 May 2015, when the rebel barons were admitted within its walls. It already had a track record of supporting rebellion, indeed had an eye for the main chance. After Henry I's death in 1135, London sided with Stephen of Blois against Henry's daughter Matilda and, when she captured the City, succeeded in forcing her out. When Richard I came to the throne in 1189, he almost immediately departed on crusade, leaving his Chancellor, William Longchamps, at the head of the government. When John and a party of barons opposed his rule, the citizens of London supported John and recognised him as supreme governor of the realm; they swore that if Richard died without issue they would support John's claim to the throne.[39] In return he recognised their commune.[40] When Richard returned from the Holy Land, the citizens politically offered 1,500 marks towards his ransom.[41] In 1215 they again turned turtle and supported the baronial rebels against John.

Clause 13 of the Charter provides that

> the city of London is to have all its ancient liberties and free customs both by land and water. Furthermore we will and grant that all other cities, boroughs, towns and ports [*civitates, burgi, ville, portus*] shall have all their liberties and free customs.

The Charter does not seek to define the liberties of cities, no doubt because they were individual to particular Charters. So far as London is concerned we may deduce from earlier grants that the citizens would have intended it to cover the right to elect their own sheriffs and now mayor; the right to have their own husting; the right to appoint their own judge to deal with pleas of the Crown; freedom from pleading outside the City; freedom from paying the murdrum fine and taking part in

---

[35] S Blanshei, *Politics and Justice in late Medieval Bologna* (Edinburgh, 2012).
[36] W Stubbs, *Select Charters and other Illustrations of English Constitutional History from earliest times to the Reign of Edward I* (Oxford, 1913) 189.
[37] Williams (n 20) 168 and 173.
[38] ibid.
[39] Round (n 8) 224.
[40] ibid.
[41] Brooke and Keir (n 3) 47.

trial by battle; freedom from paying tolls throughout the kingdom; and hunting rights in land surrounding London.[42] London still has its own Recorder, who ranks as the senior Circuit Judge in the country, and sits at the Central Criminal Court, known from the street in which it stands as the Old Bailey.

Taxation of cities is dealt with rather unsatisfactorily in the Charter. Clause 12 provides that demands for aid from the City of London shall be dealt with as it is in the rest of the kingdom, that is they require the common counsel of the realm. Nothing specific is said about other cities. The comparable article in the Articles of the Barons (32) included tallage with aids, but no mention is made anywhere in the Charter of tallage. Indeed clause 25 provides that while all shires and hundreds shall be liable to the ancient farm without any increment, this should not apply to the royal *demesne* (which included chartered cities). This was to prove significant. Matthew Paris, writing about 1250 and after, describes events in 1244. He says that Henry III assembled the nobles and demanded a pecuniary aid to raise an army to attack the Welsh and pay off his debts, particularly for wine and beer and other necessaries of life. Paris commented that the King 'could scarcely show himself among his people owing to the clamorous requests of persons demanding what was due to them'. The nobles refused to the King's face to pay an aid

> as they had been often injured and deceived . . . the king, therefore, without consulting the community of the kingdom in general, at least without the advice of the nobles, shamelessly and by force extorted 1500 marks from the London citizens to be thrown away on foreigners.

This last was probably a reference to hiring mercenaries. Even allowing for an obvious degree of bias, this account demonstrates that the attempt in the Charter to limit taxation had not succeeded.

It is not entirely clear who the mayor of London named in the Charter was. There seems to be agreement that when the rebels took control of London, Serlo the Mercer was or became mayor. He was succeeded by William Hardel, who certainly swore allegiance to Prince Louis of France when he invaded England. According to the Annals of Edward I and II the previous mayor was replaced by Serlo when the rebels entered the City.[43] City records show, however, that Serlo became mayor for a year at the end of 1214, which would make it more likely he was the mayor who was a surety. What is principally important is that a mayor of London was among those who were guarantors.

At some date shortly after the grant of the Charter, a treaty was entered into in relation to the custody of London. It was called a treaty and unlike the Charter was drawn up in counterparts, bearing the seal of the barons and King respectively. The counterpart of the former survives in the National Archives.[44] It provides, in effect, that the rebel barons are to hold the custody of London and the Archbishop of

---

[42] See Williams (n 20) 1.
[43] I, 17.
[44] Chancery Miscellania 14/1/1 and see Holt (n 35) 263.

Canterbury that of the Tower until 15 August. If the King complied with the terms of the Charter by that date the custody of London would be returned to him. When that day arrived, however, it had become plain that the differences between the parties would only be decided by armed conflict.

12

Commerce

ETWEEN 1086 AND 1300 it has been estimated that the population of England rose threefold.[1] That this indicated a rising prosperity is evidenced by the increasing number of licensed fairs. Of all cities, London was best placed to take advantage.

It stood at the lowest point where the Thames could be crossed. The Romans built the first wooden bridge and made it the nodal point of their road system. Significantly, the first stone bridge was completed in 1209.[2] It was an important port. Ships from the Baltic countries brought furs. There was much trade with the Low Countries, where merchants in such cities as Ghent and Bruges were keen to buy English wool and export finished cloth. It traded also with Arras in northern France and nearby St Omer, which was an important centre for exporting wine. Through the Rhine, London had access to the western side of Germany, including the vineyards on that river and the Moselle. The wine trade is still evidenced by the Vintry on the north bank of the Thames near London Bridge. The Rhine was also a route north from Italy and the Mediterranean.[3] By the middle of the twelfth century London had developed as a money market.[4] It had a monopoly in minting coins. Under William I and Henry I the silver content remained stable and this gave rise to sterling silver.[5] From the period immediately after the Conquest, London was protected by no fewer than three castles – the Tower, castle Baynard and castle Montfichet. It was not the only city where trade flourished; the relative importance of English cities can be gauged by the tax farm, that is the annual sum of taxes required by the Crown from a particular area. So, in the reign of Henry II, London was fixed at 500 pounds, Southampton at 200–300 pounds, Lincoln at 180 pounds and Winchester at 150 pounds.[6]

The Charter contains some important provisions relating to commerce. Previous Charters granted to London had required the removal of fish weirs on the Thames and Medway, obviously because they held up navigation. Clause 33 of the Charter now extended this requirement to removing fish weirs on rivers throughout all

---

[1] L Cantor, *The English Medieval Landscape* (London, 1982) 18; WL Jordan, *The Great Famine: Northern Europe in the Early Fourteenth Century* (Princeton, NJ, 1996) 12.

[2] See G Home, *Old London Bridge* (London, 1931).

[3] On this see G Williams, *Medieval London: From Commune to Capital* (London, 1970).

[4] ibid 222.

[5] C Brooke and G Kier, *London 800–1216: The Shaping of a City* (London, 1975) 93.

[6] ibid 41.

England, except on the sea coast. The Charter, however, went much further than this to secure freedom of movement for merchants, both English and foreign. Clause 41 provided:

> All merchants are to be safe and secure in leaving and entering England and in staying and travelling in England, both by land and water, to buy and sell free from all maletotes[7] by the ancient and rightful customs, except in time of war, such as come from an enemy country. And if such are found in our country at the outbreak of war they shall be detained without damage to their persons or goods until we or our Chief Justiciar know how the merchants of our land are treated in the enemy country; and if ours are safe there, the others shall be safe in our land.

Beyond this clause 42 conferred a general right to travel overseas:

> Henceforth, anyone, saving his allegiance due to us, may leave our realm and return safe and secure by land and water, save for a short period in time of war on account of the general interest of the realm, and excepting those imprisoned and outlawed according to the law of the land and natives of an enemy country and merchants who shall be treated as aforesaid.

One of the most potentially important provisions of the Charter in 1215 was clause 35:

> [L]et there be one measure of wine throughout our kingdom and one measure of ale and one measure of corn, namely the London quarter, and one width of cloth whether dyed, russet or halberjet, namely two ells within the selvedges. Let it be the same with weights as with measures.

Russet was a rough cloth and halberjet a superior kind. The selvedge is the finished edge of cloth which prevents it unravelling – in other words it would be a straight edge. An ell was a measurement of length. Early measurements were based on parts of the body, so foot reflected the length of that member. Ell or Elf was either the arm or forearm – below the elbow. It had a Latin forebear, *ulna*, meaning elbow. Saxon and Frisian had equivalents. In fact it was standardised in different lengths in different countries. The English length was 45 inches, which would be based on the whole arm, and the Scottish just over 37 inches.[8] At some time in the latter half of the thirteenth century a document called 'the Composition of Yards and Perches' revised the standard lengths. The Charter does not indicate what the standard weights were. There were different kinds of pound weight – the troy pound used by jewellers, the London pound and the mercantile pound. This last was based on a set quantity of cereal grains.

These commercial clauses went much further than anything found in comparable grants on the continent of Europe; they were important steps on the way to economic prosperity and, in particular, the City of London's ultimate commercial role.

---

[7] A tax on wool.
[8] See *Oxford English Dictionary*.

13

Robin Hood and the Royal Forests

T HE LEGEND OF Robin Hood, outlawed in Sherwood Forest and pursued by the wicked sheriff of Nottingham, reverberates down the centuries as a symbol of opposition to oppressive government. Royal forests were the product of the Norman Conquest. King William was owner of the whole kingdom. While he passed possession of parcels of land to his followers, he nevertheless kept large tracts of land in his own possession to maintain his court. The Norman kings were great huntsmen and preserved large swathes of forest to pursue the hunt.[1] The forests were regarded as part of the royal demesne.

The Anglo Saxon Chronicle stated that the Conqueror 'established a great pece for the deer and laid down laws therefor, that whoever should slay hart or hind should be blinded'.[2] The Dialogue of the Exchequer (about 1180)[3] describes the forest of the King as 'the safe dwelling place of wild beasts, not of every kind, but of the kinds that live in woods, not in all places, but in fixed ones and ones suitable for the purpose'.[4] It also states that the forests 'are the sanctuaries of kings and their greatest delight; thither they go for the sake of hunting, having laid aside their cares for a while, so that they may be refreshed by a short rest'.[5] It also describes the basis of royal control of the royal forests and those who transgress the forest laws as being

> outside the jurisdiction of other courts, and solely dependent on the decision of the King, or of some officer specially appointed by him. The forest has its own laws, based it is said not on the Common Law of the realm, but on the arbitrary decree of the King, so what is done in accordance with the forest law is not called just absolutely, but just according to forest law.[6]

Any attempt to reduce the power of the King over the forests would challenge royal prerogative. The customary forest laws were eventually set down in writing in the Assize of Woodstock in 1184. It was said to protect the 'vert and the venison'.

---

[1] Generally on forests see R Grant, *The Royal Forests of England* (Gloucester, 1991) and CR Young, *The Royal Forests of Medieval England* (Leicester, 1979).
[2] Rolls Series I 355.
[3] BC Johnson (ed), *Dialogus de Scarario* (London, 1950).
[4] Johnson (n 3) Bk I XII.
[5] Johnson (n3) Bk I XI.
[6] Johnson (n 3) Bk I XI.

From the eleventh century the oppressive nature of the forest laws entered folk tradition. In 1087, in the Cathedral of Peterborough, the *Rime of William* was recorded, describing how William I's officers had created the New Forest by destroying villages and expelling the inhabitants.[7] Similarly, Henry of Huntingdon recorded that William

> loved the beasts of the chase as if he were their father. On account of this in the woodlands reserved for hunting, which he called the New Forest, he had villages rooted out and people removed and made it a habitation for wild beasts.[8]

John of Salisbury[9] in the mid twelfth century wrote of William's control of the forests: 'his great men bewailed it and the poor murmured thereat, but he was so obdurate that he recked not of the hatred of them all, but they must follow the king's will, if they would live or have land'.[10] We have already seen that in 1205 John appointed a man from Touraine, Peter de Roches, as Bishop of Winchester; in 1213 he was appointed Chief Justiciar.[11] A contemporary chronicle described him as taking more delight in the suffering of wild animals than the salvation of souls.[12] Clause 50 of the Charter specifically targeted a group of his followers whom John undertook to remove and disqualify from office. Amongst them was Philip Mark. He was one of a number of mercenaries from Touraine imported by John to counterbalance the power of the barons. There was no sheriff of Nottingham in 1215 (the first appointment was not until 1449), but Mark was appointed sheriff of Nottinghamshire and the royal forests in 1208; the specific provision for his removal from his offices makes him a candidate for the wicked sheriff in the Robin Hood legend.[13]

James Holt wrote an entertaining book on Robin Hood.[14] He pointed out that 'Robin Hood enjoys a unique distinction. He was accorded in the Dictionary of National Biography an article arguing that he never existed'. Written versions of the legend started to appear in the early fifteenth century, though they no doubt followed earlier oral versions. They conflate various tales, some based on Barnsdale in South Yorkshire and others on Nottingham and Sherwood Forest.[15] The two areas are not very far apart. The period when the tale is set varies between 1193 and 1283. A Scottish author, a certain John Major, wrote his *History of Britain* in 1521 and placed the relevant events in the period leading up to the return of Richard I in 1194 and this is the time scale which eventually prevailed.[16] Several points may be made

[7] WH Stevenson (ed), *Chronicum de Lanercost*, 13, cited N Vincent, *Peter de Roches: An Alien in English Politics* (Cambridge, 1996) 3.

[8] D Greenway (ed), *Historia Anglorum* (Oxford, 1996) 405.

[9] See below App A Sources.

[10] J Salisbury, 'Policraticus' in C Webb (ed), *European Political Thought: Traditions and Endurance* (New York, NY, 1978) I, 30.

[11] See above, Chapter 5.

[12] Vincent (n 7) 3.

[13] See S Painter, *The Reign of King John* (Baltimore, MD, 1949) 206.

[14] JC Holt, *Robin Hood* (London, 2010).

[15] ibid 85.

[16] ibid 39–40.

with some certainty. Royal forests were used by outlaws and robbers, who did live off the King's deer – hence harsh penalties under the forest laws. There was an outlaw called Robin Hode who operated in Yorkshire. He did so about the same time that Philip Mark was sheriff of Nottinghamshire, though a rival candidate for wicked sheriff could be Eustace of Lowdham, sheriff of South Yorkshire. Lowdham is a village in Nottinghamshire, which is only seven miles from the city of Nottingham. Nottingham was a centre of power for John and his followers. When Richard I went on crusade he granted various fiefs to his younger brother John, no doubt to secure his loyalty. One of these was the county of Nottinghamshire, from which John received a considerable income.[17] When it appeared that Richard might not return from his crusade, John attempted to set up an alternative government. When Richard did return, troops loyal to John held out in defence of Nottingham castle longer than any other of John's supporters.[18] Sheriffs were unpopular for the rigour with which they exacted taxes and for supposedly using their role for self-profit. The specific naming of the sheriff of Nottinghamshire in clause 50 at least indicates a particular hostility.

Three issues arose in relation to forests. The first was their extent. All of the Norman and Angevin kings enlarged their royal forests. Those brought within their boundaries objected. The second issue, linked to the first, was the severity of the forest laws, which were rigorously enforced by judges travelling round the counties on eyre. Poachers caught by officers of the forest had to be produced before them; in the meantime they could be kept in gaol, often for a long period since the eyres were annual. In addition, their chattels could be seized.[19] Before the eyre they could be severely amerced (fined). The third issue was the manner in which royal officers exploited their power. The liberties granted by the forest Charters apparently applied not just to freemen, but to everybody in the kingdom.

The Charter of 1215 contains only three clauses relating to forests: one deals with the extent of the forests; another with summonses to forest courts; the third sets up an enquiry into unspecified evil customs of royal servants in royal forests. When, in November 1216, the Charter was reissued by William Marshal and the papal legate, matters concerning forests and foresters were amongst the weighty or doubtful areas reserved for consideration by a full council.[20] That consideration took a year and in 1217, when the Charter was reissued, there was a separate Charter of the Forest. This dealt with forest law in much more detail than the original Charter.[21]

A forest was not necessarily a thickly wooded area. It was simply an area of land – often woodland, but also including arable land – which the King claimed as his forest. Once he had claimed land as a forest, the customary laws of the forest applied to it. Clause 10 of Henry I's Charter of Liberties rehearsed that his barons had

---

[17]   WL Warren, *King John* (New Haven, CT, 1997) 40.
[18]   See JA Giles (ed), *Flowers of History* (London, 1849) vol II, 134.
[19]   Grant (n 1) 47.
[20]   Below, Chapter 15.
[21]   Ibid.

conceded that he was entitled to the forest lands established by his father William I, thus excluding afforestation by William Rufus. Henry II greatly enlarged the area of royal forest.[22] By his death in 1189 it has been estimated that somewhere between a quarter and a third of England was royal forest.[23] John's perilous financial position caused him to free land that had been royal forest in return for money payments. For instance, in March 1204 the men of Cornwall made a fine of 2,000 marks and 20 palfreys for disafforestation of their county.[24] John also claimed fresh land as royal forest. When the rebel barons drew up their first demands in January 1215 they demanded confirmation of Henry's Charter, which would have excluded afforestation since the death of William I. Magna Carta was more restricted in its concession; clause 47 provided that forests created by King John should be immediately disafforested. In relation to the forests created by Henry II and Richard I, a stay was imposed. By taking the Cross and undertaking to crusade to the Holy Land the King could claim crusader's respite.[25] Clause 53 of the Charter provided that the King should have a crusader's respite in respect of doing justice on disafforestation of forests created by his two predecessors. It added that 'as soon as we return, or if we do not undertake our pilgrimage, we will at once do full justice to complainants in these matters'. John did not go on pilgrimage, but he swiftly repudiated the terms of the Charter; matters were unresolved at the time of his death.

There was also concern about the manner in which royal officials had enforced customary forest law in the past. Clause 48 of Magna Carta provided that:

> All evil customs of forests and foresters, warrens and warreners, sheriffs and their servants, river banks and their wardens are to be investigated at once in every county by twelve sworn knights of the same county, who are to be chosen by worthy men of the county and within forty days of the enquiry they are to be abolished by them beyond recall, provided that we, or our Justiciar if we are not in England, first know of it.

Warrens were rabbit or hare warrens and warreners those in charge of their administration. Justices in eyre already visited the counties collecting monies due to the Crown, but also examining the conduct of royal officers. In 1212 a new forest eyre was commenced, which resulted in the imprisonment of some foresters in Staffordshire.[26] In early 1213 the King dismissed his Chief Forester, ironically replacing him with Robert de Ros, who was to be a principal rebel.[27] The King also wrote to the knights of Yorkshire and Lincolnshire that he was moved by the complaints about the conduct of royal officials and was appointing an inquest of four to enquire into them.

---

[22] JC Holt, *Magna Carta* (Cambridge, 2001) 42.
[23] JA Green, 'Unity and Disunity in the Anglo Norman State' (1989) 62(148) *Historical Research* 124.
[24] Grant (n 1) 136.
[25] See above, Chapter 4.
[26] See Holt (n 22) 211–12.
[27] ibid.

This background at least indicates that the legend of Robin Hood bore a connection to reality.[28] As a footnote, once the Charter was annulled, Philip Mark, the sheriff of Nottinghamshire, remained in office, but he was dismissed as sheriff by the regency government in December 1217.[29] The proximity of this to the issue of the Charter of the Forest in the previous November suggests that the government was seeking a clean sweep of the previous forest administration. Mark did not totally fall out of royal favour, for in 1226 he was given a parcel of land by Henry III in Barton le Street in North Yorkshire.[30] He was buried at Lenten Priory in Nottingham.

---

[28] See JC Holt, 'Philip Mark and the Shrievalty of Nottinghamshire and Derbyshire' (1952) 56 *Transactions of the Thoroton Society* 18ff.

[29] PR Cross and SD Lloyd, *Thirteenth Century England* (Newcastle, 1993).

[30] W Page (ed), *A History of the County of York North Riding* 1472–6 (London, 1925).

14

Wales and Scotland

CLAUSES 56 TO 58 of the Charter make specific provision for Wales and 59 for Scotland. The relationship of the Norman and Angevin kings with these countries was complicated and beyond the scope of this book, though we deal with it now in outline.[1] The Normans did not attempt to conquer Wales, though the Domesday Book shows that south Wales was held by Riset of the King for a farm of 40 pounds and north Wales by Robert de Rudlan at the same farm.[2] The Normans' method of controlling Wales was to enter into treaties with the Welsh princes and establish powerful earldoms on the borders of Wales, called the Marches. The Marcher lords claimed and exercised exclusive rights within their lordships. The King's writ did not run in the Marches. The marcher lords had the right to wage war or make peace independently of the King and any land they took from the Welsh they kept as part of their lordship.[3] A distinction came to be drawn between Pur Wallia, ruled by the Welsh princes, and Marchia Wallia, ruled by the English lords. The Welsh princes constantly quarrelled and fought between themselves and the English on occasion intervened.

North Wales was largely covered by the principality of Gwynedd and mid Wales by that of Powys. Principal among the Welsh rulers was Llywelyn ap Iorworth, or Llewellyn the Great, who lived from about 1172 to 1240. By 1200 he was lord of Gwynedd in north Wales, had made a treaty with John and married John's illegitimate daughter, Joan. In 1208 he seized Powys. By 1210, however, relations between John and Llewelyn had deteriorated, possibly because the latter had formed an alliance with the powerful Marcher lord, William de Braose, who by then had become John's hated enemy. John may also have been concerned at the increase in Llewelyn's power. John allied himself with the other Welsh princes and invaded Gwynedd, eventually forcing Llewelyn to agree terms. He had to surrender territory, but his wife persuaded her father not to dispossess him altogether. Llewelyn swore fealty to John. He also had to pay a large tribute in cattle and horses and hand over hostages, including his illegitimate son. In August 1212 John again prepared to invade and, as we have seen,[4] executed some of the hostages. His daughter, Llewelyn's wife, wrote

---

[1] See generally AD Carr, *Medieval Wales* (Basingstoke, 1995); R Davies, *Conquest Coexistence and Change: Wales 1063–1415* (Oxford, 2006).

[2] See Carr (n 1) 54.

[3] Davies (n 1) 283–86.

[4] Above, Chapter 1.

to him warning that if he invaded he would be murdered by his own barons. He abandoned his plans. Thereafter Llewelyn contrived to gain the support of some of the Welsh princes who had opposed him. In the period when Pope Innocent III excommunicated John, the Pope released Llewelyn from his oath of fealty. By this time Llewelyn had made himself spokesman for all the Welsh princes and in this guise made an alliance with Philip Augustus of France. When the English lords rebelled, Llewelyn took the opportunity to invade Shropshire and in May 1215 he took Shrewsbury castle. Clause 56 of the Charter provides:

> If we have disseised or deprived Welshman of lands or liberties or other things without lawful judgment of their peers, in England or Wales, they are to be returned to them at once; and if a dispute arises over this it shall be settled in the Marches by judgement of their peers, for tenements in England according to the law of England, for tenements in Wales according to the law of Wales, for tenements in the March according to the law of the March. The Welsh are to do the same by us and ours.

As this demonstrates, the three areas had distinct laws. By clause 57 unlawful disseisins by Henry II were to be dealt with on John's return from crusade. By clause 58 the hostages given by Llewelyn, including his son, were to be returned.

Scotland was a separate kingdom, but the Constable of Scotland, Alan Galloway, is listed in the preamble to the Charter as one of those who advised the King to make the grant. William the Lion (so named from his coat of arms) ruled Scotland from 1165 to 1214.[5] He also claimed Northumbria, as he had inherited the title of earl of Northumbria from his father.[6] He was compelled to surrender the title to Henry II, but this led to continuing incursions by the Scots into the area. In 1174 William invaded England. At the battle of Alnwick he was taken prisoner and eventually imprisoned in Falaise in Normandy. He agreed in the Treaty of Falaise to swear fealty to the King, which he did at York in 1175. In 1189, in return for 10,000 silver marks, Richard I, who needed the money for his crusade, released William from his oath. When Richard I died, William offered to do homage to John, if Northumbria were given to him. It was not and in 1200 he swore fealty without any such promise. In 1209 he entered into a treaty with John, under which he agreed to pay 15,000 marks to the English king, to hand over hostages for swift payment and to hand his daughters Margaret and Isabella to John. They were not hostages, but in due course Margaret was to be married to John's son Henry and Isabella to an English noble of rank. William's son Alexander was born in 1198 and in 1212 John agreed to provide a wife for him within six years. John knighted Alexander. The political end of all this was obviously to draw the two kingdoms closer together.

Alexander succeeded his father on 6 December 1214. He allied himself with the rebels, two of whom (Eustace de Vesci and Robert de Ros) were his brothers in law. Clause 59 of the Charter undertook in respect of Alexander's liberties and rights that they would be dealt with in the same manner as the King dealt with the English

---

[5] Generally see AAM Duncan, *Scotland: The Making of the Kingdom* (Edinburgh, 1975).
[6] See AAM Duncan, 'John King of England and the Kings of Scots' in SD Church (ed), *King John: New Interpretations* (Woodbridge, 1999) 245.

barons. Any disputes were to be determined in the King's court by Alexander's peers. Alexander's sisters were to be returned to Scotland.

In September 1215 a judgment of the barons in England gave Alexander the baronies of Northumbria, Westmorland and Cumberland. In January 1216 John invaded Scotland and took and burned various lowland towns, but retreated after 10 days. In August 1216 Alexander marched south, took Carlisle and eventually reached London, where he entered into a treaty with the City, both parties describing themselves as being against John. He met and did homage to Prince Louis. After Louis had surrendered his claim and left England, Alexander entered into a peace treaty with the regency government and married John's daughter Joan.

15

The Charter Restored

J OHN'S DEATH ON the night of 18/19 October 1216 must have seemed disastrous to the royal party. We have already noted that they moved swiftly to crown the young King Henry III and set up a regency government under William Marshal.[1] In less than a month, on 12 November, a version of Magna Carta was reissued. It was expressed to be made by the King on the advice of the new papal legate, Gualo, nine bishops and 23 barons. Among them were the regent, William Marshal, the Chief Justiciar, Hubert de Burgh, and four bishops, all of whom were named as advisors in the original Charter. By this time Innocent III was dead, Pandulf the papal legate in 1215 had returned to Rome and been replaced by Gualo and Stephen Langton was out of the country. No doubt it was seen as a time for a new start. The first clause granted freedom of the Church; it made no mention of the formal consent by the Crown to church appointments referred to in John's Charter of November 1214. Clause 2 granted the underwritten liberties to the freemen of the kingdom. Since the King did not as yet have a seal, those of the papal legate and the regent were used to authenticate it.

The original Charter, however, was very much cut down to size. There were now only 40 clauses. The former clause 61, which established the committee of 25 to enforce the terms of the Charter, and clause 62, which pardoned former rebels, went. In general those clauses which dealt with feudal incidents or the administration of justice remained; those that intruded on the Crown's powers to administer the country went. In clause 40 of the new Charter certain weighty and doubtful matters were reserved until a full council could consider them. The topics were scutages and assessment of aids, debts to Jews, liberty to enter and leave the kingdom, and matters concerning forests and rivers. Meanwhile the clauses which referred to these topics in the 1215 Charter were omitted, in particular clauses 12 and 14, which required the consent of the council to the levying of scutages and aids and set up a mechanism for obtaining that consent. No doubt part of the reasoning behind the swift reissue of the Charter was to encourage the rebels still in the field to swear allegiance to the new King. Nevertheless a copy was sent to Ireland, which may indicate that the Charter in its new form was regarded as a binding constitutional document.[2]

---

[1] Above, Chapter 2.
[2] See G Richardson, 'Magna Carta Hibernia' *Irish Historical Studies* III, 31-3; cited JC Holt, *Magna Carta* (Cambridge, 2001) 382.

After the defeat of the rebels in 1217, the regency government was clearly in control of the country. The Charter of 1216 had purported to be valid in perpetuity, though under English custom a minor could not makes grants in perpetuity.[3] It may be that this was one of the reasons for the reissue of the Charter on 6 November 1217. The form followed that of the 1216 Charter, though this time the advisors referred to by name were simply the papal legate, the Archbishop of York, the Bishop of London and the regent William Marshal. There were some amendments. Three new clauses were added to the 1216 version. Clause 23 limited the powers of bailiffs. Clause 41 provided that scutage from henceforth should be taken as it was accustomed to be taken in the time of Henry II. Clause 43 provided for the destruction of castles built during the civil war. With one exception, nothing of consequence emerged from consideration by the council of the weighty matters reserved to them. There were some practical amendments. The visits by royal judges to the counties, which under clause 18 of the 1215 Charter were to be four times a year, were now reduced under clause 13 to once a year. The original four visits per year must have proved unworkable. Other smaller practical changes were made.

The one area reserved to the council that did bear fruit was control of the royal forests. The 1215 Charter dealt only cursorily with forest laws. Now a separate Charter of the Forest was granted on the same day as the reissue of Magna Carta itself. It provided a comprehensive regime for control of the royal forests.[4] No doubt the fact that the King was in his minority made it easier to deal with the unpopular aspects of forest law, which would have affected the barons as adversely as everyone else. The constitutional significance of the grant of Forest Charter was that it represented a large incursion into an area of law which had previously been subject only to royal will. It took a year to draft. Much of its language is abstruse – it speaks of waste and assart and pannage, of regarders, agisters and verderers, of swanmotes, of fawning of beasts and expeditating dogs. Careful study, however, reveals the importance given to the various issues and the nature of the grievances which led to its drafting. It was reissued in 1225 along with the main Charter. In 1297 both documents were entered on to the statute book. Parts of the Charter of the Forest remained in force until it was finally replaced in 1971 by the Wild Creatures and Forest Laws Act 1971.

Clause 3 of the Charter of the Forest 1225 required the disafforestation of all forests created by Richard I or John.[5] Clause 1 provided that forest created by Henry II should

> be viewed by good and lawful men and if he made forest any wood that was not his demesne, to the injury of whose wood it was, it shall be disafforested. And if he made his own wood forest it shall remain forest, saving the common pasture and other things in that forest to those who are accustomed to have them previously.

---

[3] See D Carpenter, *The Minority of Henry III* (London, 1990) 23.
[4] See above, Chapter 13.
[5] The Latin text of the Charter of the Forest is to be found in the appendices to Holt (n 2) and a translation in Douglas, D (ed), *English Historical Documents* 3 No 24 (London, 1973) 337–40.

It is interesting to note that the right to common pasture is preserved even within forest in the royal demesne. Under clause 5 'regarders' were to go though the forests to discover their bounds at the time of Henry II.

Clause 10 provided that

> no one shall henceforth lose life or limb because of our venison, but if anyone has been arrested and convicted of taking venison he shall he be fined heavily if he have the means; and if he has not the means he shall lie in prison for a year and a day.

After that he had to find reliable pledges for good conduct or abjure the realm. Under clause 11, barons passing through royal forest were entitled to take two beasts, but should sound their horn to show they were not acting furtively. Under clause 15, all who had been outlawed for a forest offence since the coronation of Henry II were to be released from their outlawry without legal proceedings and 'shall find reliable pledges that they will not do wrong to us in the future in respect of our forest'.

Freeholders did hold land within the royal forests, but under customary forest law their right to deal with their land without royal licence was heavily limited. Waste involved felling of trees or clearing land, assart its enclosure, pannage a tax payable for grazing pigs other than in the autumn. Anyone committing waste or assart without royal licence would be subject to heavy pecuniary penalties. Under the Charter of the Forest, the rights of freeholders within the forest were now protected in respect of land they had enclosed without royal licence, or cultivated, or culled wood within, provided they had done so over a long period. They were entitled to construct a mill or pond on their land and keep hunting birds there. A swanimote was to be held consisting of freeholders within the forest to determine offences against forest law. Amongst those matters they were to view was 'expeditating' of dogs. Under customary forest law, those who kept dogs within the forest had to remove their claws and the balls of their feet. Those who failed to do so were punished. The purpose of this law must have been to prevent the dogs killing wild animals wanted for royal hunting. The Forest Charter in clause 6 provided that anyone found not to have 'expeditated' his dog should be amerced of three shillings, but in future no one should lose an ox as a penalty. It might also be regarded as a forest dogs Charter, since it restricted the disabling of dogs to three claws of the forefoot – removal of the ball of the foot was banned.

A further significance of the sudden emergence of the Forest Charter is that it must have been discussed, prepared and a text provided over a period of time, possibly as far back as Henry III's accession. The obvious candidates for drafting would be the clerks in royal employ and possibly the judges. Ecclesiastical clerks would have had little interest or possibly expertise in drafting secular clauses. This in turn may throw light on the drafting of the original Charter. On the face of it, in 1215 the King would not have wanted to provide royal clerks to assist the rebels in refining their demands. The form of the barons' first demands in January 1215 was, however, fairly simplistic, which suggests they did not have draftsmen of their own readily available. The Articles of the Barons showed a step change in legal expertise. The most obvious candidates who possessed this were the royal clerks.

On 11 February 1225 the two Charters were again reissued and this was the form in which they settled and eventually were placed on the statute book. Henry had not at this stage achieved his majority. There was no clear precedent in English custom for the age of majority. Clause 3 of the 1216 Charter had fixed it for the heirs of barons at 21. Henry was still some way short of that and indeed was not yet 18 in the early part of 1225. As feudal lord, the new Pope, Honorius III, would in the end be the one to decide at what point Henry succeeded. On 13 April 1223, having noted Henry's progress in prudence and discretion, he wrote to the chief ministers (De Burgh, De Roches and Brewer) requiring them to deliver to the King 'the free and undisturbed disposition of his kingdom'. He also wrote to the keeper of the great seal, Ralph de Neville, ordering him to use it at the King's will. Failure to obey these demands would result in excommunication.[6] The wording of this reissued Charter stressed the voluntary nature of the grant. It was said to be made spontaneously and of free will (*spontanea et voluntate nostra*). Whereas previous Charters had simply granted liberties, now a phrase 'given and granted' (*dedimus and concessimus*) was used, as if to underline the strength of the gift. Nothing is said specifically about the grant being made on advice, but at the end there is a long list of witnesses – some 31 senior clergy and 30 barons. Nine of the latter had been members of the committee of 25 drawn from the rebel party in 1215 and given powers to enforce the original Charter. A large assembly such as this plainly mirrored the council of advisors going back to Anglo Saxon times. The presence of former loyalists and rebels indicated a desire to draw a line under the conflicts of recent years, to reunite the community of the realm. It was probably the settlement that Stephen Langton had worked for all along.

Amendments made in the 1225 Charter to the 1217 Magna Carta text were relatively minor. The number of clauses was reduced to 37, achieved in part by amalgamation (clauses 39 and 40 of the 1215 Charter were now in one clause 29) and also by omission (for instance clauses 23 and 4 of the 1216 version, dealing with the powers of bailiffs, were omitted). A new clause 36 dealt with what looked like a form of tax avoidance, whereby a landowner gave land to a religious house and took the land to hold of the same house. Such deals were annulled. The clause on scutage was amended to protect exemptions to which the military orders, magnates and church had previously been entitled. Plainly none of these changes were earth shattering. The principal reason for the reissue was the Crown's requirement for money to defend Gascony.[7]

1225 marked the end of the thirteenth-century amendments to the original Charter. As the 1225 Charter had been granted when the King was underage, doubts seem to have remained about its validity. Eventually in 1237 Henry agreed to make

---

[6] See Carpenter (n 3) 301.
[7] Below, Chapter 16.

a short confirmation of the Charter, confirming its terms were granted in perpetuity 'notwithstanding that these charters were completed when we were a minor'. In 1225 Stephen Langton and in 1237 Edmund of Abingdon pronounced a sentence of excommunication on anyone who violated the terms of the Charter. By 1253 the Church considered that Henry himself had violated the terms. He made a further confirmation in Westminster Hall.[8] There was a further one in 1258.

When Edward I issued his *Confirmatio Cartorum* in 1297, it stated that the Charter of Liberties and of the Forest 'which were made in the time of King Henry our father, shall be kept in every point without breach'. The Charters were to be sent to all royal officers under the King's seal and to be read to the people twice a year.

> Our justices, sheriffs, mayors and other ministers, which under us have the laws of our land to guide, shall allow the said charters pleaded before them in judgement in all their points, that is to wit, the Great Charter as the common law and the Charter of the Forest for the wealth of our realm.

Any judgment contrary to the Charters 'shall be undone and holden for nought'. This confirmation was recorded in the King's statute book.

All these Charters were expressed to be granted in perpetuity and to bind the heirs of the grantor. Nevertheless successive monarchs, up to Henry V, were asked to and did confirm the Charter. The reasons for this may be various. One might have been because the monarch or government were seen as having breached its terms, as in the case of Henry III in 1253. There may have been doubts whether one king could bind his successors. It may simply be because of the importance successive generations attached to the Charter.

An annalist wrote in 1219 that the itinerant justices went round the country watching over the restoration of the laws and causing them to be observed in their pleas according to the Charter of John.[9] Bracton, when in about 1250 he came to collect the decisions of his predecessors, seemed to regard the period after the Charter of 1215 as a golden age:

> [L]aws and customs are often misapplied by the unwise and unlearned who ascend the judgement seat before thay have learned the laws . . . who decide cases according to their own will rather than by the authority of the law. I, Henry de Bracton, to instruct lesser judges if no one else, have turned my mind to the ancient judgements of just men . . . and have collected therein what I find worthy of note . . . to be preserved for posterity for ever.[10]

Faith Thompson, in her thesis 'The First Century of Magna Carta: Why It Persisted as a Document', recorded some 58 instances in the records of the royal courts of the Charter being cited. A famous instance occurred some 10 years after the Charter in

---

[8] See Carpenter, D, 'Magna Carta 1253' (2013) 86(232) *Bulletin of the Institute of Historical Research*.
[9] *Annales Monasticti*, cited D Stenton, *After Runnymede: Magna Carta in the Middle Ages* (Virginia, 1965).
[10] Thorne, SE (ed), *The Laws and Customs of England* II (Cambridge, MA, 1977), intro, f, 1a.

the case of the knights of Lincolnshire.[11] Clause 35 of the 1225 Charter provided that no sheriff shall 'keep his turn in the hundred but twice in the year'. The hundred court was the lowest ranking local court and in Lincolnshire the term used for a hundred was a wapentake. Under clauses 18 and 19 of the 1215 Charter the assizes were to be held in the shire or county court in the course of one day. If business was left over, some of the local knights and freeholders were to finish the business without the judge (who would have moved on) the following day. Under clause 12 of the 1225 Charter, unfinished business was to be determined by the judge elsewhere on his circuit. In this instance, the pleas had been heard from dawn to dusk and the sheriff then adjourned the unfinished business to the next day in the local courts of the wapentakes. When the business was to be started there, the local knights objected on the ground that it should be heard in the county court. Their representatives were summoned before the Justices of the Royal Bench and called in aid the Charter of Liberties, which could not be departed from without the consent of the King and the magnates of the realm. The result is not recorded, but the knights were plainly well informed on the provisions of the Charter and felt confident to cite it.

[11] See Curia Regis Rolls XII 312 and 2142; Pollock, F and FW Maitland, *The History of English Law to the Time of Edward I* I (Cambridge, 1895) 549–50; JR Maddicott, 'Magna Carta and the Local Community 1215–1259' (1984) 102(1) *Past and Present* 25–65.

16

Towards Democracy

In his authoritative *Origins of the English Parliament*, JR Maddicott writes:

> Henry III's minority had established the great council as a leading force in politics and confirmed its alignment with the liberties now guaranteed in the Charters. In the middle part of his reign the English parliament emerged from this conciliar matrix to take on the shape which, with some variations, it was to maintain for the rest of the middle ages.[1]

The route taken might be described as two steps forward, one step back – Plantagenet monarchs did not lightly give up their prerogative powers.

One of the main reasons for the acceptance of the 'conciliar matrix' was the coincidence that before and after the 1215 Charter, there were periods when there was no effective king in place. Richard I became King in the summer of 1189 and by the following summer he had departed on crusade. He was either fighting or imprisoned for the next four years. He did not appoint a regent, but left his Chancellor, William Longchamps, in charge. The Chronicler William of Newburgh recorded that this was done without the counsel or consent of the nobles. As we have already noted, Longchamps swiftly became unpopular and was forced to flee to the continent. Richard was informed and appointed Walter, Bishop of Coutances in Normandy, in Longchamps' stead, this time with the assent of the bishop, earls and barons in a meeting in St Paul's.[2] As regent, Walter frequently summoned and relied on the royal council. Another relevant period occurred during the minority of Henry III. William Marshal, as regent from 1216, could not hope to have the authority of an adult king. Probably as a result, he frequently sought the approval of a general council and this pattern was followed after his death in 1219. Between 1216 and 1225, 25 great councils of the realm were summoned.[3] This inevitably influenced the development of forms of government. Over the next decades the idea of an assembly that was more representative developed. In the 1230s the term *parliamentum* came into use.[4] An *assize* was a place where you sat together; a parliament (derived from the French *parlement*) was somewhere you came to talk.

The most crucial of the councils was that early in 1225. It was here that the council bargained supply of money for confirmation of the Charter. We have already

---

[1] JR Maddicott, *Origins of the English Parliament, 924–1327* (Oxford, 2002) 157.
[2] See ibid 109–10.
[3] They are listed in the index to D Carpenter, *The Minority of Henry III* (London, 1990) 449–50.
[4] Maddicott (n 1) 154; it had on rare occasions been used under Henry II.

noted that, although Henry III had not attained his majority at this date, the Pope, as his feudal lord, had granted him some greater role in the conduct of government.[5] On 2 February 1225 a great council was called in London.[6] Prince Louis of France, who had invaded England in 1216, was now King Louis VIII. He had recently occupied Poitou and now threatened Gascony, another territory of the English Crown; he might decide to invade England. On 2 February 1225 a council of over 60 senior clergy and barons was summoned by the Justiciar, Hubert de Burgh, who requested a levy of one-fifteenth of the value of moveables for the defence of the realm. Roger of Wendover described what happened: the Justiciar 'set out the losses and injuries which the King had suffered in the transmarine provinces; by which not only the king, but also many barons and earls had been deprived of their inheritances; and, since many were concerned in the business, the assistance of many would be necessary. He therefore asked the advice and assistance of all as to the means by which the English Crown could regain its lost dignities and old rights; in order to effect this properly, he believed that it would be sufficient if the fifteenth part of all moveable property throughout England be granted to the king, alike from clergy and laity. This proposal having been made the archbishop and all the assembly of bishops, earls and barons, abbots and priors, after some deliberation, gave for their answer, that they would willingly accede to the king's demands if he would grant them their long-sought liberties. The king therefore was induced by covetousness to grant their request.'[7] Agreement was not finally reached until the 11 February. The end result was certainly to the advantage of the Crown. The huge sum of £40,000 was raised. Gascony was retained and became the centre of a valuable wine trade with England. On the other hand the barons may have thought it was important to obtain a fresh grant at a time when it was recognised that the King was sufficiently mature to participate in government. Whatever the motivation, this grant set a precedent when the Crown later sought supply. The importance of a grant of tax in return for other legislation is obvious. Just as the crisis of 1215 had arisen in large part from the Crown's demands for money, so over the next 150 years, successive monarchs bargained taxes for confirmation of the Charter.

When he attained his majority, Henry's requirements for money outdid his father's. He too fought expensive and unsuccessful wars attempting to regain lost lands in France. He lavished patronage on his half brothers, the Lusignans, in the hope that their lands close to Poitou could be a base for military operations.[8] He rebuilt Westminster Abbey as a tribute to Edward the Confessor. He sought the throne of Sicily for his son Edmund (the rival candidate was the son of the Holy Roman Emperor) and this led to the Pope demanding huge sums for his support of Edmund's claim. The council, even when it agreed to make a supply, established committees to ensure that the money was spent for the purpose for which it was

[5] Above, Chapter 15.
[6] See Maddicott (n 1) 107.
[7] JA Giles (ed), *Flowers of History* II, 455
[8] Maddicott (n 1) 170.

granted.[9] They tried to have a say in royal appointments, something which Henry strongly opposed.[10] In 1258 his financial position was so dire that he sought consent for a tax on one-third of the value of both moveable and immoveable property. This aroused such opposition that he had to agree to the appointment of a committee of 24, who were to consider reforming the realm. This in turn led to a 'parliament' at Oxford in the same year, which produced the so-called Provisions of Oxford. An inner council was to be created, consisting of 15 members, some appointed by the King and some by the barons. They would have the power to appoint ministers. The greater council or parliament was to meet three times a year and the 15 were to attend to review the state of the realm and deal with its common business, with the King.[11] This was followed by the Provisions of Westminster in 1259, which addressed and reformed baronial grievances. The see-saw of power continued. In 1261 Henry obtained papal dispensation from his oath to observe the Provisions and reasserted his power. This led to a period of civil war and in May 1264 a rebel army, led by Simon de Montfort, defeated the royal army at Lewes and took Henry prisoner. The tables were turned in August 1265 at the Battle of Evesham, where de Montfort was killed.[12] Nevertheless there had been an attempt to follow the precedent of 1215.

We have seen that clauses 12 and 14 of the 1215 Charter, dealing with consent to taxation and summoning the council to give that consent, were omitted from the later reissues of the Charter, yet in practice these clauses were far from being a dead letter.[13] The government frequently sought consent to taxation. Moreover, in October 1255, when Henry asked the council to grant supply, the magnates refused to give it on the ground that they had not been summoned in accordance with the Charter. Clause 14 provided for the lesser tenants in chief to be summoned by proc-lamation and there is evidence that they did attend on a number of occasions when taxation was sought.[14] They become known by the general label of knights. In April 1254, when Henry was seeking to raise money for a campaign in Gascony, letters were sent to the sheriffs requiring them to appear before the council at Westminster with two knights from each county chosen in place of each and all in their counties. So here they are being summoned as representatives of the counties to agree on behalf of them to a level of taxation.[15] In June 1264 the government of de Montfort issued orders for the election of four knights for each county to be elected to attend parliament to discuss the business of the realm.[16] In January 1265 burgesses were summoned.

Summoning representatives of local communities may have been a convenient way of ensuring the payment of any taxes granted, but these representatives did play

[9] ibid 182.
[10] ibid 178ff.
[11] ibid 237.
[12] ibid 254ff.
[13] ibid 198–99.
[14] ibid.
[15] ibid 212.
[16] ibid 255.

a wider part. Edward I came to the throne in 1272. In April 1275 parliament at Westminster agreed a lengthy piece of legislation, which became known as the first Statute of Westminster. The preamble stated that

> these be the Acts of King Edward, son of King Henry at his first parliament general after his Coronation . . . by his Council and by the Assent of Archbishops, Bishops, Abbots, Priors, Earls, Barons and all the Community of the land (*la comminalte de la terre*) thither summoned, because our lord the King had great zeal and desire to redress the state of the kingdom in such things as required amendment.

There is no evidence that knights or burgesses attended, but the preamble seems to state that. There follow some 51 clauses covering a large number of legal subjects. In form and to some extent in content, they owe a lot to Magna Carta. Clause 1, for instance, provides that those who commit trespass shall be fined according to the quantity and manner of the trespass and be liable to pay damages to the victim. Clause 6 provides that amercements must be made for reasonable cause and be proportionate to the wealth of the offender. Clause 9 provides that all men must be ready to pursue felons when the sheriff demands their aid. Clause 13 provides for those convicted of rape to be imprisoned for two years. It is, therefore, a wide-ranging legal code. Interestingly, clause 5 provides that elections ought to be free and not disturbed by force of arms, malice or menace. This could refer to church elections, but also possibly elections in the county court of knights to attend parliament. The statute is so technical that those attending parliament would have been unlikely to have had any input into its drafting; their role would have been to recognise its terms and no doubt take them back to their counties. The preamble distinguishes between the council and the assent of the generality.

Whilst this statute indicates a desire on the part of the government to include representatives of the whole realm in general law making, those summoned to parliament had most political leverage when granting taxes. As Henry's and Edward's reigns progressed, they sought consent increasingly for a tax on moveables. There were precedents for such a tax. One such was the 'Saladin tax' of 10 per cent of moveables, levied by Henry II in 1187 to recover Jerusalem. Another occurred in 1190 when Richard I levied a tenth part of the value of moveables for his crusade. Roger of Wendover commented later that 'this violent extortion, which veiled the vice of rapacity under the name of charity, alarmed the priests as well as the people'.[17] In 1194, in order to raise a sum to pay a ransom for the release of Richard from captivity in Austria, a levy of 25 per cent on the value of moveable property was imposed. In 1203 King John made a similar levy, but on one-thirteenth; but this time it was to fund war against King Philip Augustus of France.[18] He made a similar levy of a thirteenth in 1207, which was expressed to be drawn on every layman of England 'from the fee of whomsoever he be'.[19] It was called an *auxilium* for the

---

[17] Giles (n 7) 129.
[18] WL Warren, *King John* (New Haven, CT, 1997) 149. Generally on this see R Bartlett, *England under the Norman and Angevin Kings*, Oxford History of England (Oxford, 2000) 165–68.
[19] Maddicott (n 1) 153.

defence of the realm, which suggested it was a feudal levy, but its extension to all the freemen of the realm took it beyond the normal feudal due. It was also said to be authorised by the common consent of the council of the realm.[20] In other words it was treated as if it were an aid given by consent. It yielded the enormous sum of £60,000, much the heaviest tax of John's reign.

A tax on moveables had further significance – it was a means of taxing not just tenants in chief through feudal levies, but all freemen. We have previously considered those taxes which derived from the feudal relationship of tenants in chief to the Crown, noting the distinction between those which could be levied as of right and those levied of grace, that is by consent. In 1215 wealth was concentrated in the hands of a small class of large landowners, mainly tenants in chief, so this was a reasonably efficient way of raising money. If, however, a way could be found to tax subtenants directly, that would further increase the Crown's revenues. Taxes on moveables are not dealt with specifically in Magna Carta. They were probably regarded as occasional taxes on rare occasions of necessity. In the 75 years after the Charter they were distinguished from scutage by the fact that they required consent.[21] Obtaining that consent was to prove the motor for constitutional change. Subsequent confirmations of the Charter followed the same pattern of bargaining. The following were granted by the council: 1232 (1/40th) 1237 (1/30th) 1269 (1/20th), 1275 (1/15th) 1283 (1/30th) 1290 (1/15th).[22] It is clear that these remained occasional and were based on national necessity. That the council felt able to judge the necessity is made clear by the fact that they refused financial support in 1242, 1244, 1248, 1257 and 1258. The tax on moveables was distinguished on occasion from aids, so that in 1253 and 1254 the council refused consent to a tax on moveables, but granted an aid. The nature of the two was sometimes elided, so that in 1245 an aid for the marriage of the King's eldest daughter and in 1253 an aid for a campaign by the Prince of Wales were granted, but levied on rear vassals.

A change came in the 1290s, when taxes on moveables were levied on a regular basis. Under Edward I there was an unprecedented period of war.[23] The years from 1294 to 1302 were dominated by war with France, Scotland and in Wales. Between 1294 and 1298 war expenditure amounted to the huge sum of £750,000. From 1294 taxes on moveables were levied in successive years. In May 1297 writs for a muster in London in July were issued. The King's intention was to raise an army and transport it to Flanders in order to attack France from there, but the writs did not state this objective. It was addressed to all men holding land worth £20 or more, which embraced a wide constituency. It was to be funded by another levy on moveables, but the levy had only been agreed by a small number of councillors. This proved the sticking point. The result was the publication of a document called the Remonstrances, complaining about the level of taxation (including indirect

---

[20] See GL Harriss, *King, Parliament and Public Finance in Medieval England* (Oxford, 1975) 17–18.
[21] ibid 27–28.
[22] ibid 29ff and index.
[23] See Maddicott (n 1) 299–302.

taxation) and the King's breaches of the Charter. The King departed in July, leaving a regency government in charge. In his absence parliament met in October and the barons issued a list of their demands in a document called *Tallagio Non Concedendo* (we do not grant a tallage); these included a requirement that future grants of subsidies should be approved not only by magnates and prelates, but also by knights and burgesses of cities and freemen. A deal was struck: the King was granted a ninth on moveables, but only on condition that he confirmed the Charter, which he did. This parliament contained not merely the nobility, but probably about 75 knights and over 200 burgesses.[24]

The parliament of March 1300 granted the King a twentieth on moveables, but imposed on him the *Articuli super Cartas* (articles upon the Charters); these required full enforcement of the Charters with special reference to disafforestation, together with other reforms in local government and legal procedure. Panels of knights were to be set up in each county to hear complaints against those who infringed the Charters. The tax was never collected, which may indicate that the King would not concede parliament's demands. There may have been extraneous reasons for this. He had made peace with France in 1299. After that, overseas trade boomed and the monies from customs dues greatly increased. Furthermore he had acquired new bankers – the Frescobaldi brothers – who were prepared to loan generously. We reach déjà vu on 29 December 1305, when the Pope issued a bull freeing Edward from his oath to observe the Confirmatio Cartarum.[25]

The liberties in the 1215 Charter were granted only to freemen. The same was true of the 1225 Charter and in particular the right to trial by peers was confined to freemen, now protected by clause 29 of the 1225 Charter. In fact, just over a century later, statutes extended the ambit of clause 29 to protect all men. In the mid-fourteenth century there was a particularly active legislative period. By the 1340s the commons consisted of members of the mercantile classes from the towns and the gentry from the country, both of whom had grown rich on the wool trade.[26] They began to sit together in parliament in a separate House from the Lords. In 1337 the Hundred Years War between England and France commenced. Edward III found himself in dire need of funding. He acted arbitrarily. Parliament became more and more concerned at the level of taxation. Statutes were passed requiring the consent of parliament to the levying of aids and (except in the case of tenants in chief) service or taxation for the King's wars.[27]

Edward had come to the throne in 1327. During his minority England was ruled by his mother Isabella and her lover Roger Mortimore, a powerful Marcher lord. They had his father, Edward II, deposed and then murdered. Roger seized lands and acted arbitrarily. In 1330, when he was 18, Edward III arrested Mortimore. He was nominally tried by his peers, though the case against him was said to be self-evident,

---

[24] ibid 316.
[25] ibid.
[26] M Ormrod, Edward III (Oxford, 2012) 365.
[27] ibid 367.

and he was hanged at Tyburn.[28] Against this background the first of the so-called Six Statutes was passed, adding to Magna Carta.[29] We say added to the Charter as they did not, as a modern statute would, say 'delete this' and 'substitute this'; they existed alongside the Charter. The first of these was passed in November 1331, providing that 'no man from henceforth be attached by any accusation nor forjudged of life or limb, nor his lands, tenements, goods nor chattels seised into the King's hands against the form of the Great Charter and the Law of the land'.[30] The man no longer had to be free.

[28] ibid.
[29] RV Turner, *Magna Carta* (Harlow, 2003) 123.
[30] ibid 123.

17

Due Process

AFTER THE FOURTH Lateran Council had forbidden clerks in holy orders to take part in trial by ordeal, the religious validation for such procedures had been destroyed. The royal judges had to find an alternative method of deciding the truth of an accusation. The uncertainty as to how to proceed is demonstrated by a writ of 1219 addressed to the royal judges, directing them to hold those suspected of crime in prison if they might commit evil again. Soon there is evidence that the judges are turning to the inquest as a means of establishing the truth. An example is the case in 1219 where Hamo accused Elias Piggun of stealing his mare in his common pasture 'wickedly feloniously and in larceny'.[1] The royal judge sitting at Waltham put Elias to his oath. Elias swore an oath the mare was his and produced warrantors as to their belief in its truth. Hamo objected to them because he said they were hired and offered the King one mark to have an inquest. The judge questioned the parties about their assertions. Hamo told the court the foal was stolen from his field at Easter 1219 and he could recognise her from a mark. Elias said that the foal was given to him in Cardiff by a man to whom he had given fencing lessons. The judge swore four eight-man juries and sent them to make enquiries locally. On the due date they returned and swore as to their finding. The men of Waltham swore that they believed the mare belonged to Hamo. Cheshunt said they did not know if it was foaled to Hamo, but would rather think it was not. Wormly did not know if it was foaled to Hamo or not. Enfield believed the mare was Hamo's. The judge found this sufficient to convict Elias and order that he lose his foot, pointing out that he was being dealt with leniently. It may be noted that the jury are really being used as investigators – they are not assessing evidence called in court. The transformation to that kind of trial took more than a hundred years.

By the time of Edward I, decisions of the royal court were recorded in Year Books. Those for the 30th to the 31st year of his reign (1302–03) record a case where a presenting jury accused a knight of crime. He objected on two grounds to the same jurors trying his guilt or innocence: first, they were his accusers and could not be his judges; secondly, he was entitled to be tried by a jury of knights. The judge agreed with both arguments and a jury of knights was empanelled. The first ground would

---

[1] FW Maitland, *Select Pleas of the Crown* (London, 1881) (Selden Society no 192; quoted in T Plucknett, *A Concise History of the Common Law* (Indianapolis, IN, 2010) 112).

now be regarded as a basic requirement of a fair trial. The second appears to have equated trial by peers with trial by petty jury.[2]

Trial by jury, however, was only one aspect of criminal procedure. The very active legislative period in the mid-fourteenth century extended the protection of due process. Again this was precipitated by the King's need for money to fund continental campaigns. In 1337 Philip VI of France confiscated Aquitaine on the ground that Edward III held it as his vassal and as such had failed to perform his duties. Edward responded by claiming the throne of France and the Hundred Years War started. Edward allied himself with Flanders and in 1340 sailed there with a large fleet, which defeated the French fleet in the Battle of Sluys in June of that year. In his absence he had left John de Stratford, Archbishop of Canterbury, as chief minister in charge of the government. Edward demanded supplies of money and when these were not forthcoming he returned in fury to England and dismissed some of his ministers. He drew up 22 articles charging Stratford with misconduct, including treason. De Stratford fled to Canterbury and there wrote a letter to the King.[3] He complained that clerks, peers and other persons had been seized, 'an unseemly process against the law of the land and the great charter'. He requested an enquiry into his financial management during the King's absence and trial by his peers in parliament: 'for god's sake be unwilling to believe of us and of your good people anything but good, before you know the truth, for if folk shall be punished without answer, judgment of the good and of the evil shall be all one' – an eloquent statement of the presumption of innocence.

The quarrel between King and Stratford was eventually patched up, but concerns about the government's arbitrary actions remained. The Crown had started to use special commissions and prerogative courts to enforce order. This led to a statute in 1351 which curbed imprisonment or dispossession 'by petition or suggestion made to our lord the king or to his council'. Such sanctions could only follow 'indictment of good and lawful people of the same neighbourhood, where such deed be done, in the manner or by the process made by writ original at the common law'. Then most importantly in 1354 an Act was passed providing that 'no man of what estate or condition whatsoever shall be put out of his land or tenement nor taken nor imprisoned nor disinherited nor put to death without being brought in answer by due process of law' (in law French *saunz ester mesne en repons p dues pses de loi*).[4] The use of the words 'any condition' seems to indicate that the statute applies to all subjects of the King and so turns a privilege into a general right. De Stratford's complaint about 'unseemly process' is now cured by a requirement for 'due process', a principle now recognised as an essential foundation for the rights and liberties of the citizen.

---

[2] F Pollock and FW Maitland, *The History of English Law to the Time of Edward I* (Cambridge, 1895) vol II, 625n.
[3] D Douglas (ed), *English Historical Documents* (London, 1973) IV no 23 p 72.
[4] 28 Ed III.

18

The Charter Survives

S
O FAR AS the Constitution is concerned, the influence of Magna Carta waned during the fifteenth and sixteenth centuries. Express royal confirmation of the charters at the meetings of parliament gradually came to an end, the last being Henry V's in 1416. This may initially have been because further confirmation was otiose, though the disorders which followed his reign and led to the Wars of the Roses may simply have deflected attention away from it.

The new century started with a new King, the first drawn from the Lancastrian side of the Plantagenets. Henry Bolingbroke was crowned Henry IV in October 1399. He had deposed Richard II and his claim to the throne was even more fragile than some of his forbears. In that month, the Westminster Parliament, seeking to justify his assumption of the Crown, promulgated Articles of Deposition heavily critical of Richard II's reign; they focused on a number of matters which were regarded as of specific importance during the revival of interest in the 'ancient' Constitution in the early seventeenth century. The criticisms included the King's refusal to do justice according to law: 'with a stern and forbidding countenance', he frequently asserted 'that his laws were in his mouth, or sometimes in his breast: and that he alone could alter and create the laws of his realm'.[1] As we shall see, the great debate in the seventeenth century was whether, indeed, *rex est lex* or *rex est lex loquens* (the king is the law or the king is the voice of the law). Another Article deprecated the secret meetings held by Richard with the judges some 12 years earlier, not simply seeking their views, but persuading them to a much broader view of the extent of prerogative rights. Again we shall see that this was a source of considerable anxiety to Sir Edward Coke. Finally, the Articles of Deposition made a clarion call to Magna Carta; the King had 'wilfully contravened the statute of his realm' which provided that 'no free man should be arrested etc., or in any way destroyed, nor should the King proceed, or order any process against him, unless by lawful judgment of his peers, or by the law of the land'.

One of the new King's main spokesmen in the Westminster Parliament was Archbishop Arundel. He had been exiled by Richard, but returned with Bolingbroke's army and was reinstated as Archbishop of Canterbury. He explained that the new King would no longer allow the country to be 'ruled and governed by

---

[1] All quotations taken from Parliament Rolls of Medieval England 1275–1504, VIII Henry IV 1399–1413, 9ff.

children, and by the advice of widows'. Rather it was his will 'to be advised and ruled by the honourable, wise and prudent people of his realm' and by their 'common advice, counsel and consent'. Of course, this Parliament was called and expected to endorse the change of regime from Richard II to Henry IV. It is nevertheless not without significance that first, Henry IV, and then Richard III and Henry VII after him, thought it appropriate or necessary to seek parliamentary support for his accession; second, that Magna Carta continued to be treated as a statute; and third, perhaps of most significance in the present context, that the contravention of Magna Carta was included at all. So plainly, nearly 200 years or so after it was first sealed, it was embedded in the national consciousness.

We do not attempt a detailed history of constitutional issues in the fifteenth century. The stark reality was that after the glories of Agincourt, the reign of the infant Henry VI was followed by a civil war, which provided the excuse for the belligerent descendants of Edward III to fight for the Crown. In the turmoil of civil war and the disarray consequent upon it, we can now discern the decline of the medieval world in which Magna Carta had had its origins. It was a period when there was very little room for sophisticated arguments about constitutionality. Nevertheless, in this period one of our great legal treatises was written by Chief Justice Fortescue. He was appointed Chief Justice of the King's Bench in 1442. Like that of William Marshal, his life was hardly sedentary. He fought on the Lancastrian side at the bloody Battle of Towton. After exile as a supporter of Queen Margaret of Anjou, he returned to England and fought again at the Battle of Tewksbury, where he was taken prisoner. Perhaps because of his age, but more likely because he had never previously been pardoned by Edward IV, he was not included among the supporters of the House of Lancaster who were executed after the battle.

He wrote his treatise *In Praise of the Laws of England* (*De Laudibus Legum Angliae*) in the form of an instruction to the young prince Edward.

> The King of England cannot alter nor change the lawes of his Realm at his pleasure. For why hee governeth his people by power, not only royall, but also politique. If his power over them were royal only, then he might change the Lawes of his realm and charge his subjects with Tallage and other burdens without their consent; such is the dominion that the civill Law purports when they say, The Prince his pleasure hath the force of a Law. But from this, much differeth the power of a King, whose government over his people is politique, for he can neither change Lawes without the consent of his subjects, nor yet charge them with strange impositions against their wils. Wherefore his people do . . . freely enjoy and occupy their own goods, being ruled by such lawes as they themselves desire . . . the power Royall is restrained by power politique.[2]

He continued that 'statutes cannot thus passe in England, for so much as they are made not only by the Princes pleasure, but also by the assent of the whole Realm'. Deprecating the use of torture, and lauding the verdict of a jury of 12 about the

---

[2] All quotations taken from the translation of *De Laudibus* by J Selden, *Notes to Fortescue's De Laudibus Legem Angliae* (London, 1660).

'veritie of the issue', Fortescue exhorts the Prince not to marvel 'if the Law, whereby the truth is sifted out in England bee not frequented and used in other nations, for they are not able to make sufficient and like Juries, as bee made in England'. He reflects personally that 'I would rather with twenty evill doers to escape death through pittie, then one man to bee unjustly condemned'. *De Laudibus* was not printed until 1543. The same theme was developed by Fortescue in *Difference Between an Absolute and Limited Monarchy*,[3] where he repeated that 'a King may not rule his people by other laws than such as they assent to'.

No express reference is made by Fortescue to Magna Carta. Nevertheless, by asserting that the King cannot change the laws at 'his pleasure' he was endorsing the fundamental principle, which grew from Magna Carta, about the relationship between the monarch and his people. Fortescue was not a voice crying in the wilderness. In the case of the Rector of Edington,[4] Chief Baron Faye asserted that 'the law is the greatest inheritance that the King has for the law he himself and all his subjects are governed by, and if this law did not exist, there would be no King and no inheritance'.

It would be something of an exaggeration to describe any one of the Tudor monarchs as a democrat, and we rather doubt whether any of them would have recited the clauses of Magna Carta to lull themselves to sleep at night. After the publication of *The Prince* in 1519, Machiavelli would always have trumped Magna Carta. Once the monarch became the Head of the English Church, the freedoms of the Church embodied in the Charter issued from the Temple in 1214, and clause 1 of Magna Carta itself, were subsumed in the broad authority and responsibility of the monarch for the governance of the Church.

This revolution was established with parliamentary support. In the *Oxford History of the Laws of England*, Professor Sir John Baker underlines that, following the break with Rome and the huge widening of the ambit of the law of treason, 'the changes were wrought by Parliament rather than the judges'. He explains that 'the Reformation Parliament . . . finally established the legislative supremacy of the King in Parliament over its only serious rival, supposedly the catholic Church . . . Henry VIII . . . exalted Parliament by goading it into new feats of sovereignty; and Parliament, in return magnified Henry'.[5] Even the notorious 1539 Act of Proclamations, which gave the force of statute to royal proclamations, did not apply to proclamations relating to life, limb or forfeiture, and so still represented the constitutional primacy of the King in Parliament; the repeal of this pernicious Act by subsequent statute at the outset of Edward VI's reign underlined it.

The first of many political trials in Henry VIII's reign, the populist prosecution of his father's ministers, Empson and Dudley, included charges that they had contravened Magna Carta. These charges were misdemeanours rather than felonies and

---

[3] Published in C Plummer (ed), *Governance of England, John Fortescue* (Oxford, 1885) 347.
[4] [1441] YB pas 19 Hen VI f 1063 Pl 1; quoted in JH Baker, *The Common Law Tradition: Lawyers, Books and the Law* (London, 2000) 347.
[5] JH Baker, *Oxford History of the Laws of England, vol VI 1483–1558* (Oxford, 2003) 36.

were not pursued once they had been convicted of treason.[6] Perhaps Henry VIII did not need Machiavelli at all, as this trial took place 10 years before the publication of *The Prince*. Professor Baker observes that 'for the remainder of the period the law officers, and the judges, were careful to ensure that treason charges fell within the law, and if the law needed to be extended, it was done by legislation rather than legal fiction':[7] hence the rise in the alarming attainder processes, which in effect, again with parliamentary agreement, deprived the defendant of trial by his peers.

In the meantime Magna Carta's profile was diminished rather than extinguished. The invention of printing (our ancestors' experience of a new world of communication) gave wider access to the world of ideas, at a time when questions were being raised about what were once thought to be 'self-evident truths' about matters of religious faith. As far as we can ascertain, the first printed version of the Charter was published as *Magna Carta cum Aliis Antiquis Statutis* by Richard Pynson in 1508, and in the *Great Abridgment*, published by John Rastell in 1527, some 24 clauses of the Charter were included. In 1534 the full text of the Charter was published in an English translation by a common lawyer, George Ferrers. In 1576 Tottell published a version of the Charter for his edition of *Antiqua Statuta*. What these repeated publications demonstrate is that although the Charter was never deployed in the high constitutional, religious or political conflicts of the age, it continued to have a distinctive resonance. Like modern publishers, the early printers had potential sales in mind. They were not motivated by altruistic desire to preserve the Charter: rather they perceived a market in the way in which the law was taught and practised and applied. They fed the market largely by looking back at old law, and no doubt contributed to the development of our devotion to legal precedent.

At the Inns of Court, there were abundant 'readings' (effectively, lectures on which the education at the Inns of Court was based) directed to different aspects of Magna Carta. Edmund Plowden, the revered Treasurer of Middle Temple who oversaw the building of the glorious Hall and was one of the first law reporters, cites references to Magna Carta in five of the cases included in his Commentaries and Reports. His references were not directed to constitutional issues, but they demonstrate that Magna Carta was still thought to have practical application. Moreover, in the context of the later dispute between the common law courts and the Conciliar courts such as the Star Chamber and Privy Council, occasional defiant voices were raised against procedures which were said to interfere with common law principles.

A series of actions started in the Court of King's Bench and the Court of Common Pleas, described by Professor Baker as a 'stream', included arguments on Magna Carta and subsequent statutes relating to 'due process'.[8] Perhaps more significant, in actions in trespass for false imprisonment and applications for release under habeas corpus, Magna Carta was cited in support of actions for damages or to chal-

---

[6] Baker (n 5) 88 and 593.
[7] ibid 583.
[8] ibid 192.

lenge the imprisonment. Some of these examples related to what we might reasonably describe as incarceration by or on behalf of the authorities of the State. Sir Humphrey Browne, a King's Serjeant, relied on Magna Carta to support his argument that his imprisonment on the King's orders in 1532 was illegal.[9] In 1546 two criminals were committed to the Tower 'by order of the King's Council', but were removed into the King's Bench by habeas corpus. One of Elizabeth I's Chief Justices of the King's Bench, Dyer CJ, who had examined all the relevant authorities during the earlier Tudor period, concluded that they established

> the authority of the King's Bench to examine the cause of imprisonment of any prisoner in the realm, even if committed by the Council, and to commit, bail, or enlarge him as they thought expedient, . . . the courts had found an effective means of curbing arbitrary power, whether exercised by ministers of the Crown or by any other person exercising an authority or jurisdiction which deprived the subject of his liberty.[10]

In *Bradshawe v Brooke*[11] the judges ruled against a 'General Warrant' issued by the Recorder of London, insisting that unless a warrant to arrest specified the cause, it was invalid.

In 1591 they were consulted by the Council about committal on the basis of an order or direction by the Council or the Queen. The issue was whether, if an individual was detained by order of the Council, the common law courts would admit him to bail if no cause for detention was specified. Maitland points out that two differing versions of the judicial resolution were reported, both 'singularly obscure – perhaps they are intentionally obscure'.[12] An attempt to analyse this resolution was made in the habeas corpus proceedings brought in the *Five Knights* case in the reign of Charles I. This resolution apart, however, habeas corpus was developing into a powerful remedy against unlawful detention.

The temper of Elizabeth's reign may be gauged by the fact that in 1596 or thereabouts, Shakespeare's King John says not a word about Magna Carta. That sometimes leads to suggestions that Elizabethan England had lost interest in it. Such a judgement overrates Shakespeare's value as a historian. Like films about historical events produced in Hollywood, his interest was the box office. He was a playwright. He found the dramatic action of this play in Arthur's murder, the French invasion and the defiance of the Pope, reflecting Elizabethan concepts of English nationalism which neither the royalist nor the rebel barons in 1215 would have begun to understand. We can rapidly gain some idea of what Shakespeare had in mind from Act 3, scene 1:

> Tell him this tale; and from the mouth of England
> Add thus much more, that no Italian priest
> Shall tithe or told in our dominions;
> But as we, under heaven our supreme head
> So under him that great supremacy,
> where we do reign, we will alone uphold; . . .

[9] ibid 91.
[10] ibid (n 5), 93, 94.
[11] *Bradshawe v Brooke* [1579] BL MS Add 35941 FO 56 v, referred to by Baker (n 4).
[12] FW Maitland, *The Constitutional History of England* (Cambridge, 1948) 274.

These last lines would have drawn a thunderous round of applause from post-Armada English audiences, who would have been perfectly well aware that their Queen, Elizabeth, had been a target for assassination by papal decree.

By Elizabeth I's death our constitutional arrangements were encapsulated in the response given by the Lord Keeper, Puckering, to the House of Commons in 1593. The Commons asserted their 'ancient right' of freedom of speech. Speaking in the presence of the Queen, Puckering said that she granted them 'liberal but not licentious speech, liberty therefore but with due limitations'.[13] Members were warned off any absurd notion that this ancient right might entitle them to consider ecclesiastical or constitutional arrangements. There was not much doubt that Elizabeth understood that there were limits to freedom of speech in Parliament, and although from time to time individual Members of Parliament, like the puritan Peter Wentworth, might challenge her view, whether by state craft, or habit, or affection and respect for the ageing monarch, the serious confrontations which occurred in the subsequent reigns were avoided.

By the end of the century there were rumblings which presaged the constitutional storm that lay ahead in the next century and the arrival of the Stuart dynasty. Elizabeth, dealing with increasingly truculent Parliaments, facing pressures building up from religious dissent by the Puritans and more broad anxiety about the succession, had by the end of her reign come to woo and encourage Parliament. An independence of spirit was beginning to emerge in Parliament, and in the Commons in particular. The precise ambit of the privileges of Parliament, and the methods of enforcement of the obligation of the monarch to abide by the law, and the rights of citizens if and when she failed to do so, were never tested to destruction. The spirit of independence had not developed sufficiently for there to be any real risk that the wishes of the monarch would be defied. So long as the relationship reflected a coincidence of interest, it never became necessary to address the constitutional problem that lurked below the political surface.

---

[13] C Drinker Bowen, *The Lion and the Throne, The Life and Times of Sir Edward Coke* (London, 1957) 18, 19

19

The Rule of Law

ELIZABETH I DIED on 24 March 1603. In early April, James VI of Scotland made his royal progress to London to become James I of England. At Newark he dispensed royal justice, ordering the execution of a cutpurse, without a hearing or a trial. The Scots had a phrase, Jeddart Justice, which derived from an incident at Jedburgh in the Lowlands where a member of a criminal gang was hanged first and tried later. This indeed was Jeddart Justice. The new King was flying in the face of English principle and practice. Sir John Harington, Queen Elizabeth's philosopher godson and inventor of the flush toilet, commented 'tis strangely done: now if the winde bloweth thus, why may not a man be tried before he hath offended?' The incident attracted some passing popular interest but little criticism of the King. This was the first new government for 45 years and, as today, it was no doubt allowed a honeymoon period. It was nevertheless hardly a propitious start.

Those who had read James's writings would have seen his action at Newark as all of a piece with his political views. In 1598 he had published his treatise *The Trew Law of Free Monarchies*, articulating his conviction that the monarchy was free of constitutional restrictions. This was the divine right of kings, regal authority bestowed by God on the monarch, a God to whom alone the monarch was answerable. The idea that a monarch, chosen by God, should be subject to legal constraints, the very concept enshrined in Magna Carta, was the precise antithesis of what James believed his function to be. No immediate problems arose. The honeymoon period was followed by the conference at Hampton Court, which eventually culminated in the glories of the Authorised Version of the Bible, and the alarms of Gunpowder Plot. Nevertheless it was not very long before issue was joined between the King and Sir Edward Coke, recently appointed as Chief Justice of the Common Pleas.

Coke was born in Norfolk in 1562 into a family with strong legal connections. He was called to the Bar by the Inner Temple on 20 April 1578. His stepfather advised him to 'loathe concealers, prefer godly men and briskly do business with willing clients'.[1] He became a Member of Parliament for Aldeburgh in Suffolk for the first time in 1589. In 1593 he was made Speaker of the House and in 1592 and 1594 successively Solicitor General and Attorney-General. In Elizabeth's reign he prosecuted, amongst others, the Earl of Essex, and after his reappointment by James as Attorney-General

---

[1] AD Boyer, *Sir Edward Coke and the Elizabethan Age* (Stanford, CA, 2003) 11.

he prosecuted the gunpowder conspirators, and Sir Walter Raleigh for treason. His conduct of this trial in particular was disgraceful. His description of Raleigh as a 'notorious traitor, a vile viper and a damnable atheist' exemplified his misuse of prejudicial and emotive language to compensate for the paucity of evidence. In 1606 he was appointed Chief Justice of the Common Pleas, no doubt in the confident expectation that he would continue to support the Crown and uphold the prerogative after his appointment as he had before. Perhaps no one understood the significance of his motto *Lex est tutissima cassis* – the law is the safest shield; as he put it later, 'the surest sanctuary . . . the strongest fortress to protect the weakest of all'.[2]

This happened to be the moment when conflict between the common law and prerogative courts was developing. One immediate problem was the extent, if any, of the powers of the Court of High Commission, a prerogative court entrusted with supervision of ecclesiastical matters, to order arrest and detention. Coke believed that it was his duty to resist any encroachment on the jurisdiction of the common law courts and he and the judges of the Common Pleas decided that any such practice was contrary to Magna Carta and that arrest could be resisted. Where the High Commission proposed to act, the Court would grant an order of prohibition.

In late 1608 James decided that he would adjudicate between the rival contentions. Coke questioned the King's jurisdiction to do so. Archbishop Bancroft asserted that the King could judge whatever cause he pleased. The authority of the King to act as a judge belonged to him by the Word of God. Coke responded that the Word of God required that 'The laws even in heathen countries must be obeyed' – Magna Carta and the subsequent statutes required due process according to ancient law. Different versions of what then happened are available, but they are all to the same effect.[3] The King told the Chief Justice that he 'spoke foolishly'. While relying on his prerogative, the King would also 'ever protect the common law'. Coke responded that 'the common law protecteth the King'. The royal rejoinder was alarming. The King exploded, 'Then I am to be under the law, which is treason to affirm' – the King protected the law and not the law the King. This dangerous moment for Coke is vividly brought home by the report that the King shook his fist at him, and took great offence at the suggestion that he should be subject to the law. Coke quoted from Bracton, '*Quod rex non debet esse sub homine, sed sub Deo et Lege*' (the King ought not to be subject to man, but subject to God and the Law). Given the King's assertion that Coke was speaking treason, this was a remarkable response. In some accounts, Coke fell flat on his knees, and the Lord Treasurer, Lord Cecil, intervened to pacify the situation. Nevertheless, on the following day a new prohibition was sent to the High Commission from the Court of Common Pleas, with Coke's seal on it.[4]

---

[2] Quoted in C Drinker Bowen, *The Lion and the Throne: The Life and Times of Sir Edward Coke* (London, 1957) 241.

[3] Coke, 12 Rep, 64–65; Drinker Bowen (n 2) 261–64; J Campbell, *The Lives of the Chief Justices of England* (London, 1849) 271ff.

[4] Drinker Bowen (n 2) 264.

Perhaps this meeting was still in James's mind in March 1610, when he addressed Parliament:

> The state of monarchy is the supremest thing upon earth . . . (Kings) exercise a manner or resemblance of divine power upon earth . . . God hath power to create or destroy, make or unmake at his pleasure, give life or send death, to judge all and to be judged accountable to none. Kings make and unmake their subjects; they have power of raising and casting down, of life and of death . . . and make of their subjects like men at the chess.[5]

Thus within a few years of ascending the throne, James was offering an unequivocal challenge to the position of Parliament, and indeed the courts. Throughout the Tudor Age, although Parliament was subservient to Henry VIII, and became increasingly truculent but nevertheless persuadable by Elizabeth, the King-in-Parliament was established as the appropriate constitutional model. If, however, the King was above the law, he could make it, or alter it, without reference to or complaint from either. He could indeed make or unmake his subjects, and he could extend his prerogative, including the powers of the prerogative courts, at will. Expressly, he was unaccountable, to any subject, or any institution. Nevertheless, however provocative this language may have seemed, the King was still perceived to be integral to the constitutional arrangements. It was recognised that the King had royal prerogatives as well as royal responsibilities. As it developed the real dispute was whether the time-honoured phrase the 'King-in-Parliament' meant 'the King, in Parliament', that is with the laws made by the King after he had taken the advice of Parliament, but ultimately irrespective of whether Parliament consented or not, or whether it meant 'the King-in-Parliament', reflecting authority shared between the King and Parliament.[6] In modern statutory language, the distinction was between mere consultation by the King with Parliament and a requirement of parliamentary concurrence.

The Petition of Grievances by the Commons in response reflected on the diminution of their ancient rights. Lost in its list of carefully worded complaints, it spoke of how

> amongst many other points of happiness and freedom which Your Majesty's subjects have enjoyed under your royal progenitors . . . there is none which they have accounted more dear and precious than this, to be guided and governed by the certain rule of law which giveth both to the head and members that which of right belongeth to them and not by any uncertain or arbitrary form of government.[7]

This represented a substantial development of a phrase in use in the courts to indicate a principle or rule of law[8] into a declaration of constitutionality with which we have now become familiar. The 'rule of law' is not a newly minted aspiration nor a phrase created by AV Dicey in the nineteenth century.

---

[5] For the whole speech, see James I, *The Works of the Most High and Mighty Prince* (London, 1616) 528–31.

[6] J Goldsworthy, *The Sovereignty of Parliament, History and Philosophy* (Oxford, 2010) 8.

[7] Quoted in H Hallam, *The Constitutional History of England* (vol1) (London, 1973) 441.

[8] F Thompson, *Magna Carta: Its Role in the Making of the English Constitution* (Minneapolis, MN, 1948) 295.

To address what steadily became intractable differences between the monarch and his subjects, Magna Carta was revivified. Those who supported a measure of constraint on the King's powers harked back to history, and the resuscitation of ideas from antiquity which were said to have been present in Britain since Roman times and culminated in Magna Carta and the subsequent statutory provisions which reinforced it. Even if much of this history was fictitious, and no one was entirely clear about the differences between the 1215 Charter, or the 1216 or 1217 reissues, or the 1225 Charter, there could be no denying Magna Carta. There was, equally, no denying that, whether in consequence of the Charter or a now centuries-old convention which had its genesis in the Charter, taxation and subsidy required parliamentary consent. And finally, although not articulated in the early stages of the argument, if the prerogative courts were ever dismantled, the ancient common law rules of due process by the Charter and the subsequent statutes would be universally applied.

The support for Magna Carta was far from unanimous. There was a substantial body of opinion, not confined to sycophants or placemen, which rejected the pre-eminence attached to it by Coke and others. It was, after all, a document extracted from the King at Runnymede by force, certainly under coercion. This thinking is exemplified in *Patriarcha* by Robert Filmer, probably written in the 1620s but published many years after the Civil War in 1680:[9] Magna Carta 'first had an obscure birth by usurpation, and was secondly fostered and showed to the world by rebellion'.[10] When Francis Bacon explained, in his well-known phrase, how judges were lions under the throne, the objective was to show that the judges rested, if not quite cowered, at the monarch's feet, and symbolically that the position in which the King sat demonstrated that he was superior to the law. For those of this frame of mind it was eminently sensible for the King to take the advice of Parliament, but in doing so he 'subjected his law-making power to a procedural restraint, but not to a substantive one'.[11]

Magna Carta was the banner carried by those who were concerned at any extension of the royal prerogative or any diminution in what they believed to be their rights and the rights of Parliament. For them Magna Carta was not an archaeological, entombed relic, now conveniently available to be resurrected in argument; in modern language it was a living instrument. The question was whether, and if so how, it should apply to the changed seventeenth-century world.

For those who adhered to the King-in-Parliament theory of the Constitution in the seventeenth century, the historic link made between their situation and Magna Carta reflected the legacy of political theory described, amongst others, by Bracton and Fortescue. Furthermore, the protections offered by Magna Carta against the imposition of penal sanctions without trial and in accordance with law came to sup-

---

[9] See JM Wallace, 'The Date of Sir Robert Filmer's *Patriarcha*' (1980) 23(1) *The Historical Journal* 155–65.

[10] Quoted in RV Turner, *Magna Carta* (Harlow, 2003) 165.

[11] Goldsworthy (n 6) 89.

port the privileges of Parliament. If a Member of Parliament was entitled as a matter of lawful *right* to speak freely and exercise his other responsibilities, no offence could be committed when he did so. The liberty provisions of Magna Carta, as we shall call them, became linked to the right to exercise parliamentary privileges which by 'the King, in Parliament' theory only proceeded as a matter of royal grace. If there was no legal *right* to exercise privileges, then any attempt to do so against the wishes of the King could be and was seen as an unlawful interference with, and an offence against, the royal prerogative; if, however, they were indeed privileges, they would be protected by Magna Carta. As these various considerations gradually entwined, Magna Carta came to be treated as the foundation for liberties of every kind.

In the meantime Coke was writing his Reports which were published serially in eleven parts between 1600 and 1615. The Second Report speaks of the 'auncient Law of England, declared by the Great Charter and spoken in the person of the King; *Nulli Vendemus, Nulli Negabimus, Aut Differemus Justicum Vel Rectum*'. The title page of the Eighth Report repeats these words from Magna Carta. After 1628 he set about writing his *Institutes*, his personal instruction in the laws of England, with his unashamed admiration for, and continuing commitment to, Magna Carta encapsulated in the *Second Institute*. Not the least crumb should be overlooked. Among others who took inspiration from Coke's works were John Lilburne and William Penn and generations yet unborn in the future United States of America.

John Selden was another member of the Inner Temple, called to the Bar in 1612. He was to become a significant player in the contest between Parliament and the Crown in the 1620s. He was fascinated by, and wrote about, legal history and deployed his learning in his professional work as an advocate and in Parliament. It is an indication of his continuing reputation as a legal scholar and historian that when towards the end of the nineteenth century it was proposed to establish a society to encourage the study and advance the knowledge of the history of English Law, it was named after Selden, who was described by Lord Coleridge CJ at the inaugural meeting 'as a mountain of learning'.[12] The Selden Society continues to thrive.

In 1616 Selden published a new edition of Fortescue. He then added some notes of his own, saying what should be

> truely understood . . . of the grand Charter, cap. 29- *nec super eum ibimus nec super eum mittemus, nisi per legali judicium Parium Suorum vel per legem terrae*, I would capitally English it thus: neither will we enter on his possession nor commit him . . . but by legal judgment of his Peers or men of his condition (that is by Jury).[13]

Like Coke's Reports, the new edition, and this comment at this particular time, cannot have been coincidental.

---

[12] Selden Society, *Centenary Guide to Publications* (London, 1987) 4, n 11.
[13] J Selden, *Notes to Fortescue's De Laudibus Legem Angliae* (London, 1660) 27.

Coke and Selden were lawyers and parliamentarians. Both ended up in the Tower. They were by no means the only ones to do so. By contrast, a number of scholars of the history and principles of our Constitution flourished during Tudor times. One was William Lambarde, who regarded the Great Charter of the Liberties of England as the 'first Letters of Manumission of the People of this Realme'. Another was Richard Hooker, himself Master of the Temple Church, who declared in his *Treatise on the Laws of Ecclesiastical Polity* that 'a law is the deed of the whole body politic'. However by the early seventeenth century members of the House of Commons and holders of judicial office were being forced to decide where they stood in what were no longer matters of constitutional theory and scholarly debate.

Probably to make it more difficult for him to battle against the prerogative, and in the face of his own objections, but as 'a kind of discipline to him for' his opposition to the King,[14] in 1613 Coke was elevated to be Chief Justice of the King's Bench, the highest judicial office in the land. Despite the objective he was uncurbed. In 1616 he was required to consider the right of the Crown to grant a benefice *in commendam*, that is, an arrangement by which the beneficiary received payment while the responsibilities were performed by a deputy. When a claim to prohibit the process was brought, the judges were ordered by the King to stay the proceedings. Coke led the judges to refuse, arguing before the King that 'the stay required by your Majesty was a delay of justice and therefore contrary to law and the judges' oath'. Coke declined to respond to a hypothetical case which might arise if the King asked for proceedings to be stayed, saying that 'when the case should be, he would do that which should be fit for a judge to do'.[15] There is no clearer statement of judicial responsibility.

A few days later, James asserted that it was 'atheism and blasphemy to dispute what God can do; so it is presumption and high contempt in a subject to dispute what a King can do, or say that a king cannot do this or that'. He ordered the judges 'not to meddle with things against the King's prerogative or honour'. There then followed an attempt to force Coke, in effect, to censor his own reports, to remove from them references which might be unfavourable to the King and the prerogative. Coke offered five minimal changes. He was dismissed. He was not the only Chief Justice to be summarily dismissed by the early Stuarts.

Coke returned to Parliament in 1621 and renewed the battle from the House of Commons. He was very much an elder statesman, who joined a generation of men who entered the Commons at a particularly young age – including Phelips at 18, Eliot at 21, Selden at 22, Holles at 25, Hampden and Digges at 27 and Pym at 30. They came from different parts of the country and different backgrounds, but what at first united them was their dislike of the King's favourite, Sir George Villiers – later Duke of Buckingham – and the corrupt and high-handed way he acted on behalf of the King. Typically, many of the young men who challenged 'the King, in Parliament' theory of the Constitution were lawyers or had studied law at the Inns

---

[14] Bacon's August 1613 letter to the King, quoted in Drinker Bowen (n 2) 293.
[15] Quoted in Drinker Bowen (n 2) 322.

of Court, which were then regarded as the Third University of England. For example, like Coke and Selden, Hampden was a member of the Inner Temple, Sandys, Pym and Phelips were members of the Middle Temple, and Digges of Gray's Inn.

Coke was appointed Chairman of the Parliamentary Committee for Grievances. A Petition of Grievance was presented and the royal response was unsurprising. It asserted that parliamentary privileges were based on toleration and grace rather than inheritance and right. Coke's response echoes down the years:

> If my sovereign will not allow me my inheritance, I must fly to Magna Charter and entreat explanation of his Majesty. Magna Charter is called Charter *Libertatis quia liberos facit* . . . The Charter of liberty. . . when the King says he cannot allow our liberties of right, this strikes at the root. We serve here for thousands and ten thousands.[16]

In Coke's ringing language, Magna Carta was not merely a constitutional document, rather it was the foundation for the rights and liberties of the nation represented in Parliament. Coke urged the Commons to make a protestation. When Parliament was adjourned, Coke appeared before the Privy Council. He was committed by prerogative order in close confinement to the Tower. Phelips and Mallory followed him. Selden twice ended up in custody, again by prerogative order. So did Edwin Sandys, of the Middle Temple, the creator of the 'Great Charter' (surely not a title chosen by accident) of Virginia, which expressly preserved for the new colonists their rights and liberties as Englishmen, a pattern which was repeated throughout the development of new colonies in North America. The detention of Sandys was challenged by Guy Palmes, who commended the way in which 'our ancestors' had preserved 'the privileges of this Land by Magna Carta and many laws since'.[17] As to Selden's detention, he himself was later to write of his second period of detention that he was

> committed to custody for certain parliamentary matters with some leading statesmen who were lovers of the prerogative of the sovereign as well as the true liberty of their country, not because I had acted rashly, but because I mingled with them as a counsellor.[18]

They were all victims of an alarming and developing pattern, detention without trial and effective house arrest for those who challenged the King.

In the meantime, the grievance of monopolies, many granted in Elizabeth's reign, and the abuse by monopolists of their patents became a focus of anger. A royal grant to a single favoured individual of a monopoly to exploit a specific trade, like the playing card monopoly granted to Raleigh, was inevitably unpopular, but particular criticism was directed at monopolies which enabled the beneficiaries to arrest and imprison those alleged to have infringed their rights. In the debates Coke condemned a patent for the 'sole engrossing of wills and infantries' and a different patent 'for making all bills at York' as contrary to Magna Carta. SR Gardiner, in his 10-volume *History of England from the Accession of James I to the Outbreak of the*

---

[16] Quoted ibid 391.
[17] Thompson (n 8) 299–309.
[18] D Berkowitz, *John Selden's Formative Years* (Washington, DC, 1989) 55ff.

Civil War, 1603–1642, explained 'the champions of the common law were justly dissatisfied with the creation of an arbitrary tribunal which sent men to prison without the interference of a jury'.[19] We pause to note that during the course of this Parliament, the Commons were concerned with the huge number of offences for which the death penalty was ordered, and a Bill was proposed to reduce the number of such offences, and replace them with periods of public services.[20] Today that would be called community service.

The 1624 Parliament was the last of James's reign. He opened the proceedings by inviting the free advice of Parliament on foreign affairs. Eliot warned against any compromise with the vindication of privileges, and Edward Alford used Magna Carta to emphasise the entitlement to parliamentary freedoms. A Bill was advanced 'to secure the subject from wrongful imprisonment, and deprivation of their trades and occupations, 29th chapter of the statute of Magna Carta'. An attack was also directed against impositions, which were, in effect, a form of taxation. By the Great Charter, as Coke patiently explained, taxation required common consent as expressed in Parliament. By the end of this reign, in short, Magna Carta had been extended to protect both the liberty of individual citizens from unlawful arrest and the broad constitutional position of Parliament.

The mood of Parliament, buoyed by the failure of negotiations for the marriage of the Prince of Wales to a Spanish Infanta, suddenly changed and the legislative programme was rapidly carried. Resolution of the issue, 'the King, in Parliament' or 'the King-in-Parliament' was postponed to the next reign.

---

[19] SR Gardiner, *History of England from the Accession of James I to the Outbreak of the Civil War, 1603–1642*, vol 4, 48, quoted in Thompson (n 8) 301.
[20] Drinker Bowen (n 2) 382.

20

'Reason of State'

A T CHARLES I'S first Parliament the immediate response in the Commons was to see if a new start could be made. But this honeymoon period was very short indeed. Suspicion of the King's intentions flared over preparations for war. An inadequate subsidy was unenthusiastically voted. Tonnage and poundage, essentially a form of levy on goods, was limited to one year. The King believed, with reason, that these funds were insufficient.

In the meantime the plague flourished and Charles ordered Parliament to meet in Oxford. Unhappily for him, it emerged that the English navy was to be deployed by the King of France in his military endeavours against the Huguenots. The Commons refused to vote to 'engraft subsidies upon subsidies'. Robert Phelips observed: 'We are the last monarchy in Christendom that retain our original rights and constitutions. Let us not perish now'.[1] At that time he cannot have appreciated that the Estates General in France, which last met in 1614, was not to meet again until 1789, but he certainly understood that parliamentary assemblies were in decline everywhere on the continent. For the protagonists of the 'King-in-Parliament', support had to be found at home, not abroad. Faced with an attack on his favourite, Buckingham, Charles dissolved this Parliament.

Coke was missing from the 1626 Parliament. So, too, were the leading adherents of the King-in-Parliament principle, including Phelips, Alford and Palmes. The device that excluded them was their appointments as High Sheriff, which bound them to stay within their counties for their shrieval years. Buckingham was impeached. One charge against him was the sale of honours in contravention of the prohibition on the sale of justice in Magna Carta. Dudley Digges proposed the impeachment, and Eliot, in effect supporting the prosecution, closed the debate. Selden and Pym, among others, supported them in reporting the Articles of Impeachment to the House of Lords. On the next day Eliot and Digges were removed to the Tower.

The Commons refused to address the subsidy issue until both were released. The assertion that Eliot's detention arose from crimes committed outside Parliament was brushed aside. A speech by a member called Browne linked Habeas Corpus with Magna Carta. According to one report he said, 'the King cannot detaine anyone in prison above 24-howers without showing the cause of his emprisonment

---

[1] C Drinker Bowen, *The Lion and the Throne: The Life and Times of Sir Edward Coke* (London, 1957) 406.

if it be demanded'.[2] Charles dissolved Parliament and the issue of the lawfulness of the detention of members was postponed. In the meantime he needed funds. A variety of devices was created – free gifts, forced loans and, as a method of encouragement to agree to the loans, billeting of soldiers in private homes, and finally imprisonment or house arrest for numerous 'gentlemen recusants' (in our language 'refuseniks'). All this was remarkably ill-judged and indeed, when the King sought the views of the judges, they were prepared to make the loans themselves, but not to endorse their legality. To make an example of him, the Chief Justice of the King's Bench, Ranulph Crewe (or Crew) was dismissed, rejoicing that he 'had done his duty, and that he was delivered from temptation'.[3] Earlier in his career, Crewe had recognised the unpredictability of human affairs in one of the great judgments of the common law.[4]

So to the great case of the *Five Knights*: applications for Habeas Corpus were made in the King's Bench by five of those imprisoned for refusal to pay a forced loan. To this day these applications have a continuing resonance. The return to the applications asserted that the committal was by His Majesty's special commandment. Darnel withdrew, but Hebbeningham, Earle, Corbet and Edward Hampden nevertheless continued their applications. Selden and Noye argued for the applicants, with submissions based on Magna Carta and the subsequent statutes of Edward III. The special command of the King did not provide a sufficient basis for refusing bail. Magna Carta postulated that no freeman should be imprisoned without due process of law, that is, by acknowledged forms of process, presentment or indictment. The Attorney-General, Heath, relied on the King's authority, which vested him with an absolute power to commit when necessary in the overall interest and general welfare. It was 'reason of State' exercised on the basis of the King's judgment, and it was not open to challenge.[5] This argument would have justified the use of *lettres de cachet* – unchallengeable, sealed orders from the King, which commanded immediate obedience – which disfigured the absolute monarchy in France. Heath also sought to rely on one of the reports of the resolution of the judges in Elizabeth's reign to the effect that where a person was committed at the King's command, the cause need not be shown on the warrant. The remedy was by petition to the King. Selden found the second record of the resolution of the judges to different effect,[6] but in any event, as far as we are aware, this was the first occasion when reason of State, or State necessity, was advanced on behalf of the executive. This

---

[2] Quoted in F Thompson, *Magna Carta: Its Role in the Making of the British Constitution* (Minneapolis, MN, 1948) 325–26.

[3] J Campbell, *The Lives of the Chief Justices of England* (London, 1849) 375.

[4] We recognise that his observations have nothing to do with Magna Carta, but we cannot resist this quotation from the judgment in the *Oxford Peerage* case, 1626, taken from the *Oxford Dictionary of Quotations* 244–45: 'And yet time hath his revolutions; there must be a period and an end to all temporal things, *finis rerum*, an end of names and dignities and whatsoever is terrene; and why not of De Vere? Where is Bohun? Where is Mowbray? Where is Mortimer? Nay, which is more and most of all, where is Plantagenet? They are entombed in the urns and sepulchres of mortality'.

[5] Thompson (n 2) 130–33.

[6] D Berkowitz, *John Selden's Formative Years* (Washington, DC, 1989) 141–46 and 137.

line of argument remains familiar to this day. Carried to its logical conclusion, reason of State can very quickly degenerate into detention at the behest of the executive, and the courts continue to be deeply concerned when arguments justifying detention or imprisonment are said to be based on State necessity.

Without Chief Justice Crewe to lead them, the immediate decision of the court was that the applicants should continue to be remanded. Whether deliberately or not, the decision was misunderstood, as if it were a final decision. In fact it was not a final judgment, and, consistently with what they had informed the King, the judges subsequently made clear that it was not. Nevertheless, their decision appeared to confirm, and certainly the perception was, that an arrest on the basis of the King's special command (that is, without any further reason provided) was a permissible feature of his prerogative. As it was, events moved very quickly and the litigation before the court became subsumed in a new Parliament.

The 1628 Parliament was undoubtedly one of the most important Parliaments in our history. By the time the writ for the election was issued the High Sheriffs for the year had been appointed, and the device to prevent the election of potentially uncooperative members by appointing them to this office was not available. Given how vociferous the lawyers had been in support of Magna Carta, Charles was minded to prohibit the election of lawyers, but he backed away from that idea. The issue about who may be allowed to stand for election, or be elected, would itself have generated a crisis. More important, Charles was unable to prevent the election of 27 members who had refused to pay the loan and, like the five knights, had been imprisoned without trial. Many of those excluded from the 1626 Parliament by the shrieval device, including Coke and Alford, were elected. Among the other members, Selden and Noye, together with Pym, Digges, Eliot, Phelips, John Hampden, whose fame lay a few years ahead, and Oliver Cromwell, whose yet greater fame lay even further ahead, were elected. Charles and his ministers faced formidable opposition. The membership included too many men, or their relatives or friends, who had been imprisoned without trial, in effect for defying the King. Yet Charles could not or would not and never did change, or even begin to appreciate the need for a rethink. In surely the most dignified moment of his life, facing death on the scaffold in 1649, he repeated 'For the people . . . their liberty and freedom consists in having government . . . it is not in having share in government . . . that is nothing pertaining to them'.[7] For him the only viable constitutional principle was and, uncompromisingly remained, 'the King, in Parliament'.

The new Parliament was opened by Charles I on 17 March 1628.[8] On 21 March Coke preferred a bill 'against long and unjust detainment of men in prison'. It was

[7] See CV Wedgwood, *The Trial of Charles I* (Harmondsworth, 1983) 195ff.

[8] There are a number of detailed accounts of this Parliament, all based on the original sources. We highlight in particular the work of Drinker Bowen (n 1); Thompson (n 2); J Goldsworthy, *The Sovereignty of Parliament, History and Philosophy* (Oxford, 2010); Berkowitz (n 6); P Christianson, *Discourse on History, Law and Governance in the Public Career of John Selden* (Toronto, 1996); and H Hulme, *The Life of Sir John Eliot* (London, 1957). The quotations of direct speech appear in one or other, or more usually, in more than one of them. Our narrative represents a distillation of these detailed accounts.

the first of many speeches of remarkable quality which addressed the prerogative of the Crown and the liberties, literally, of the subject, and the relationship of the King with Parliament. A few days later the Committee of the whole House voted unanimously that property could not be taken without the assent of Parliament. When challenged to show how Magna Carta applied to admitting individuals to bail, Selden emphasised that according to Magna Carta freemen could not be imprisoned at pleasure. A few days later, Coke intervened to attack discretionary imprisonment, which went against the reason of the common law. In equally vivid language Eliot, gradually assuming a crucial role in the opposition, urged what he had written to the King while in custody, seeking to explain why the forced loan was contrary to statute, and why its enforcement by imprisonment contravened Magna Carta. Eliot was not educated at the Inns of Court, but his arguments show that Magna Carta was common currency, standing for something much more potent than tiresome lawyerly grandstanding.

There was a determined attempt to establish precisely how best to avoid any interference with the rights of Parliament and indeed the liberties of the subject. It is difficult to convey the level of determination and energy which infused the proceedings in the Commons. This was not a smooth journey to a preordained destination. As against the issues identified in the Commons, the King was getting increasingly desperate for his supply and he was not without adherents. A number of subsidies were agreed, but 'this gift is upon assurance that the King will settle the fundamental liberties of the subject'. Sir Thomas Wentworth urged that 'grievances and supply go hand in hand, and the subjects' liberties go hand in hand together'. He sought a 'Bill for our liberties'.[9] The time had not yet come, but in 1689 the Bill of Rights became one of the essential documents of our partly written Constitution, and later Bills of Rights assumed equal importance in the United States of America.

The attitude of the Lords undermined the preparation of the proposals advanced by the Commons. The Lords suggested the addition of the words 'His Majesty would be graciously pleased to declare . . .'. Coke would have none of it: 'When the King doth a thing of grace, it implies that it is not our right'. There was no 'intrinsic prerogative. It is a word we find not much in the law. Admit this intrinsic prerogative and all our laws are out'. His devastating attack was summarised in six words – 'reason of state lames Magna Carta'. He also insisted that 'cause should be found before any commitment' and that cause found afterwards 'was fearful'.[10] This was not an academic issue. It still goes to the heart of our judicial processes. It is an elementary principle that the citizen cannot be detained without cause. Any such detention is unlawful.

The King declared that Magna Carta and the other statutes relating to taxation remained in force and his subjects would be maintained in their 'just' freedoms. His

---

[9] Hulme (n 8) 191–92 and 202–10; Berkowitz (n 6) 148–49. The development of the idea of a 'bill' to this effect is narrated in Hulme (n 8) in the chapter entitled 'The Defeat of a Bill of Rights' 184–224 and 202–10.

[10] Drinker Bowen (n 1) 124 and notes at 514–15.

royal word was as strong as any law that Parliament could make. That begged the question, pertinently asked by Eliot, who would 'expound' what was 'just'? The King suggested that the Commons should rely on his royal promise. For the opposition, messages, even messages of love, were not good enough. The King was being gracious, but the issue was the law. Digges first suggested a Petition of Right. Coke took up the cause, but even so it took time to gain acceptance. Wentworth abandoned his original suggestion of a Bill of Rights, and came to support the Petition of Rights.[11] Eliot himself was unenthusiastic about a Petition of Right.

We must briefly pause. What the dry narrative can never fully convey is the intensity of the fevered atmosphere of the times. As we have explained, the royal prerogative did not lack for support. The opposition consisted of a disparate group of individuals. Their most obvious characteristic was a determined and robust sense of independence. The issues being addressed on all sides mattered way beyond forensic squabbles or posturing. Those of the conflicting persuasions who attended meetings with others who shared their general approach to the issues, but who were opposed to the King, were not a political party in any sense that we might understand. There was no loyal opposition. At their meetings there was discussion, disagreement and compromise about parliamentary tactics. What is more, in a way that is more difficult for our secular age, less steeped in the Bible, to understand, all of them will have been familiar with the direction in Ecclesiastes 'Curse not the King, nor not in thy thought'.[12] They would all certainly have understood , and none better than Coke, the law of treason and misprision of treason and the ease with which it might be proved. There is no doubt that when they met they were planning to obstruct the King's wishes. In Tudor and Stuart England this was a dangerous occupation.

The dangers of speaking in merely disparaging terms of the King are illustrated by the now forgotten case of Hugh Pyne, formerly Treasurer of Lincoln's Inn. In 1627 he was charged with treason for suggesting that Charles was no more fit to be King than a well-known local simpleton, whom he named. When the Attorney-General sought the views of the judges, they were agreed that

> the mere speaking of the words, although they were as wicked as might be, did not amount to treason; for it had been adjudged to charge the King with a personal vice, as to say of him, 'he is the greatest whoremonger or drunkard in the Kingdom,' is no treason.[13]

Although Pyne avoided a trial for treason, he remained in custody for eight months on the order of the Star Chamber until the case, together with his practice, eventually collapsed.

Many of those adhering to the 'King-in-Parliament' principle, or their families or friends, had been in prison without trial or cause shown. The shadow of the prerogative courts was deepening. As we have seen, judges who failed to agree with the King were liable to be dismissed. With this background those who were opposed to

---

[11] Hulme (n 8) 227.
[12] Authorised Version, Ecclesiastes 10:20.
[13] D Cressy, *Dangerous Talk: Scandalous, Seditious and Treasonable Speech in Pre-Modern England* (Oxford, 2010); Campbell (n 3) 116–31.

the idea of the 'King, in Parliament' cannot have doubted, and later events proved them right, that they were taking serious personal risks. We should be doing less than justice to them if we did not notice the sustained courage they were called on to display under the banner of Magna Carta.

The story of the Petition of Right exemplifies much of the toing and froing between the two Houses as these issues of great principle were discussed. When the terms of the Petition were sent to the Lords, the two Houses became enmeshed in conflict about them. The King gave an assurance that there would be no imprisonment for refusal to lend money 'or for any cause which within our conscience doth not concern the State, the public good and safety of us and our people'. As to stating the cause of imprisonment, that would always be done as soon as convenient and safe. In short, reason of State was reiterated, and the King should be trusted. The courts have become accustomed to addressing emollient assurances of this kind, and they give them such weight as they merit. In 1628 the assurance of the anointed King had to be approached with considerable respect, and as we have underlined, caution too. Any forthright language rejecting the King's good faith could readily be followed by detention, and even if words critical of the King did not themselves constitute treason, ill-tempered words could be used as evidence to demonstrate conspiracy to commit treason.

Coke presented the draft Petition of Right to the House of Lords. The Lords were content to 'leave entire that Sovereign Power, wherewith your Majesty is trusted' and required these words to be included in the text. This embellishment may not have seemed very important, but the opposition were alert to the implications. Coke knew that

> prerogative is part of the law, but *Sovereign Power* is no parliamentary word. Should we now add it, we shall weaken the foundation of the law . . . Take heed what we yield unto! Magna Carta is such a fellow that he will have no sovereign.[14]

The word 'sovereign' was neither in Magna Carta nor in any of its subsequent confirmations. This was a Petition of Right, based on the law.

There has been some dispute about precisely what Coke meant by these words and even whether he said them, at any rate in the way they have come down to us.[15] Given everything we know about what Coke did say, the words attributed to him do not surprise us. We believe that his comment should be read as a response to the opinion of the Lords that the Petition should be qualified by reference to the sovereign power of the King. Put in context, what we believe Coke was saying was that there was no royal sovereign or prerogative power fit or appropriate to undermine Magna Carta.

Eventually the Petition of Right drafted by the Commons was accepted by the Lords. In due course it was read aloud in Parliament. The King did no more than he had promised all along. He would do right 'according to the laws and customs of

---

[14] RV Turner, *Magna Carta* (Harlow, 2003) 157.
[15] Goldsworthy (n 8) 114.

the realm' and he would take no action which was contrary to the just rights and liberties of his subjects. This represented the failure of the Petition. The Commons tried again and, after a conference between them and the Lords, the King returned to Parliament. He still needed his subsidy. The Petition was read again. At the end of the reading the Commons burst into applause. The King pronounced the traditional words of royal assent, '*soit droit fait comme il est desire*'.

The Petition of Right drew on and, consistently with the assertion that its terms were declaratory of existing rights, made deliberate reference to history. It prohibited forced loans and the billeting of soldiers on reluctant citizens. It protected against detention by the King's 'special commandment' without charge. And with its reference to the common consent of the kingdom through Parliament and the requirement of due process of law, we emphasise, 'whatever the estate or condition' of the citizen, and its rejection of detention without charge, the 'statute called the Great Charter of the Liberties of England', Magna Carta, was reclothed for the seventeenth century. The ancient liberties, or perhaps more accurately, the seventeenth-century view of the ancient liberties, had been confirmed. 'The King-in-Parliament' principle had prevailed.

Not for long – it soon emerged that, when first published, the Petition of Right included the King's first response and omitted the crucial second response, *soit droit fait* . . . When explanation was sought, the King's printer responded 'by warrant either immediately under the King's hand or from the Clerk of Parliament'[16], and unsurprisingly another parliamentary crisis exploded. The King sought to direct the order of the debate, and required the House to consider tonnage and poundage. Parliament was summoned by his prerogative, and he therefore could direct the order of its proceedings. The House instead chose to address religion and a claim for parliamentary privilege by Rolle, a member who refused to pay tonnage and poundage which had not been granted by Parliament.[17] The Commons proceeded against the customs men responsible for the collection, and the King treated this as an attack on his honour and assumed full responsibility for what the customs officers had done to collect the tax. So once again sovereignty and privilege were in conflict. A meeting of the opposition was arranged, but somehow word of it reached the ear of the King. He decided that the session should be ended.

Next morning there was another dramatic and historic event. On the King's instructions, the Speaker announced the end of the session. There were cries in opposition. The Speaker attempted to leave the chair. He was restrained by Holles and Valentine. There was a minor scuffle to hold him there. Was the Speaker the King's official or the servant of the House? Parliament was dissolved, the King referring to the disobedient vipers who 'must look for their reward of punishment', and he issued a declaration attacking their 'secret designs . . . to abate the powers of our crown and bring our Government into obloquy'. Action was immediately taken.[18]

---

[16] Berkowitz (n 6) 205.
[17] F Thompson (n 2) 349–51.
[18] Berkowitz (n 6) 232.

Warrants were issued in the Privy Council summoning nine members of the Commons before it. Eliot, Selden, Coryton, Holles and Valentine were committed in custody to the Tower, and Hobart and Haymon committed to the Fleet and the Gatehouse respectively. Long and Strode were arrested and detained later, and detained at the King's pleasure and commandment. Parliament was not recalled until 1640.

21

Ship Money

THE ATTORNEY-GENERAL CONSULTED the judges about the extent and limits of parliamentary privilege, but unhappy with their responses, he proceeded in the Star Chamber. Selden applied for habeas corpus, joined by Holles, Valentine, Hobart, Long and Strode, relying on Magna Carta.[1] The judges were summoned by the King, and he saw each one of them individually, seeking their opinion whether the Star Chamber had jurisdiction over parliamentary offences. Seven of the judges offered to subscribe their opinion that there was no such jurisdiction, the other five dissented, but refused to subscribe.

In the meantime, seeking habeas corpus in the King's Bench, the prisoners relied on the Petition of Right. The Attorney-General responded that the Petition was not a law, and merely confirmed the legal position as it had always stood. In other words, he was relying on the King's answer given after the first reading of the Petition of Right. The judges should consult the King and he would let them know of the danger of admitting the defendants to bail. So, again, state necessity would trump Magna Carta.

The judges concluded that the prisoners should be bailed. They advised the King accordingly, but perhaps to sweeten the pill, respectfully suggested that if he sent a direction that the prisoners should be bailed, the law would be upheld on all sides to his advantage. This approach failed. Those responsible for holding the prisoners were ordered not to produce them in answer to habeas corpus. The King then changed his mind and agreed to give an indication that it was his pleasure that on the first day of the next legal term, the prisoners should be admitted to bail. In the theme with which everyone had become familiar, this offer of bail came as a matter of his grace, rather than of their right. He wanted to know what the judges' response would be. They indicated that they would implement the King's request, but they would not alter the basis of their decision that the order for bail would reflect the rights of the prisoner rather than the generosity of the King. The King responded that if the prisoners refused the bail offered as a matter of his grace, his indication that he was prepared to allow them to be admitted to bail would be recalled. When the case came on, the judges admitted the prisoners to bail on the provision of sureties for their good behaviour. Even that was too much for the prisoners who refused

---

[1] The progress of these proceedings is fully set out in D Berkowitz, *John Selden's Formative Years* (Washington, DC, 1989) 240–65.

to accept any conditions. They were taking their stand on the rights and privileges of Parliament. Accordingly their remand in custody continued.

In the end, Eliot, Holles and Valentine were prosecuted in the King's Bench for conspiring to frustrate the royal order to the Speaker for an adjournment of the House, and the consequent assault and restraint of the Speaker, which caused a breach of peace in the House. The prisoners offered no response. They refused to accept the jurisdiction of the court. In a paper prepared by Eliot, recognising that his silence would be treated as a confession, he underlined that he remained silent as a matter of duty to Parliament.[2] Holles and Valentine took the same view. Inevitably the prisoners were convicted, and then fined and sentenced to imprisonment during the King's pleasure, and there indeed they languished. Eliot died of ill health in the Tower in late 1632. Holles and Valentine remained in custody for 11 years, and were not released until a new Parliament was summoned.

The proceedings against the remaining prisoners gradually lapsed. In a gesture of support, while he was subject to custody, Selden was appointed one of the stewards for the Annual Reader's Dinner at the Inner Temple. In late 1634 Selden, still unconvicted of any offence, was persuaded to petition the King for his discharge. This was granted in February 1635. He was the last of the 'unconvicted' prisoners to be released by royal command.

By the time of Selden's release, the country was enmeshed in 'Ship Money' controversy. In the absence of Parliament, there was no supply. Fresh sources of revenue had to be found. Ship Money represented payment by the coastal towns for their defence from sea attacks. Charles proposed that, as the entire country benefited from the defence of the coast from invasion, the financial responsibility for protecting the coast should be extended to all regions. Quite whether there was any imminent threat to the nation at that date is open to question, but to us today, the principle is plain enough. The cost of defence is part of public expenditure met out of taxation. John Hampden refused to pay Ship Money just as he had refused to pay the forced loan. He saw Ship Money, as many of his contemporaries did, as a new form of taxation. Taxation needed Parliamentary consent.

Mindful of the potential problems, Charles had sought an opinion privately of the judges on two questions:

> 1. Whether, in cases of danger to the good and safety of the kingdom, the King may not impose Ship Money for its defence and safeguard, and by law compel payment from those who refuse?
> 2. Whether the King be not the sole judge both of the danger, and when and how it is to be prevented?[3]

At their private meetings the judges unanimously indicated their agreement with both propositions, that is, that Ship Money could be raised as the King saw appropriate in the event of national danger.

---

[2] H Hulme, *The Life of Sir John Eliot* (London, 1957) 335.
[3] State Trials, ed Hargreaves (London, 1776) vol 1, 509–10.

No doubt to the surprise of the judges, and no doubt, equally, to the discouragement of Hampden's counsel, the views expressed privately by the judges were made public, when the issue came for resolution in open court in the Exchequer Chamber. Even today, the arguments on both sides, and the appeals to history and tradition and precedent, remain, at any rate to us as lawyers, remarkably impressive.[4] Considerable weight was attached on behalf of Hampden to what is described in the report as 'The Statute of Running Mead', with reference to clause 12 of Magna Carta – in short, that there was no requirement to pay scutage or aid without the consent of the community. In essence it was argued that the scutage provision remained in force even though it was not included in the later reissues, and that was because it was simply declaratory of the common law. Accordingly, as the Ship Money obligation had not been agreed by Parliament, Hampden was not liable to pay or to be penalised for not paying.

The majority of the judges rejected this submission. They accepted that the defence of the kingdom required the King to take all necessary steps. However, of the 12 judges, four dissented, and the Chief Justice, while agreeing that Ship Money could be raised throughout the country, would have given judgment for Hampden on a technicality. The dissenting judges relied on Magna Carta as a confirmation of the liberty of the subject and the requirement of Parliamentary assent to taxation. Hutton J roundly asserted that 'the subjects of England are free men, not slaves, free men, not villeins'. When he had completed his judgment, he was confronted at the bar of the court by a clergyman called Harrison, who accused him of high treason for giving a judgment that encouraged the stubbornness of those who refused to pay Ship Money.[5] Harrison was subsequently convicted of contempt of court, but his intervention demonstrates that it was not simply judicial opinion that was divided on this issue.

In short, the majority of the court had given a view of Ship Money with which those who supported the King-in-Parliament principle disagreed. This view, not by any means legally outrageous, was based on the proposition that defence and declarations of war were part of the prerogative and had been so regarded for centuries. In 1939 Mr Chamberlain did not seek parliamentary approval for the declaration of war and when, in August 2013, Mr Cameron took a vote in the House of Commons on the possibility of armed conflict with Syria, this was emphatically not a legislative process. Nevertheless, some of the judgments in the Ship Money case were profoundly royalist, and ardently embraced 'the King, in Parliament' view of the Constitution. Statements of political rather than juridical opinion were made, conveying the impression that the decision was not based on legal principle. Echoing what was alleged against Richard II in the Articles of Deposition, Berkeley J said 'I never read or heard that *lex* was *Rex*; but it is common and most true that *Rex* is *lex* for he is *lex loquens*, a living, a speaking, an acting law'. Crawley J considered that 'the first regal prerogative . . . contains all the rest, that the King may give laws to his

---

[4] ibid 506–719.
[5] *R v Harrison*, ibid 719–22.

subjects, and this does not detract from him when he does it in Parliament'. Coke would have revolved in his grave.

The Ship Money issue was re-examined in the case of Lord Say in the King's Bench. Bramston LCJ said that the judgment should stand 'until it were reversed in Parliament'. The significant feature of this observation was that it proceeded on the basis that as between the courts and Parliament, the last word rested with Parliament. By the time it was made, the principle was well understood that even Magna Carta itself could be overruled by an Act of Parliament.

The issue had been addressed in the broad context of the dispute about the ambit of Parliament's authority. The realisation that an Act of Parliament could overrule Magna Carta was not perceived as diminishing the authority of Magna Carta, but rather acknowledged that Magna Carta was itself a legislative provision. Thus Selden, who lauded Magna Carta throughout his career, noted that 'an act of Parliament may alter any part of Magna Carta'.[6] The judiciary, too, was subject to Parliament, as 'executors' not 'executioners' of statute, as Oliver St John, a future Chief Justice, was vividly to comment in the prosecution of the Ship Money judges.[7] Where did all this leave Coke's famous observation in *Bonham's Case* in 1610 that 'when an act of parliament is against common right and reason . . . the common law will control it and adjudge such Act to be void'?[8] As we shall see, the observation assumed huge importance to the constitutional arrangements which developed in North America during the next century. Quite what Coke meant, and indeed why he said it, has been debated ever since, but what he believed the constitutional position to be is summarised in the *Second Institute*, which includes his commentary on Magna Carta itself: 'the highest and most binding laws are the statutes which are established by Parliament'.[9] When he wrote these words Coke would have thought it inconceivable that any parliament would ever seek to repeal the liberty and taxation provisions of Magna Carta. In any event, although widely celebrated in North America, his observation had nothing to do with the case in hand, where a different principle, that no man could be a judge in his own cause, was engaged and upheld.

The Assembly in Maryland would have offered Coke some solace against the distress likely to have been caused him by the royalist judicial observations in the Ship Money case. In 1636 it passed legislation which provided that the inhabitants 'shall have all their rights and liberties according to the great charter of England'.[10] Unsurprisingly the legislation did not receive royal assent, not least because the King was advised by the Attorney-General that this might not be agreeable with the royal prerogative. The King might have thought that one out for himself.

---

[6] J Goldsworthy, *The Sovereignty of Parliament, History and Philosophy* (Oxford, 2010) 128.
[7] State Trials (n 3).
[8] *Dr Bonham's Case* 8 Co Rep 116.
[9] Quoted in Goldsworthy (n 6) 123.
[10] HD Hazeltine, 'The Influence of Magna Carta on American Constitutional Development' in HE Malden (ed), *Magna Carta Commemoration Essays* (London, 1917) 195.

At the same time Massachusetts was framing a constitutional structure, 'a body of grounds of law in resemblance to a Magna Carta', according to John Winthrop in his *History of New England*, which took final legislative form in 1641 in the Body of Liberties.[11] The language that sanctions must not be imposed unless there was a contravention of 'some express law . . . warranting it' is happily familiar today. In 1647 the Governor and Assistants in Massachusetts ordered the importation of two copies each of Coke's *Second Institute*. As in early seventeenth-century England, from their earliest days these newly established communities regarded Magna Carta as the foundation for the liberties which they espoused and as late as 1732 the Charter of Georgia, the last of the 13 States founded before the War of Independence, copied the Massachusetts documents. As we shall see, the day came when the 13 States were to question the sovereignty of Parliament, which sought to impose unacceptable legislation on them. The ways parted. Nevertheless the genesis of two distinctive constitutional democracies was the same twelfth-century parchment.

Parliament was summoned in 1640. The position was that there would be no vote of supply until Magna Carta and its confirmation by the Petition of Right were secured. This Short Parliament was dissolved after three weeks. It was followed by the Long Parliament. From the outset, the deadlock between the King and Parliament was unbroken. Holles and Valentine were released from custody and Berkeley and Crawley JJ and the judges who decided for the King in the Ship Money case were impeached for treasons and misdemeanours. These proceedings were expressly political. The judges had given a view of the Ship Money issue which Parliament utterly rejected. They were said to have 'set themselves up above Parliament leaving the citizen without hope of redress' and had, in effect, undermined Parliament, giving 'much offence to the nation' and occasioning 'great heart-burns in the House of Commons'.[12] Judicial independence awaited the Act of Settlement 1701. These judges were, however, more fortunate than Thomas Wentworth (now Earl of Strafford). Although they were detained, unlike him they were not executed. When Wentworth's prosecution for treason before the House of Lords seemed doomed to failure, it was replaced by attainder proceedings. It is one of the ironies of the political tumult which eventually culminated in the Civil War, that Strafford, whose support for Magna Carta when in the Commons was clear and unequivocal, should find himself subjected to attainder proceedings by the newly invigorated Parliament, no longer reliant on, nor too deeply concerned about, the right granted by Magna Carta to trial by one's peers.

The Long Parliament was the last Parliament elected before the Restoration in 1660. Its proceedings included the notorious attempt by the king in person to arrest members of the Commons ('I see the birds have flown'); with express reference to Magna Carta, the Star Chamber and the prerogative courts were abolished; Pride's Purge sought to expel those members who failed sufficiently to recognise that the

[11] ibid 192.
[12] State Trials (n 3) 695; and see Goldsworthy n 6 128–30.

King could not be trusted to negotiate any diminution in his prerogative. It continued thereafter as a Rump, until its peremptory dismissal by a dictator, Oliver Cromwell.

22

Independence of the Jury and the Right to Silence

INEVITABLY THE PASSIONATE debates about constitutional principle and complaints about the lawfulness of the exercise of royal prerogatives and proceedings before the prerogative courts were silenced by the march to civil war. Charles raised his standard at Nottingham in August 1642. In their propaganda material, the Parliamentarians focused heavily on Magna Carta, which, according to them , took 'clean away the King's pretended absolute negative voice' to parliamentary bills.[1] Nearly seven years later Charles was tried for, and convicted of, High Treason for levying war on Parliament and his people. It is beyond the scope of this book to examine the story of the Civil War and the events which culminated in the trial and execution of the King.[2]

Oliver Cromwell was described as the Protector, yet he wielded power as ruthlessly as any Stuart monarch. When in 1656 legal objection on the basis of Magna Carta was taken against custom duty imposed by the Protectorate, Cromwell charmlessly reacted, 'your magna farta cannot control actions taken for the safety of the Commonwealth'.[3] Counsel who advanced the argument were committed to the Tower. On this occasion, reason of state did not merely lame Magna Carta, it tore it up. Chief Justice Rolle resigned.[4] Lamentably, a few years later, on an occasion when reliance was being placed on Magna Carta against arbitrary commitment, the same description was applied to the Charter by a Restoration Chief Justice, John Kelynge. His main qualification for office appears to have been that he was a 'violent cavalier' and a friend of the Duchess of Cleveland.[5] When charged by the Commons with vilifying the Charter, he sought unconvincing refuge in the need for judicial efficiency on the basis that the reference to Magna Carta had 'nothing to

[1] RV Turner, *Magna Carta* (Harlow, 2003) 150.

[2] For detailed accounts, see State Trials, ed Hargreaves (London, 1776), vol I, 985–1044; The Tryal of the Regicides, 1739; CV Wedgewood, *The Trial of Charles I* (Harmondsworth, 1983), where the main focus of attention is the King himself; G Robertson, *The Tyrannicide Brief* (London, 2005), focusing on the prosecutor, John Cooke; and R Bradshaw, *God's Battle Axe* (Manhattan Beach, CA, 2010), focusing on Bradshaw, the President of the Court.

[3] J Campbell, *The Lives of the Chief Justices* (London, 1849) vol 1, 432, 433, quoting Clarendon, *History of the Rebellion*.

[4] Campbell (n 3) 433.

[5] ibid 503–11.

do with business'.[6] We reflect that in his own comments on the proceedings Samuel Pepys described Magna Carta as 'the great preserver of our lives, freedoms and property'.[7]

If Cromwell behaved autocratically, others like the Levellers espoused egalitarian principles. In brief, their stance, as explained in the *Agreement of the People*, was the requirement for a written constitution, with legislative authority exclusively vested in elected representatives. Their most famous adherent, John Lilburne, attacked the monarchy in unequivocal terms in 1647 in *Regal Tyranny Discovered*.[8] His thesis was that Charles was the very worst of kingly tyrants, the 'greatest delinquent'. He must be brought to justice and executed; not, however, by a military tribunal or the Parliamentary Rump of which Lilburne was deeply mistrustful. In August 1649, not long after the execution of Charles I, he wrote *An Impeachment of High Treason against Oliver Cromwell*. In essence, faced with a choice between a military dictatorship and the Prince, as he described Charles II, the better choice would be the King.[9] It was even feared that the Levellers might make common cause with him.[10]

In October 1649 Lilburne was brought to trial for high treason. It was not the first time he had faced trial, and indeed it was not to be the last. He was a master of forensic strategy and a brilliant natural advocate. To this day his words leap vividly off the printed pages of State Trials.[11] He claimed the 'indubitable birthright and inheritance' due to him as a free-born Englishman. These were derived from and based on Magna Carta and legislation made contrary to Magna Carta was null and void. 'The great Oracle' was Coke. Quite what Coke would have made of such commendation from someone he would have regarded as a dangerous revolutionary is open to question.

Among a number of highlights of the trial, we identify how Lilburne demanded open justice, which indeed, as the court pointed out, was provided before he sought it – a reflection of the fact that the prerogative courts had been abolished. He refused to plead to the indictment, not only because he claimed that it was difficult for him to understand, but because, to plead at all might lead to self-incrimination. It is sometimes said that Lilburne was the first person to identify a privilege against self-incrimination, but the contention had been made earlier, for example by Robert Beale in Elizabeth's reign: 'Whereby I do infer that by the statute of Magna Charter and the older Laws of this realm, this oath for a man to accuse himself was and is utterly inhibited'. Beale also contended that no one should be proceeded against without 'better proof' than his own bare saying.[12] Nevertheless, it was Lilburne who

---

[6] A Pallister, *Magna Carta, The Heritage of Liberty* (Oxford, 1971) 30.

[7] *The Diary of Samuel Pepys*, vol 8, 577.

[8] P Gregg, *Free-born John: A Biography of John Lilburne* (London, 2000) 285.

[9] A Sharp, 'The Levellers and the End of Charles I' in J Peacey (ed), *The Regicides and the Execution of Charles I* (London, 1999) 197.

[10] Gregg (n 8) 291.

[11] State Trials (n 2) vol 2, 19–79.

[12] F Thompson, *Magna Carta: Its Role in the Making of the British Constitution* (Minneapolis, MN, 1948) 221–23.

gave energy to these ideas. He also objected to the prosecutor having any discussion with the bench in what he describes as 'hugger-mugger' fashion: this, too, we take for granted. He suggested to the jury that they should be judges of the law as well as the facts. This contention, unsustainable in law, did not prevent the jury from triumphantly acquitting him.

It was not the end of Lilburne's clashes with the authorities. In late 1651/early 1652 he was sentenced without charge and without trial by Parliament to fine, damages and banishment. Shortly after Cromwell had disbanded the Rump in 1653, Lilburne defied an order of banishment and returned to England. The penalty was death. He was prosecuted. Once again his skill as a forensic strategist was on display. In law Lilburne had no defence. Again he relied on Coke. He took a subtle but appealing line. Either he was condemned as a result of the work of the Rump Parliament, a body which had been dissolved for injustice and maladministration, or alternatively, if it was indeed to be treated as a lawful Parliament, then the first defendant should be Cromwell himself, who had organised what, on this basis, would have been its unjust dissolution.[13] The verdict was astounding: not guilty of any crime worthy of death. Even before the famous case of *Penn and Mead*, and as far as we know for the very first time, the jury refused to apply the law when they did not believe that the sentence, the death penalty, bore any just relationship to the crime. Whether this verdict amounted to a conviction or an acquittal, Lilburne's detention continued 'for the peace of this Nation'.[14] Thereafter he was removed in custody to the Channel Islands.

The independence of the jury was finally established in the case of the two Quakers, Penn and Mead, in 1670.[15] The defendants faced a charge of riotous assembly, for preaching to the great disturbance of the peace. William Penn relied on Coke and Magna Carta: 'Lord Coke tells us, that Common-Law is Common Right and that Common Right is the Great Charter-Privileges'. He appealed to the jury that he was pleading for the fundamental laws of England. If they were not 'indispensably maintained and observed, who can say he has the right to the coat on his back?' He protested that the jury were not to be menaced and that 'their verdict should be free, and not compelled'. The Recorder of London directed the jury to convict. When they acquitted he expressed, in intimidating language, his regret that they had followed their own opinion. Penn sought his discharge, but he was fined and imprisoned until the fine was paid. He protested that the order contravened Magna Carta, both clauses 14 and 29 of the 1225 Charter. His protest was rejected. The jury, too, were fined and imprisoned until the fine was paid. An application for habeas corpus on their behalf was made before the Court of Common Pleas and, led by John Vaughan, the Chief Justice, the court ordered their release. 'The writ of habeas corpus is now the most usual remedy by which a man is restored again to his

---

[13] Gregg (n 8) 332.
[14] ibid 333.
[15] State Trials (n 2) vol 2, 610–16.

liberty, if he have, against law, been deprived of it'. Even when the verdict was not to the judge's 'opinion and liking' it must nevertheless be accepted.

Bushell's Case, as it is known,[16] established beyond question that the jury is and must be free to return its own verdict. In later centuries, faced with trials which led to the death penalty if the value of the goods allegedly stolen exceeded a prescribed level, juries followed the jury in Lilburne's case and returned verdicts that the value of the property was just below the level which would be followed by the death penalty. To this day the independence of the jury remains sacrosanct. However inescapable the defendant's guilt may appear to the judge, the jury cannot be directed to convict him.[17] These principles are not found in the language of Magna Carta, but it was Magna Carta and Coke who gave Lilburne and Penn their voices at their trials. Penn was released, and eventually made his way to North America. In 1681 he founded the new colony of Pennsylvania, where, in 1687, as part of a tract extolling the privilege of enjoying the birthright of being a free-born subject of England, Magna Carta and the 1297 Confirmation were published.

Lilburne died in 1657, and Cromwell in 1658. The Protectorate came to an end.

---

[16] *Bushell's Case* (1670) Vaughan 135, 124 ER 1006.
[17] *R v Wang* [2005] 1 WLR 661.

23

Towards an Independent Judiciary

IN 1660 THE monarchy was restored under Charles II. At his first Parliament, the son of Charles I was offered gratitude and congratulations by the Speaker 'for restoring to us our Magna Carta liberties'.[1] Charles II and Clarendon, his Lord Chancellor, were careful not to test the relationship between the King and Parliament to destruction, but the mood of the Cavalier Parliament elected amid the euphoria of the Restoration steadily soured over the years until its dissolution in 1678. In the meantime, as Charles's marriage remained childless, the succession of his brother, James, Duke of York, a convert to Roman Catholicism, became increasingly likely. This was a period in our history when politics and religion could and did produce an explosive mixture of polarised intolerance. In the end, James II succeeded in 1685. Less politically sensitive than his brother, his short reign ended in 1688. For present purposes we shall examine these two reigns together as a developing whole.

One line of royalist thought reinvigorated 'the King, in Parliament' theory of the Constitution. Magna Carta came under renewed attack. It neither illustrated nor encapsulated the common law. It was 'only a relaxation of the feudal military law'.[2] Other royalist thinkers, perhaps with greater sensitivity to the strategy of persuasion, accepted the 1225 Charter and directed their criticism at clause 61 of the 1215 Charter, as a concession extracted by force. 'Rebellion is a very ill bottom to found our liberties upon'.[3] As events unfolded Magna Carta remained at the heart of the continuing debate about the Constitution, and assumed importance in the dispute whether James should be excluded from the succession. Ironically, the supporters of his right to do so relied on Magna Carta, arguing that his exclusion would contravene the Charter by stripping him of his rightful inheritance. In law this was a more appealing argument than the opposing reliance on the Charter by associating the Duke of York's 'popery' with absolutism or despotism, as support for the conclusion that the liberties of the Charter would be lost if he succeeded to the throne.[4] The Test Acts 1673 and 1678 underlined the religious divide. With the objective that Roman Catholics should be excluded from any form of civil or military office, all those appointed were required to swear the oath of Supremacy and Allegiance and,

---

[1] Quoted in A Pallister, *Magna Carta: The Heritage of Liberty* (Oxford, 1971) 26.
[2] Brady, *Complete History of England 1688*, quoted in Pallister (n 1) 34.
[3] Collier, *Vindiciae Juris Regii*, quoted in Pallister (n 1) 33.
[4] Pallister (n 1) 37–38.

as Roman Catholics, to betray their faith by rejecting the doctrine of transubstantiation. These Acts also bore heavily on Nonconformists, who rejected any form of oath taking, but they at any rate would have had no difficulty on the doctrinal issue.

In the decade before 1688, between 1679 and 1688, Parliament met five times, doing business for 171 days. It was prorogued in late 1685, and did not meet again while James II was King. A number of developments caused increasing concern. Apart from the absence of Parliament itself, the military power of the King substantially increased. The Petition of Right and the Disbanding Act 1679 precluded forced billeting, but after very large forces were enrolled to defeat Monmouth's rebellion, a substantial body of soldiers remained. This was a standing army, and soldiers were sometimes billeted in private houses, sometimes in public places.[5] There were inevitable troubles. At the same time, the judges were under constant pressure to comply with royal wishes. In the last years of Charles II's reign, between 1676 and 1685, no fewer than 11 judges were removed from the bench.[6] This pattern persisted during the next reign. What is more, the later Stuart judges were led by a group which included four of the worst Chief Justices of the King's Bench in our history. Apart from Kelynge, they included Scroggs, Jeffreys and Wright, perhaps less of a merciless bully than the other three, but equally servile and blind to even the remotest risk of his own fallibility. Sir Francis Winnington, an exclusionist, condemned Scroggs's decision to discharge the Grand Jury considering whether the Duke of York should be indicted as a recusant and observed

> we are come to the old times again, when the judges pretended they had a rule of government, as well as a rule of law. . . if they never did read Magna Charta, I think they are not fit to be judges; if they had read Magna Charta, and do thus so contrary, they deserve severe chastisement[7]

Judges should be, he later argued, 'the great barrier' of impartiality between the monarch and any attack on the fundamental laws.[8]

The further feature of this period, although beyond the ambit of this book, was that 'the Restoration held back the freedom of the English press for another generation'.[9] The judicially authorised murder of a bookseller, John Twyn, in 1664 was mirrored by the execution of innocent Catholics who were victims of Titus Oates. These were not the best of times for our liberties.

Amid this turmoil, one valuable piece of legislation effectively prevented the withering of habeas corpus. After several unsuccessful efforts, the Habeas Corpus Amendment Act 1679 was enacted to defeat attempts by the executive to undermine habeas corpus principles by incarcerating prisoners, in effect, beyond the jurisdiction of the courts. The Act simultaneously gave statutory force to the principle that detention was unlawful unless cause was shown. Thus it was, deriving from argu-

---

[5] T Harris, *Revolution: The Great Crisis of the British Monarchy 1685–1688* (Oxford, 2006) 188–91.
[6] AF Havinghurst, 'James II and the Men in Scarlet' (1953) 69 LQR 524.
[7] Quoted in Pallister (n 1) 31.
[8] State Trials, ed Hargreaves (London, 1776) vol 1, Preface and vol 3, 222.
[9] R Hargreaves, *The First Freedom: A History of Free Speech* (Stroud, 2002) 102–17.

ments based on Magna Carta in the Five Knights Case and the 1628 Parliament, the medieval writ of habeas corpus became entrenched as a protection against arbitrary imprisonment. In the next century William Blackstone described the Act as 'a great bulwark of our constitution . . . a second Magna Carta, as beneficial and effectual as that of Running Mead'.[10] In his *History of His Own Time* Bishop Burnet reported that the legislation was only carried in the House of Lords by 57 to 55 votes when one of the tellers counted a rather rotund peer as 10 votes.[11] If so, it was one of the greatest jests of our history. To this day it remains a tradition that an application for bail should be heard before any other business, because a bail application involves the liberty of the subject.

The deepest crisis of government was postponed until James II succeeded his brother. James inherited his father's inability to discern political realities. His brief reign has been much studied.[12] Notwithstanding the anti-popery frenzy which disfigured the later years of his brother's reign, James II would not have forfeited his throne if he had practised his religion privately. Unfortunately, believing that his royal powers were unfettered, James immediately embarked on a policy to promote the interests of his Catholic co-religionists in violation of the law. In doing so,

> he provoked opposition from those very people who had been the chief supporters of the monarchy during the final years of his brother's reign . . . He fell because he failed to understand the realities of power within the restoration policy and the (limited) ways in which royal authority could be effectively exercised.[13]

Even earlier in his reign than his grandfather, he created alarm when he publicly attended Mass within days of ascending the throne, observing that he would not have broken the laws if he had been a subject, but he was now the King and above the executive force of the law.[14] Protestant sentiment cannot have been improved by the revocation of the Edict of Nantes by Louis XIV. Anti-Catholic feeling was rife and its mood was violent. The linkage of 'popery' and 'slavery' had proved to be effective propaganda. By April 1686 the trained bands of London were unable, in good conscience, to hinder a crowd 'pulling down popery'[15] – and at much the same time a jury in Bristol acquitted a defendant who, armed with a blunderbuss, disrupted a service in a Catholic church.[16]

In the absence of Parliament, and with Monmouth's rebellion crushed but the royal army not yet disbanded, in 1686 James II established his new Ecclesiastical Commission. This was not quite the Court of High Commission with which Coke

---

[10] W Blackstone, *Commentaries on the Laws of England*, vol 4 (Dublin, 1769) 451.

[11] T Bingham, *The Rule of Law* (London, 2011) 22.

[12] Competing views can be found in GM Trevelyan, *The English Revolution, 1688–1689* (London, 1939); JR Jones, *The Revolution of 1688 in England* (London, 1984); J Miller, *James II: A Study in Kingship* (London, 2000); and Harris (n 5).

[13] Harris (n 5) 30.

[14] ibid 46.

[15] ibid 201.

[16] ibid.

had become entangled, and which had disappeared with the prerogative courts in 1641, but Jeffreys was appointed to preside over it and he referred to it as a court.[17] At much the same time the King's Bench decided *Godden v Hales*, in which it was required to address the royal power to dispense with the restrictions of the Test Acts.

Hales was a Catholic associate of James, who was appointed as colonel of a foot regiment in Kent. He did not take the oath required by the Test Acts. His coachman, Godden, informed against Hales, who appeared at Rochester Assizes and was fined. As the informant, Godden was entitled to receive the amount of any fine, and when Hales refused to pay it, Godden brought an action of debt against him in the King's Bench. Hales relied on letters patent granted by the King, which allowed him to hold the military position without taking the required oaths. Before the case was heard the King sought the views of the judges. Six indicated their opinion that it was not open to him to dispense with the provisions of the Test Acts. They were removed, and six new judges, more amenable to the King's wishes, were appointed.[18] The Chief Justice of the Common Pleas, Thomas Jones, was one of those who declined to support the King, and when the King said that he would have 12 judges of his opinion, Jones replied that he may find 12 judges but they would scarcely be lawyers.[19] Jones was among the judges who were dismissed. The judges ruled in favour of the dispensing power by a majority of 11 to 1. They ruled 'the Kings of England were absolute sovereigns; that the laws were the King's laws; that the King had power to dispense with . . . laws as he saw the necessity for it; that he was the sole judge of necessity'.[20] This sounded like Ship Money revived.

The threat of removal from judicial office and the imposition of sanctions on judges came from another source. When Parliament was in the ascendancy and wished to make a protest against a judicial decision with which it disagreed, as we have seen in the Ship Money case, royalist judges were prosecuted for misconduct. During this later Stuart period, Kelynge was obliged to apologise publicly to the House of Lords; Scroggs faced proceedings for impeachment, and was saved by the dissolution of Parliament; Jeffreys died in the Tower and Wright died in Newgate. Having been dismissed by James II, Jones himself was committed to prison in 1689 for a decision said to constitute a breach of the privileges of the House of Commons made six years earlier with Chief Justice Pemberton. Pemberton in his turn had been discharged by Charles II at the behest of Scroggs, then shortly afterwards appointed to replace him as Chief Justice, then dismissed again because he was not sufficiently favourable to the Crown, and then, with Jones, committed to prison by the Convention Parliament.[21]

---

[17] ibid 204.
[18] ibid 192.
[19] E Foss, *A Biographical Dictionary of the Judges of England* (London, 1870) 378.
[20] J Campbell, *The Lives of the Chief Justices of England* (London, 1849) 87–88
[21] Foss (n 19) 373, 378, 382, 507, 599, 765.

The process of pre-hearing interviews between the King and judges to see whether they would be favourably disposed to James's wishes was accompanied in late 1686 by a series of interviews with members of both Houses of Parliament, again with the object of discovering whether they would be agreeable to the repeal of the Test Acts. After this proved unpromising, and 18 months since it last sat, Parliament was dissolved in July 1687. James also embarked on what we shall describe as an electoral campaign to secure the return of favourable members if he summoned a new Parliament, but without success, and Parliament was not summoned again. Similarly, polls of office holders, such as justices of the peace and officers of livery companies, were organised. The results were so unsatisfactory from the King's point of view that a 'wholesale purge' took place.[22]

In early 1687 the first Declaration of Indulgence in England was issued, a few weeks after the issue of a similar Declaration in Scotland, and this was followed in late 1688 by a second Declaration of Indulgence. This went to the heart of the argument. The Declarations purported to have what we should regard as the laudable aim of freedom to worship according to one's faith, and royalist supporters described how they represented 'Magna Charta for liberty of conscience'.[23] In fact, the Declarations were issued as emanations of the royal prerogative, that the penal statutes relating to ecclesiastical matters should be suspended. As to Parliament, the King expected that Parliament, whenever he decided it should be summoned, would assent to his decision. The question whether these Declarations represented or were as a matter of law examples of the exercise of a suspending rather than a dispensing power can be discussed at length. Dispensing with the impact of a statute on an individual or group of individuals was, in constitutional terms, less dramatic than its wholesale suspension by royal decree. In the context in which James exercised either or both these powers, they nevertheless represented a direct route back to 'the King, in Parliament' and despotism.

As with the exclusion dispute it was not royalists alone who appealed to Magna Carta. In his *Letter to a Dissenter*, Halifax, who had supported the accession of James to the throne, invited non-Catholic dissenters to recognise the hidden danger in this more tolerant approach to religion. There was no prerogative right in the King to set aside the law. To make any such concession would make them look 'like counsel retained by the Prerogative against your old friend Magna Charta, who hath done nothing to deserve her falling thus under your displeasure'.[24]

By now, therefore, Magna Carta was being proclaimed and relied on in support of rights and liberties by protagonists who took diametrically opposed views of their contemporary constitutional arrangements and the role of the monarch in them. Without any diminution in the potency of the ideas for which it stood, the appeals to Magna Carta had become remote from the specific provisions of its

[22] Harris (n 5) 230–35.
[23] Pallister (n 1) 38.
[24] ibid 39.

clauses. Nevertheless the influence of the Charter on contemporary thinking was undiminished.

These disputes were highlighted by James's insistence that the bishops should order the reading of the second Declaration in church on successive Sundays. If they agreed, of course, that would be interpreted as support for the Declaration. Seven of the bishops, including the Archbishop of Canterbury, petitioned, in effect, against the use, or misuse, of the dispensing power. They were summoned to explain themselves, and protested that 'no subject was bound to accuse himself'. In due course they were tried for the publication of their petition to the King, the publication taking the form of presenting him with it. The arguments advanced on their behalf were complex, but are perhaps best summarised in the submission by John Somers, then a junior counsel, that the petition presented to the King was not designed to diminish the prerogative, 'because the King hath no such prerogative'.[25] To widespread rejoicing the bishops were acquitted. Two of the judges who agreed with the arguments on their behalf were summarily dismissed. On the day of the acquittals of the seven bishops a group of magnates invited William of Orange to intervene. It was less than 30 years since the Restoration.

A little noticed feature of the journey towards despotism was James's proposal to create the Dominion of New England, which would have abolished the representative assemblies of each of the different colonies.[26] In effect, all would be subsumed into one. Perhaps if carried through, this proposal would have united the colonies into making a much earlier Declaration of Independence. As it was, one important consequence of the Revolution of 1688 was that each colony survived with a degree of autonomy which, in due course, ensured their survival as independent states within the United States of America.

---

[25] Hargreaves State Trials (n 8) IV 303-395 at 383.
[26] J Hoppit, *A Land of Liberty? England 1689–1727* (Oxford, 2000) 271.

24

The Bill of Rights

WILLIAM OF ORANGE and his wife Mary, James II's daughter, were assuredly Protestant. With a well-timed declaration, which condemned the subversion of established laws and liberties, and the contravention of Magna Carta 'that no man shall lose life or goods but by the law of the land', William invaded England at the head of a professional army. Without deploying his own substantial forces, James II abjectly fled. In England this revolution was virtually bloodless. In Ireland much blood was shed in a war the memories of which still re-echo to this day.

In England a Commission of peers and members of the earlier Parliaments organised elections to what was described as the Convention Parliament. The throne was declared vacant. James was deemed to have abdicated. Mary refused to reign on her own and William declined to act as 'regent'. In February 1689 the Crown was vested in joint sovereigns, William and Mary. William was later described in the Bill of Rights as the 'glorious Instrument of Delivering this Kingdom from Popery and Arbitrary Power'.[1] Thus, the Divine Right of Kings was consigned to the scrap heap. The source of regal authority was earthbound. The King 'was tied up to the law as well as we' wrote John Somers, one of the architects of the settlement.[2] It also followed from the constitutional settlement that the law would be defined by the King-in-Parliament.

One much-debated question was whether there should be a new Magna Carta. 'It was therefore thought necessary to frame this Instrument so, it could be like a new Magna Charta'.[3] And in reality that was achieved. It 'was our second Magna Carta'.[4] The first Parliament of the new reign began work on 13 February 1689, and the 'Act declareing the Rights and Liberties of the Subject and Settleing the Succession of the Crowne' received Royal Assent in December 1689. We know this document as the Bill of Rights 1689.

Like Magna Carta, the Bill of Rights is one of our crucial constitutional documents, the end product of the turbulence of the previous century, and like Magna

---

[1] The Recital, Bill of Rights.
[2] Quoted T Harris, *Revolution: The Great Crisis of the British Monarchy 1685–1720* (London, 2006) 354.
[3] Bishop Burnet, *History of His Own Times*, quoted in A Pallister, *Magna Carta: The Heritage of Liberty* (Oxford, 1971) 41.
[4] Bolingbroke, quoted in Pallister (n 3) 41.

Carta, without proclaiming any high-flown constitutional theories, it pragmatically identified the grievances against the exercise of royal power which occurred in James's reign, and forbade their repetition. Indeed it began by criticising the King and his Counsellors who had endeavoured 'to subvert and extirpate the Protestant religion and the Lawes and the Liberties of this Kingdom'.

The Bill of Rights is a very short document, including only 13 substantive clauses. Interestingly, in view of the controversy at the end of the last reign, the first two clauses declared that suspending or dispensing with the laws or their execution without parliamentary consent is unlawful. The Court of Ecclesiastical Causes and levying money by 'pretense of Prerogative without Grant' were illegal. The right to petition the Crown was maintained. Without parliamentary consent, the raising or keeping of a standing army was illegal, but provided they were 'Protestants', citizens were entitled to carry arms for their defence. The election of Members of Parliament 'ought to be free' and freedom of speech in Parliament was not open to question in any court or, indeed, anywhere but within Parliament itself, thus enabling the unconstrained fulfilment by Members of their representative functions. Parliament should be called frequently so that grievances might be redressed and the laws strengthened and preserved. Excessive bail was prohibited, so were excessive fines and 'cruell and unusuall Punishments'. Jurors must be properly empanelled.

In a series of subsequent statutes, principles that we now take for granted, such as regular parliamentary elections,[5] parliamentary control of the armed forces,[6] and judicial security of tenure[7] were fixed, in effect beyond argument, and open to change only by later parliamentary enactment, but never by royal assertion or proclamation.

The result of the Glorious Revolution was that although our constitutional arrangements nominally remained 'the King-in-Parliament', Parliament had achieved primacy. Not yet a true democracy, this constitutional arrangement nevertheless underlined that those who ruled the country were themselves subject to the law, that changes to the law required community assent in Parliament, and that citizens enjoyed rights which were based not on authority's grace but on their own entitlement.

Magna Carta, or more accurately, the ideas for which Magna Carta was the inspiration, had triumphed.

---

[5] The Triennial Act 1694.

[6] The Mutiny Acts 1689 and 1703.

[7] The Act of Settlement 1701. For as long as they did not misconduct themselves ('quamdie se bene gesserint') judges held office from which they could not be removed without an address of both Houses of Parliament. No High Court or Court of Appeal judge in England has ever been removed from office under this power.

25

Rebellion in America

THE BIRTHRIGHTS ENJOYED in England were equally enjoyed, or understood to be enjoyed, in each of the new colonies in North America. Unlike the colonies founded in North America by Spain and France, a distinctive element of self-government by their own assemblies was a general characteristic of the colonies originating from England. In his *Commentaries on the Laws of England* Blackstone described the process by which English law operated in the colonies. Basing himself on a decision of the Privy Council in 1722,[1] he observed 'if an uninhabited country be discovered and planted by English subjects, all the English laws then in being, which are the birthright of every subject, are immediately then in force'.[2] Whether rightly or wrongly, the eastern seaboard of North America was treated as unsettled land. The colonists' view of their position was summarised in 1764 by James Otis, just before the notorious Stamp Act was enacted:

> Every British subject born on the continent of America is, by the laws of God and Nature, by the Common Law, and by Act of Parliament entitled to all the natural, inherent, and inseparable rights of our fellow subjects in Great Britain.[3]

There was, however, one critical omission from the catalogue of shared rights. The colonists were disenfranchised from parliamentary elections in London. Few inhabitants in England were entitled to vote in elections to the House of Commons, but no one living in any colony could do so.

Within this broad context each colony possessed its own legal characteristics, anticipating the time when each would become a fully fledged State. By way of brief example, unlike Virginia, Massachusetts Bay did not have and was not required to have headquarters in London. And, like England, none of the other colonies offered the freedom of worship permitted in New York after the surrender of the New Netherlands in 1674 and positively encouraged in Pennsylvania. We have already indicated earlier in the narrative the Bill in the Maryland Assembly in 1638 to recognise Magna Carta as part of the law of the colony, and the adoption of the Body of Liberties in Massachusetts Bay.[4] Rhode Island adopted its code of laws in 1647, which was prefaced by reference to Chapter 29 of Magna Carta. 'Quotations from

---

[1] 2 *Peer Williams* 75; 24 ER 646.
[2] W Blackstone, *Commentaries on the Laws of England*, 3rd edn (Dublin, 1769) I, 106–08.
[3] Quoted in HD Hazeltine, 'The Influence of Magna Carta on American Constitutional Development' in HE Malden (ed), *Magna Carta Commemoration Essays* (London, 1917) 211, n 3.
[4] Above, Chapter 21.

or echoes of the Charter occur in the laws of South Carolina, Virginia, Pennsylvania and New Jersey'.[5] As a foretaste of things to come, there was resistance in New York in 1680 to taxation which was 'contrary to Magna Carta and the Petition of Right'.[6] The colonists were not isolated from events in England, and Magna Carta, but also the Petition of Right, the Habeas Corpus Amendment Act and the Bill of Rights, were all documents with which the colonists were entirely familiar. The history being made in seventeenth-century England was their history in the making too.

The eventual triumph of the common law over the prerogative courts was an inherent part of their heritage. Thus in Virginia, in 1677, the assembly decreed that 'no law (could) compel a man to swere against himselfe in any manner wherein he is lyable to corporall punishment'.[7] Trial by jury, with the defendant who pleaded not guilty seeking trial 'by God and my country' was the customary method of trial of criminal offences. In a trial arising from unusual events in 1684, one Talbot sought to rely on Coke's *Institutes* when taking a jurisdiction point. He successfully blinded the General Court of Virginia to the fact that Coke, rather than supporting his argument, provided authority against him.[8]

Following Penn in 1687, in 1721 Henry Care's *English Liberties or the Freeborn Subjects' Inheritance* was one of the first books separately printed in the colonies. This publication included Magna Carta, the Petition of Right, and the Habeas Corpus Act within the text, and provided an account of the liberties of the subject, including trial by jury.[9] The first catalogue of the Harvard College Library of 1723 included Coke's first and second *Institutes*. When John Adams was a law student he was advised to 'conquer the Institutes'.[10] Thomas Jefferson paid Coke the compliment of noting that 'a sounder Whig never wrote nor profounder learning in the orthodox doctrines of British liberties'.[11] After Coke came Blackstone, first with his work on Magna Carta and then his *Commentaries*, more structured and therefore easier to study than Coke, 'a handbook clarifying the law for lawyers and laymen alike'.[12]

The first American edition of Blackstone's *Commentaries* was published in 1772. One of the Charter subscribers was Thomas Marshall, father of the future Chief Justice. Blackstone 'had a significant influence on the legal profession in Britain, but it was in North America that his work made its greatest impression'.[13] For some

    [5] HM Cam, 'Magna Carta – Event or Document?', the Selden Society Lecture 1965, published in *The Selden Society Lectures 1952–2001* (Buffalo, NY, 2003).
    [6] ibid 325.
    [7] W Billings, *A Little Parliament: The Virginia General Assembly in the 17th Century* (Virginia, 1948) 156.
    [8] ibid 162–64.
    [9] Hazeltine (n 3) 206.
    [10] C Drinker Bowen, *The Lion and the Throne: The Life and Times of Sir Edward Coke* (London, 1957) 443.
    [11] ibid 444.
    [12] JE Smith, *John Marshall: Definer of a Nation* (New York, NY, 1998) 76.
    [13] ibid 77.

time before its publication at home, numerous young Americans had come to London for their education and joined the Inns of Court for this purpose. According to Edmund Burke, like Blackstone himself a member of the Middle Temple, in his speech seeking to reconcile the colonies with Britain, 'in no country in the world was the law so generally studied as in America . . . as many copies of Blackstone had been sold there as in England'.[14] We can be quite sure that these young men would have understood Blackstone's opinion that three crucial rights of the individual – life, liberty and property – should be attributed to Magna Carta, and that the Habeas Corpus Amendment Act 1679 was 'a second Magna Carta'.

At the same time as these young Americans were attending the Inns of Court as part of their education, Magna Carta had once again come to the forefront of public discussion in England. The press, or some elements of it, were proving troublesome to the government in London. That weapon of authoritarianism, the general warrant, was once again revived and deployed in support of allegations of seditious criminal libel. One radical, Arthur Beardmore, knowing that his arrest was imminent, arranged to be found teaching his son about Magna Carta at the moment of his arrest in 1762. He subsequently established that his arrest was wrongful, and a popular print was published, in which he is shown pointing out Chapter 29 of Magna Carta to his young son. More significant, *No 45 of the North Briton* was published by John Wilkes at much the same time and in 1763 he was arrested and imprisoned on a general warrant. He sought his release on the basis that Magna Carta was a 'glorious inheritance . . . a distinguishing characteristic' of England',[15] and that his prosecution threatened the liberty of every subject. He, too, was discharged. Like Lilburne, with whom he has frequently been compared, Wilkes returned to public attention, this time taking on the House of Commons itself when, after his election by the county of Middlesex, he was expelled by the House. Again like Lilburne, he successfully elevated his treatment into a broad and popular claim to the liberties of every Englishman. He was determined that popular security could 'only be obtained by the most wholesome laws . . . built on the firm basis of Magna Carta, the great preserver of our lives, freedom, and property'.[16]

The populist cry of 'Wilkes and Liberty', particularly when Wilkes was expelled from the House of Commons after he had been duly elected, placed Magna Carta back in the forefront of popular thinking. The young American students at the Inns of Court would have absorbed something of the ferment of these issues. Whether they did or not, the Middle Temple is proud of the contribution made by its members to the creation of the United States of America and its constitutional arrangements. That, however, lay in the future.

---

[14] E Stockdale and R Holland, *Middle Temple Lawyers and the American Revolution* (Eagan, MN, 2007) 15.

[15] Quoted in RV Turner, *Magna Carta* (Harlow, 2003) 176–77.

[16] ibid 177.

It is difficult to comprehend how the joint success of British and colonial forces during the Seven Years War, or the French and Indian Wars as they are known in the United States, which ended in 1763, could possibly have developed just over a decade later into the Declaration of Independence in 1776, and victory to the new United States of America in 1783.

The trouble began with money. Like all wars, this war had been highly expensive. During the struggle the colonists had sacrificed many men and sustained heavy casualties, but the general funding had been provided by London. In March 1765, two years after the Treaty of Paris, Parliament in London enacted the Stamp Act. We have not found any evidence to suggest that when they were fighting the French, the colonists were also warned that they would in due course be expected to bankroll, or help to bankroll, the financial cost of the war. As part of their history, the colonies had expected to pay duty on their successful trade dealings, but the Stamp Act, for the first time, imposed direct taxation on them.

The Stamp Act is an extraordinary statute, rather anticipating some modern legislation in its length and complexity. It has nothing whatever to do with postage stamps in the now familiar sense. Even a cursory glance at its terms underlines the intrusive nature of its provisions into the ordinary functioning of society, involving a tax on documents such as mortgages, contracts and wills, and indeed any documents other than private correspondence, with its consequent blunting effect on commercial energy. No less important, it interfered with the right to trial by jury.

Representatives from nine of the 13 colonies met in New York in October 1765 and petitioned the King for the repeal of the Stamp Act. In a Declaration drafted by John Dickinson,*[17] the colonists took their stand on the simple principle 'that only the representatives of the people of these colonies are persons chosen therein by themselves and no taxes ever have been, or can be constitutionally imposed on them, but by their respective legislatures'.[18] No taxation without representation: it was the principle which, in England, reached back to Magna Carta itself, and had sustained and invigorated the constitutional struggles of the previous centuries. For the colonies the legislation represented arbitrary diktat. Typically, the Massachusetts Bay assembly declared that the Act was invalid as it was 'against Magna Charta and the natural rights of Englishmen, and therefore, according to Lord Coke, null and void'.[19]

The argument by the Stamp Act Congress was well supported in England. The question was asked: 'If the people of Britain are not to be taxed by Parliament, does it not directly follow that the colonists cannot, according to Magna Carta and the Bill of Rights, be taxed by Parliament, so long as they continue unrepresented?'[20] Lord Camden declared 'taxation and representation are inseparably united; God

---

[17] Those asterisked were members of the Middle Temple.
[18] Quoted in D Reynolds, *America, Empire of Liberty* (London, 2009) 58–59.
[19] Quoted in Drinker Bowen (n 10) 272.
[20] James Burgh, *Political Disquisitions*, quoted in A Pallister, *Magna Carta: The Heritage of Liberty* (Oxford, 1971) 56–57.

hath joined them, no British Parliament can separate them'.[21] Quite whether the same principle was being advocated on both sides of the Atlantic is open to question, because the view expressed in the Congress was that taxation on the colonies could only be imposed by a parliament of the colonies, or indeed each colony.

The Stamp Act did not survive long and was quickly repealed. The jubilation had hardly died away before it came to be appreciated that the Declaratory Act 1766, which repealed it and bore the title 'An Act for the better securing of the Dependency of His Majesty's Dominions in America upon the Crown and Parliament of Great Britain', asserted in unequivocal terms the authority of the British Parliament to legislate 'to bind the colonies and people of America in all cases whatsoever'.[22] No wonder Barbara Tuchman identified the behaviour of successive governments in London as a prime example of the march of folly.[23]

The Declaratory Act identified 'the underlying issue . . . Britain wanted more revenue from America whereas the colonists claimed that this could be raised only with the consent of their legislatures'.[24] And so, instead of documents, duties were imposed on different items, including, notoriously, tea, which culminated in December 1773 in the Boston Tea Party. In the meantime, the colonists struggled hard to achieve what they regarded as the constitutional rights they had brought with them from England. These are exemplified in the Massachusetts Circular Letter of 1768, the Virginia Resolutions of 1769, and ultimately the Declaration of the First Continental Congress of 1774. This Congress met to identify and declare the rights of the colonies which had been infringed since 1762. John Adams described the Congress as 'a nursery of American Statesmen'.[25] At this first meeting in Philadelphia the interaction between the representatives of the different colonies 'helped to make them Americans'.[26] The first President of the Congress was Peyton Randolph*. It was still hoped that the unacceptable legislation would be repealed, but in England, notwithstanding Burke's historical reference to the fact that Magna Carta had been promulgated in Ireland and should not be confined to England, his attempt to persuade the Commons that the colonists should be given 'English privileges' was heavily defeated. As in England, in the early 1640s, the issue was decided by war.

The Declaration of Independence 1776 is one of the world's great documents, approved on 4 July, with 12 of the 13 colonies voting in favour, and New York abstaining.[27] The Continental Congress did not govern the United States; there was no central government. The former colonies produced Constitutions which reflected their independence, independence not simply of Britain, but of each other. Thus, in

[21] Pallister (n 20) 57, n 1.
[22] Reynolds (n 18) 59.
[23] B Tuchman, *March of Folly: From Troy to Vietnam* (London, 1984).
[24] Reynolds (n 18) 59.
[25] Quoted in ibid 62.
[26] ibid 62.
[27] The signatures of the Declaration included five Middle Templars, Edward Rutledge, Thomas Heyward Jnr, Thomas McKian, Thomas Lynch Jnr and Arthur Middleton, as well as William Packer of the Inner Temple.

1777 the Constitution of New York provided that the common and statute law of Great Britain and the Acts of the Colony of New York, as they stood on 19 April 1775, continued to be the law of the State, subject to the right of the legislature to amend it. More significantly perhaps, within their own Constitutions, a number of colonies included a 'bill of rights to secure the liberties of the citizens of the new states', which included the essence of Chapter 29 of Magna Carta.[28] In the meantime, at Yorktown in 1781, George Washington's representative at the negotiations which culminated in the surrender of the British was John Laurens*. The Americans had won, and by the Treaty of Paris, Britain accepted the independence of the United States.[29]

The Constitutional Convention culminated in the signing of the new Constitution of the United States in September 1787.[30] In due course, the Constitution was ratified by the individual States, not always without controversy, and not always without a significant minority vote to the contrary. Then, in 1791, a Bill of Rights was formally adopted into the Constitution as 'the legitimate child of Magna Carta'.[31] Between them, these constitutional documents make provision for the constitutional efficacy of the ideas derived from Magna Carta. The Fifth Amendment simply represents the development of Chapter 29 over the centuries. 'Nor shall any person be deprived of life, liberty or property, without due process of law', a principle reaffirmed after the Civil War in the United States by the Fourteenth Amendment 1868 that 'no state shall deprive any person of life, liberty or property, without due process of law'. The Eighth Amendment follows in a direct line from the English Bill of Rights 1689 by providing that 'excessive bail shall not be required nor excessive fines imposed nor cruel or unusual punishments inflicted'. We find irresistible the suggestion that the very language of the constitutional documents, in particular those which deal with the rights of the individual, would be 'literally meaningless without an understanding of the common law'.[32] Words and phrases retain their common law meaning and implications. They include 'convicted, 'indictment', 'privilege of the Writ of Habeas Corpus', 'Bill of Attainder'; and in the Bill of Rights, attention is drawn to 'searches and seizures', 'warrants', 'due process of law', 'right to a speedy and public trial by an impartial jury' and, expressly, 'no fact tried by a jury shall be otherwise re-examined in any court of the United States than according to the rules of common law'.[33]

In summary, during the War of Independence, the Americans were seeking to uphold established constitutional principles which formed part of their heritage. In

---

[28] Cam (n 5) 325.

[29] The story of the war is, like the stories of most wars, extremely complex, and the views of historians on both the broad issues and the details vary hugely. For a readily understood narrative account, we refer to Reynolds (n 18) 56–73.

[30] Seven members of the Middle Temple signed the Constitution, William Livingstone, John Blair, John Dickinson, John Rutledge, Charles Cotesworth, Charles Ingersoll and Charles Pinckney.

[31] Cam (n 5) 325.

[32] Frederick Wiener, 'The Uses and Abuses of Legal History', The Selden Society Lecture 1962, published in *The Selden Society Lectures 1952–2001* (Buffalo, NY, 2003) 276.

[33] This passage is taken directly from a footnote in ibid 276.

seventeenth-century England, from which their ancestors had departed, the obstruction to constitutional and personal rights was the unfettered power of the monarch. The response to the Divine Right of Kings was the increased authority steadily asserted and gradually vested in Parliament, that is, the legislature. Once the 'King-in-Parliament' principle was finally established, the danger of royal despotism disappeared.

The problems faced by the American colonists stemmed from the practical consequences which the assertion of parliamentary sovereignty would have had over them. Success in the War of Independence obviously defeated any prospect of the future sovereignty of any British Parliament. In one sense, therefore, it would have been possible for the new country simply to have adopted the basic British model, save and except that sovereignty would be vested not in a Parliament in London, but in a new Parliament (given the same, or a different name like Congress) based in the United States. That possibility was rejected. There was, indeed, much argument about and reflection on Coke's observation in *Bonham's Case* and the constitutional possibility of declaring that an Act of Parliament was null and void. But in England, by the middle of the eighteenth century, any suggestion that the courts could nullify an Act of Parliament was of academic interest only. To protect the new Constitution from subsequent legislative interference, a new structure had to be found. Consciously or otherwise, refuge was found in Coke's motto that the law is the safest shield. Thus the Constitution of the United States sets out propositions of fundamental law and vested the judiciary with power to reject even properly enacted legislation which conflicted with the Constitution. Complex provision is made to enable amendments of the Constitution, but the entitlement of the electorate to remove from office any government responsible for legislation which undermines or damages the liberties of the citizens is not, in the United States, regarded as a sufficient source of protection for them.

The result is that two constitutional arrangements, based on centuries of shared history, have diverged. Yet the spirit of Magna Carta, and the constitutional struggles of the seventeenth century in England, live on in provisions like the Fifth Amendment and the Fourteenth Amendment and the Eighth Amendment. Notwithstanding this divergence, Magna Carta has always been and remains the first Great Charter of American liberties as it is of those we enjoy here. Over the years we have witnessed for ourselves the profound devotion and respect in which lawyers and citizens from all parts of the United States regard Magna Carta. It is a document which carries meaning in each individual State, and in the country as a whole. Thus Magna Carta and our Bill of Rights 1689 live on, effectively immune from change.

Epilogue

With the entrenchment of parliamentary sovereignty here and the establishment of the new constitutional arrangements in the United States of America, we have reached our chosen destination. Neither, however, was the end of Magna Carta's worldwide journey, largely, but not exclusively, a bequest of the expansion of British influence overseas.

Perhaps surprisingly to common lawyers, the immediate impact occurred in Revolutionary France. Thomas Jefferson was appointed the Minister for the United States of America in France in 1785. In the ordinary exercise of his responsibilities he should, of course, have maintained a neutral distance from the disturbing events which culminated in the French Revolution. However, he was and remained a close friend of Lafayette, and no doubt in acknowledgement of Lafayette's contribution to the success of the War of Independence at home, Jefferson was willing to help him achieve an orderly dismantling of absolutist monarchy in France.

In June 1789 he proposed 'a Charter of Rights solemnly established by the King and nation' to be signed by the King and members of each of the three Estates General which had now been convened. Clause 4 of this draft is of particular interest. It provides:

> No person shall be restrained of his liberty, but by regular process from a court of justice, authorised by a general law . . . on complaint of an unlawful imprisonment, to any judge whatever, he shall have the prisoner immediately brought before him, and shall discharge him, if his imprisonment be unlawful.

The echoes of Magna Carta and the habeas corpus legislation are obvious.[34] Years later, in 1815, referring to the 'Tennis Court Oath' in 1789, Jefferson reminded Lafayette of how he had urged a constitutional 'compact with the King, securing freedom of religion, freedom of the press, trial by jury, habeas corpus, and a national legislature'.[35]

In August 1789 the Estates General approved the Declaration of the Rights of Man and the Citizen. Apart from upholding the presumption of innocence and prohibiting punishments which were not strictly and obviously necessary, Article 7 provided 'no person shall be accused, arrested, or imprisoned except in the cases and according to the forms prescribed by law'. The Declaration itself continues to be included in the preamble to the Constitution of the Fifth Republic created in 1958.

---

[34] RB Bernstein (ed), *Thomas Jefferson, An Expression of the American Mind* (Folio Society, 2013) 186–88.
[35] ibid 421–27.

In the meantime, Magna Carta and the constitutional struggles in England and the United States of America have impacted on numerous countries which once formed part of the British Empire. The manner in which Britain divested itself of imperial power was somewhat haphazard. Not every moment was glorious, and in some countries the fight for independence resulted in the shedding of blood. After independence was achieved, the new constitutional arrangements in the former colonies drew on and largely reflected the now long-established principles with which we have become familiar. The influence of British legal thinking on many of those at the sharp end of these principled struggles is best exemplified by the fact that Mohandas Gandhi was called to the Bar by the Inner Temple. And memorably, Nelson Mandela, in his passionate speech at his trial in Pretoria in 1964, summarised the ideals for which he wished to live but for which he was prepared to die; he spoke of the veneration in which democrats throughout the world held Magna Carta, the Petition of Right and the Bill of Rights. The continuing attachment to English legal tradition is seen daily on our television screens in the trial of Oscar Pistorius (still continuing as we write) in Pretoria. The robes worn by Mrs Justice Masipa are identical to those worn daily by High Court Judges trying serious criminal cases in England and Wales. In different ways, the principles of the common law have been established all over the world. We offer three examples from the end of Empire.

Canada, in the late eighteenth century included five provinces that were treated as 'settled colonies', which automatically received the common law. In another five provinces, reception statutes were enacted. Initially, at any rate, the Constitution could properly be described as a federalised British Constitution, and subject to the same unwritten conventions. Equality in status between Canada and Britain was finally formalised in the Statute of Westminster 1931. In 1960 the Parliament of Canada enacted an Act for the Recognition and Protection of Human Rights and Fundamental Freedoms as a Bill of Rights, which underlined that the right to life, liberty, security of the person and enjoyment of property, and the right not to be deprived of any of them 'except by due process of law'. Arbitrary detention, imprisonment or exile, and the imposition of cruel and unusual treatment or punishment were prohibited, and among many other rights, the remedy by way of habeas corpus was reasserted. The Canadian Constitutional Act 1982 confirmed these principles.

In Australia, by contrast, although some specific individual rights, including protection against deprivation of property on unjust terms and trial by jury, are expressly protected by the Constitution, none of the legislation after the Statute of Westminster enacted a Bill of Rights. Any remaining powers left in the British Parliament to legislate for Australia are repealed, but the principles of the common law, including Magna Carta, were received into Australia and continue in force, unless and until changed by the Australian courts or Parliament. Indeed since the enactment of the Human Rights Act 1998 in this country, a number of our Australian colleagues suggest that it is Australia where the stream of the common law is found at its purest, free from exposure to extraneous influences such as the European

Convention on Human Rights. We have not detected that the liberties of the citizens of Australia have suffered any consequent diminution.

British control of India until 1858 was exercised by the commercial East India Company. The company was abolished by the Government of India Act 1858 and the territory of India was vested in the Queen of England as Empress. In the period after the First World War the Indian independence movement grew in strength and full independence was granted by the Independence of India Act 1947. A new Constitution was drafted over a period of 166 days. Its principal architect was Dr Bhimrao Ramji Ambedkar. This is probably the most beautiful Constitution in the world, hand-decorated by prominent Indian artists. It is a very far cry from the rather undistinguished parchment of Runnymede. Section 3 of the Constitution defines fundamental rights and Section 4A imposes fundamental duties. This Constitution borrows both from the common law and from the Constitution of the United States. Thus, Article 21 provides 'no person shall be deprived of his life or his personal liberty except according to procedure established by law'.

Universal or international principles are summarised in the Declaration of Human Rights by the Member States of the United Nations adopted in 1948. The preamble states that it is essential, if man is not to be compelled to have recourse, as a last resort, to rebellion against tyranny and oppression, that human rights should be protected by the rule of law. When this Declaration was submitted to the General Assembly, Eleanor Roosevelt observed 'we stand today at the threshold of a great event both in the life of the United Nations and in the life of mankind. This Declaration may well become the international Magna Carta for all men everywhere'. The drawing on this link between the great international Charter, which evolved in the immediate aftermath of the Second World War, and the meeting at Runnymede in 1215 was entirely apposite. The 'Rule of Law' has indeed come a long way since the Petition of Grievances in Parliament in 1610.

Shortly after the Declaration in 1948, the representatives of 10 nations that formed the Council of Europe met in Strasbourg to draft a European Treaty which would protect the human rights that had been treated with such horrifying contempt in Europe. The Chairman of the Legal Administrative Committee was Sir David Maxwell Fyfe QC (later Lord Kilmuir, Lord Chancellor), who had been one of the principal prosecutors at the Nuremberg war crimes tribunal. The resulting Convention, which came into force in 1953, contained a summary of rights and liberties, such as freedom from arrest without proper cause, freedom from torture, and the entitlement to a fair trial within a reasonable time, which are bred in the bone of the common law. The question whether it is open to the European Court of Human Rights to order the British Parliament to enact legislation that will ensure compliance with the Court's view of the way in which the Convention should be applied in particular circumstances has yet to be resolved.

In courts in this country and in the United States of America, to this day, questions arise which would have seemed familiar in the seventeenth and eighteenth centuries. In 1962 a man called Connelly was charged with murder in the course of a robbery. He was convicted of murder but the conviction was quashed. The Crown sought to proceed on a separate indictment of robbery. The defence argued that, in the light of the previous acquittal, it constituted an abuse of the process of the court for the second indictment to proceed. The trial judge said that he had no power to prevent the prosecution but expressed the view that the Crown should not proceed. The Crown nevertheless went ahead. Connelly was convicted of robbery. He appealed against this conviction and his appeal eventually reached the House of Lords. There was argument about the extent of the power of the courts to control the decisions of the Crown to prosecute, and the Solicitor General argued that the Crown was vested with the sole discretion whether to prosecute or not. It should be trusted not to abuse the process of the court. In his judgment Lord Devlin observed:

> Are the courts to rely on the executive to protect their process from abuse? Have they themselves not an inescapable duty to secure fair treatment for those who come or are brought before them? To questions of this sort there is only one answer. The courts cannot contemplate for a moment the transference to the executive of the responsibility for seeing that the process of law is not abused.[36]

This view was followed in later cases and established the right of the defendant to seek an order from the court to stay proceedings where the due process of the court had been abused by the prosecution. Coke would have approved.

In the United States, Paula Jones, an employee of the Kansas Industrial Development Commission, sued President Clinton on the basis that when he was State Governor he had made abhorrent sexual advances to her in a hotel during a conference she was attending at Little Rock. She alleged that her rejection of his advances led her supervisors to punish her. The President claimed that he was immune from civil suit. His motion was heard by a district judge who rejected it. In her judgment she stated:

> [N]owhere in the Constitution Congressional Acts or the writings of any judge or scholar, may any credible support for such a proposition be found. It is contrary to our form of government, which asserts as did the English in the Magna Carta and the Petition of Right, that even the sovereign is subject to God and the law.[37]

The Supreme Court of the United States affirmed that while a president may have immunity from suit in respect of his actions in the course of his office, no such immunity extended to unofficial acts committed before he took office. There were no grounds for postponing a hearing until after he had left office.

The reference to Magna Carta is entirely consistent with the way in which the Supreme Court of the United States has referred to its provisions in the course of numerous judgments. For example, in *Rasul v Bush*[38] in relation to detention in Guantanamo Bay of alleged foreign terrorists, the majority judgment explained 'executive imprisonment has been considered oppressive and lawless since King

---

[36] *Connelly v DPP* [1964] AC 1254.
[37] *Jones v Clinton*, 858 F Supp 902 (ED Ark 1994).
[38] *Rasul v Bush* 542 US 466 (2004).

John at Runny Mede pledged that no free man should be imprisoned, dispossessed, outlawed or exiled save by the judgment of his peers or the law of the land'. The remedy for unlawful detention was habeas corpus.

We return to our Introduction. There we observed 'the perception of what the Charter stood for became as important as the actual language of the original clauses'. Perhaps Magna Carta's most important legacy to us today is that it continues to symbolise our commitment to the preservation of our rights and liberties. On 12 March 1989 a British scientist working at the CERN laboratory in Switzerland published a paper advocating a hypertext database. He was encouraged and assisted to develop what we now know as the World Wide Web. Tim Burners Lee generously refused to patent his idea. Appearing very recently on the BBC Television breakfast show he expressed deep concern about the extent to which the web was used for government surveillance and commercial exploitation:

> Are we going to set up a bunch of values? Are we going to set up something like a Magna Carta for the World Wide Web, now it is so important, so much part of our lives, that it becomes on a level with human rights?

Magna Carta continues to carry huge, intuitive emotional weight in our national consciousness, rousing us when our liberties and rights appear to be threatened and symbolising our commitment to their preservation. For centuries those two Latin words, not themselves used by the self-interested barons who gathered at Runnymede in 1215, have stood for ideas and principles far beyond their parochial comprehension. It was indeed a Great Charter. In 1215 it was short lived and appeared to have no future, yet the ideas for which it was the inspiration have triumphed and are with us still.

Appendix A: Sources

The prime source is obviously the Charter itself. Four copies of the 1215 Charter survive. One is at Lincoln Cathedral; Hugh, Bishop of Lincoln, is one of those listed in the Charter as advising John to make the grant. Another is in Salisbury Cathedral; a royal official, entrusted with distributing copies, later became a canon of that Cathedral. Two are kept in the British Library; they came from the collection of the antiquarian, Sir Robert Cotton. None now bear seals (though they probably were sealed to authenticate them) and one is fire damaged. Statutes in the fourteenth century amended the original Charter.

In the period prior to the Charter there are a number of documents which throw light on the law in the twelfth century. These include Henry I's Charter of Liberties, issued about the time of his coronation; the Laws of Henry I (*Leges Henrici Primi*) a collection of laws made by an unknown hand; and the Charters of Richard I and John to the Jews. The first two have to be approached with caution, because the copies which survive are not contemporaneous and may include later additions.

There are two contemporary documents which reflect the course of negotiations leading up to the grant at Runnymede. The first historians have entitled unexcitingly 'the Unknown Charter'. It was first widely disseminated around 1900 by Professor Powicke. There has been considerable academic debate about its authenticity and date. Professor James Holt gave a detailed account of this in Appendix II to his *Magna Carta*. It consists of a repetition of Henry I's Charter, whose confirmation is sought, together with some additional clauses relating to feudal incidents. He concludes that it probably is authentic and dates from about the end of 1214 or very beginning of 1215 and marks a first attempt to formulate the barons' demands. The other document is called 'the Articles of the Barons'. This probably dates from the beginning of June 1215 and represents a text reasonably close to the eventual Charter. Most of the clauses have an equivalent or connected clause in the Charter. There may be the hand of a royal clerk in it. It is much more sophisticated than 'the Unknown Charter'. Holt discusses the provenance of the Articles in his Appendix 5.

One of the more reliable contemporary accounts is found in the letters of Pope Innocent III. He was initially in conflict with John over the latter's refusal to accept Stephen Langton as Archbishop of Canterbury. Once John had capitulated and done homage to the Pope as his feudal lord, the Pope supported his cause. Innocent does give a careful account of the progress of events. Unfortunately, because it took a long time to get a letter to Rome and receive a reply, he is frequently behind the game – events have overtaken his edicts.

Less reliable are the chronicles of monks. None is completely contemporaneous, many are biased and some love the dramatic more than the actual. Roger of

Wendover may fall into this category. He was a Benedictine monk at the abbey of St Albans. Some time in the 1220s he started a history from Creation to the thirteenth century. He died in 1235, when his fellow monk at St Albans, Matthew Paris, took over the task. Roger's work was called *Flowers of History*; we use the translation by JA Giles. Paris included it with his work in *Chronica Majora*, now in the Rolls Series, where the Latin text may be found. Mathew Paris did question a number of people who had been around at the time of the Charter, including Henry III, but he would have been eight at the time. Another more reliable account is to be found in the so-called *Barnwell Chronicles*, found in an Abbey of that name near Cambridge. They were copied by Walter de Coventria and survive in his version. Gervase was part of the Chapter at Canterbury and wrote an account of the Archbishops to 1205. A source for the reign of Richard I is Richard of Devizes.

The *Dialogus de Scaccario* is an account of the workings of the Royal Exchequer written around 1180. It is in the form of a dialogue between a high official of the Exchequer and one who seeks to learn its practice.

Also of great importance are two legal texts, both called *De Legibus et Consuetudinibuss Angliae* ('Concerning the Laws and Customs of England'). The authorship of both is uncertain. We treat the general accepted ascription as suffi-cient for our purposes. Ranulf de Glanvill was a royal judge under Henry II. The treatise given his name was probably written between 1187 and 1189 (for brevity we ascribe it in our text to 1190). There is a translation and useful introduction by GDH Hall. Henry de Bracton was another royal judge writing about 1250, but apparently distilling his statements of the law from a period going back to the Charter. There is a translation by S Thorne, again with an introduction. Both writ-ers base themselves on the various writs which commence proceedings in the royal courts. They do theorise about government and here may be on less certain ground.

In the seventeenth century, Coke's *Reports and Institutes* explain his reliance on Magna Carta to oppose the absolute rule of the early Stuarts; after he left office as Chief Justice his involvement in the Petition of Right from the House of Commons to the King demonstrates his continuing part in the struggle. The Bill of Rights in 1689 advanced the constitutional argument.

Sir William Blackstone's *Commentaries on the Laws of England*, published in 1766, raised the Charter to a constitutional pinnacle. It was widely disseminated in North America and influenced the Declaration of Independence and the Constitution of the United States. Among later text books commenting on the Charter, Pollock and Maitland's *A History of English Law to the time of Edward I*, published in 1898, should be noted.

Collections of English State Trials appeared from 1719. They give a fascinating insight into the legal concepts underpinning the trial process. We have relied on the Hargreaves 1776 edition.

In 1915, on the 700th anniversary of the grant of the Charter, a set of Magna Carta commemoration essays was published with contributions from, among others, Professors Powicke (who published a good deal of useful material on the

Charter), Vinogradoff and McKechnie (who also published a textbook on the Charter). Another collection of Magna Carta essays was published in 1965.

Pre-eminent among the modern textbooks is James Holt's *Magna Carta*, first published in 1965 and still the standard work. Other modern writers who have made a significant contribution to the learning about the Charter, include Ralph Turner, JR Maddicott, Nicholas Vincent and David Carpenter. Anyone with the slightest interest in English legal history is deeply indebted to the oracle, John Baker.

Appendix B: The Rebel Barons[1]

Eustace de Vesci

Principal among the northern rebels were two contemporaries, Eustace de Vesci (or Vescy) and Robert de Ros. Two Norman brothers, Robert and Ivo de Vassy, are reputed to have been part of the Conqueror's invasion force.[2] The name may have been corrupted in English to de Vesci. In any event, in 1090 King William granted the barony of Alnwick to Ivo de Vesci and he erected the first castle there. Eustace de Vesci was born about 1169 and in 1190 on his majority paid a fine of 1,300 marks to the King to take up his inheritance. He married an illegitimate daughter of William the Lion, King of Scotland. He was originally loyal to John, but was then accused of plotting to murder him. In 1213 John set off on a punitive expedition against the leader of the Welsh. He was informed there was a plot to murder him in the course of the campaign. He returned to London and demanded hostages for good behaviour from his barons. Eustace fled to Scotland. The leader of the East Anglian rebels, Robert Fitzwalter, fled to France. Their flight might (though not necessarily) be an indication that they had plotted against the King. In any event, both were outlawed and had their property seized, including their castles. The Pope's excommunication of John in 1209 was accompanied by an interdict freeing his subjects from allegiance. According to the *History of the Dukes of Normandy* written probably in the 1220s, both men persuaded the Pope that the reason they had fled was because they could not serve an excommunicant. In May 1213 John renewed his allegiance to the Pope. As part of the price of lifting the interdict the Pope required that all who had been exiled during the period of excommunication should be allowed to return. Both men did and their lands were restored, but their castles destroyed. When the Charter failed, Eustace set off south to declare his allegiance to Prince Louis of France, but was killed on the way whilst besieging Barnard Castle, in County Durham.

Robert de Ros

Robert de Ros was born in 1170. He too married an illegitimate daughter of the King of Scotland. He and his wife both inherited Norman properties, but through

---

[1] There are works on individual barons, which are noted below. Otherwise the sources are the *Oxford Dictionary of National Biography*; Appendix to *Simon Langton* by Powicke, Ford Lectures (Oxford, 1927); C Brooke and G Keir, *London 800–1216: The Shaping of a City* (London, 1975).

[2] JR Planche, *Somerset Herald*, London, 1874.

his father (who had been a ward of Henry II's Chief Justiciar, Ranulph de Glanvill), Robert inherited the lordship of Roos in Yorkshire. He paid 1,000 marks to enter his inheritance. We have not found a specific connection in Normandy, though there is a town which was called Ros (now Rot) near Caen and the foot of the Cotentin peninsula. Robert had been a close friend of the King, being one of his gambling companions. Maybe his marital connection to de Vesci led him to join the rebels when they assembled at Stamford in April 1215. He remained part of the rebel party until after the death of John, when he switched his allegiance to the new royal party. He was a witness to the confirmation of the Charter in 1225. He was a generous benefactor of the Knights Templar and in due course joined the order. When he died about 1227 he was buried in the Temple Church in London.

Richard de Percy

Another northern rebel was Richard de Percy. Percy is located in Normandy at the foot of the Cotentin peninsula. Richard's forbear, William de Percy, does not appear to have taken part in the invasion of England, but he came over in 1067 and played a prominent role in the suppression of the Anglo Saxons in the north of England. At the time of the Domesday Book he held 118 manors. He appears to have gone native. His nickname was 'aux gernons' – whiskery. The Normans were clean shaven and the English bearded. He married a Saxon noblewoman. He went on the First Crusade and died near Jerusalem.

Richard de Percy (1181–1244) was the son of Agnes de Percy, to whom the title and lands had descended in her own right. Richard's elder brother died in 1198 leaving a son William. When Agnes died, both Richard and William claimed the title. Richard seems to have been initially successful. He served with John on several of his early campaigns. He refused, however, to pay scutage for the campaign in Poitou, thus aligning himself with the rebel party. In December 1215 he was excommunicated by the Pope. He supported the invasion by Prince Louis. In May 1217 Henry III's Regent stripped him of his lands, which were given to his cousin William. They were restored to Richard when he submitted to the Crown in November of that year. Richard witnessed the confirmation of the Charter in 1237. The family were to become one of the most powerful in the north of England, being later granted the barony of Alnwick when the de Vesci line ran out. Shakespeare's Hotspur was a descendant.

John Fitzrobert

John was only 22 years old at the grant of Magna Carta, having come into his inheritance the previous year. He was Lord of Warkworth in Northumberland.

Warkworth Castle, which was granted to the family by Henry II, still stands near the coast, close to Alnwick. The family may be the only one of the guarantors to be present in England before the Conquest. By 1215, however, they were connected through marriage to other rebel families such as the de Lacys, Quincys, de Veres and Bigods. John himself married Margaret de Chesney, who was heiress to large estates in Norfolk. In 1213 King John went on an expedition to Northumberland, probably to intimidate the northern barons. He stayed at Warkworth Castle. The proximity of the Fitzrobert seat to Alnwick and the land held in Norfolk, together with the many connections with the families of rebels, probably led Fitzrobert into their camp. There is little information on his subsequent history, though he is known to have died in 1244.

John de Lacy

The de Lacy family came from Lassy near Calvados in Normandy. They fought at the Battle of Hastings. They became Constables of Chester and held a number of northern baronies including Pontefract in Yorkshire. Roger de Lacy swore allegiance to John in 1199 on condition that his rights were upheld. He served John loyally and went on a number of expeditions to France. His son John, who was a guarantor of the Charter, seems to have been the ultimate flip flopper. He did not succeed to his father's titles and lands until 1213. They bore 100 knights' fees. He had to pay the Crown a fine of 7,000 marks to receive his inheritance. He served in the Poitou campaign and took the Cross with John in March 1215. He did not throw in his lot with the rebels until after the fall of London. In January 1216 King John took his castle at Donington in Leicestershire. Immediately after John de Lacy made his peace with the King and repudiated the terms of Magna Carta. He fought with the King's party in Kent, but before John's death had reverted to the rebel cause. After the fall of Lincoln he reverted to the royal camp and in August 1217 swore fealty to Henry III. In 1218 he went on a pilgrimage with Ranulph Earl of Chester and Lincoln. He had married Ranulph's daughter. In 1232, through his wife, he succeeded to the title of Earl of Lincoln.

Roger de Montbegon

Roger held lands in Lincolnshire and was Lord of Hornby castle in Lancashire. Initially he was a supporter of John and held Nottingham Castle for him during Richard I's absence on crusade and in captivity. When Richard returned he surrendered the castle to him. He was one of the most vociferous opponents of scutage for the Poitou campaign. He was an early member of the rebel party and for this his lands were seized and he was excommunicated. He appears to have rejoined the royal party around the time of John's death.

William de Mowbray

William de Mowbray was lord of Axholme castle in Lincolnshire and also held land in Yorkshire at Slingsby and Thirsk. The original Mowbray family were descended from Geoffrey, Bishop of Coutances at the time of the Conquest. One of his descendants rebelled against the Conqueror's son, William Rufus, and his forfeited lands were granted to the d'Aubigny family. One of them took the name Mowbray. William Mowbray was descended from him. His land bore 100 knight's fees. He remained on the rebel side until he was captured at the siege of Lincoln. He was subsequently ransomed.

Robert Fitzwalter[3]

The East Anglian rebels were led by Robert Fitzwalter. When the rebels commenced armed rebellion they declared themselves the Army of God and the Holy Church. Robert was chosen as the Marshal of the army.[4] The family originated in lower Normandy and came over with the Conqueror. One of them was Chief Justiciar to William I. Robert's father was steward to Henry I, who granted him the lordship (subsequently converted into a barony) of Dunmow in Essex and of Baynard Castle in the City of London. The castle stood in the south-west corner of the City near the modern Queen Victoria Street. The lord of the castle bore the standard of the City and commanded the militia. Robert developed close ties with the City and was granted the right to import wine by the King. This City connection was to be vital to the success of the rebels. On his mother's side he was also related to other powerful East Anglian families, notably the de Lucys of Norfolk and the Clares of Suffolk. By 1215, through various inheritances, Robert had come to hold land bearing nearly 100 knight's fees. When his father died, his mother remarried and Robert's half brother by that marriage, Saer de Quincy, became the chief spokesperson for the rebels at Runnymede. Each of the brothers bore the arms of the other on his seal.

At first Robert was favoured by John and fought in the King's support in a number of foreign campaigns. In 1213, however, when suspected of plotting to kill the King, he fled to France. When John later submitted to the Pope, Robert was allowed to return to England at the Pope's insistence. His restoration, and that of de Vesci, was a recipe for rebellion.

---

[3] The use of 'fitz' at this time merely indicated 'son of'; it did not denote illegitimacy.
[4] See JH Round, 'King John and Robert Fitzwalter' (1904) *English Historical Review* 19.

When in 1214 John sought knight service or scutage for a campaign in Poitou, Fitzwalter refused to provide either. Additional to any concerns he had about royal taxation, he also blamed the King for depriving him of part of the de Lucy inheritance and he also felt the King should have supported a claim he made against the Abbey of St Albans. These concerns probably contributed to making him a leader of the rebels.

In May 1215 John ordered confiscation of his lands. The Army of God marched south. The City opened its doors to them. When John went back on the obligations of the Charter, Robert continued to fight with the rebels. It was he and Saer de Quincy who in early 1216 invited the French Dauphin to take the English Crown. He fought in support of Prince Louis, but was captured when William Marshal took Lincoln. The Treaty of Lambeth in 1217 granted the supporters of Louis absolution from offences and return of their lands. In October of that year he attended a meeting of the Council at Westminster and did homage to the young King. In 1225 he witnessed a confirmation of the Charter.

Saer de Quincy

The de Quincy family also had Scottish connections. They appear in Great Britain in the late twelfth century. The family name is derived from Cuincy near Bethune in the Pas de Calais. Saer de Quincy was born about 1155. Saer's father served as a knight in the service of William, King of Scotland and married the daughter of Lord Leuchars in Fife, which Saer eventually inherited. In 1173 he married the younger sister of the Earl of Leicester and Huntingdon. He served at the court of Richard I and in 1199 acknowledged John's accession. In 1200 he was present when William the Lion King did homage to King John. In 1204 his brother in law died and Quincy was given the custody of the earldom of Leicester, which carried with it the Stewardship of England. In due course the earldom went to the de Montfort family, but de Quincy, by virtue of his wife's claim, was awarded half of the lands attaching to it. In 1207 the King made him Earl of Winchester. From 1211 to 1214 he served as a royal justice and in 1212 sat as an auditor in the court of Exchequer. In 1213 he witnessed John's submission to the Pope. He therefore seemed to be at the heart of John's court.

He apparently thought, however, that he had been unjustly deprived of the castle of Montsorrel in Leicestershire. This, plus his family connection to Robert Fitzwalter, seems to have led him to join the rebel cause and thereafter to become one of the chief negotiators of Magna Carta. It was at his seat at Brackley in Northamptonshire that representatives of the King met those of the rebels in April 1215. He joined the rebels in Northamptonshire on their way to take London. When the fortunes of rebellion turned after John's repudiation of the Charter, Saer was one of those who went to France to offer the English Crown to Prince Louis. He was captured at the siege of Lincoln by William Marshal. His lands were confiscated, but when hostilities ceased in 1217 they were restored to him. He witnessed the confirmation of the Charter in 1217. In 1219 he went on a crusade and died near Acre where he was buried.

Roger Bigod/Hugh Bigod

Another powerful East Anglian family to join the rebels were the Bigods. The name may be a corruption of 'bigot', taken from the Norman habit of swearing frequently in God's name.[5] In 1055 Robert Bigod discovered plans by the Count of Mortain to overthrow William as Duke of Normandy and betrayed them to the Duke. He was reputed to have fought at Hastings, but this may not be true. In 1075 the Conqueror's brother, the Bishop of Bayeux, granted Robert's son Roger a substantial subtenancy of lands in East Anglia forfeited to the Crown by the previous owner. No doubt the family were seen as reliable. Robert became Sheriff of Norwich. He used his position to build up large estates in East Anglia. Even in the Domesday Book, the family's holdings were the 15th most valuable in the Kingdom. By 1135 Robert's son Hugh had 125 knights enfeoffed on his lands. Hugh was made an earl by King Stephen and this was confirmed in 1154 by Henry II. Hugh died on a pilgrimage in 1177.

After that there was a fierce struggle for the succession between the families of Hugh's two wives. Eventually in 1189 Roger Bigod (born about 1144) paid a fine of 1,000 marks to inherit the earldom. He was present at the coronations of both Richard and John. He fought in campaigns in Poitou in 1206 and also in Ireland. The burden of feudal dues on his large estates led him to strike a bargain with John in 1211 in which, in return for a fine of 2,000 marks, his arrears were written off. It may have been the hope of limiting his feudal liabilities which led him to join the rebels. His son Hugh was also a guarantor.

The family had built up a formidable group of castles in East Anglia, particularly at Framlingham, Walton, Thetford and Bungay. When John had renounced the Charter and defeated the rebels in the north, he turned to besiege Framlingham, where Roger led the defence. The King offered him a safe passage, no doubt in the hope he would renew allegiance, but it was refused. After the cessation of hostilities he returned to support the new government and in 1218 his lands were restored. He died in 1221.

---

[5] Camden's *Remains Concerning Britain* (1636).

William d'Aubigny

William d'Aubigny married the daughter of Roger Bigod and Alice de Tosni. The d'Aubigny family were Breton lords from near Rennes. They appear in England in the reign of Henry I, when William d'Aubigny married Cecilia, heir to the honour of Belvoir. Her ancestors were large landowners at the time of the Domesday Book and had built the first Belvoir castle in Leicestershire not long after the Conquest. The d'Aubignys did seem to have an eye for the main chance. Their son, also William, eventually inherited the Belvoir estate. He was prominent in the court of Richard I, but after John's accession gave strong support to the new King. Although he was frequently excused his liability to scutage, he nevertheless was one of those objecting to liability for service in France. He did not throw in his lot with the rebels until after the fall of London. After the granting of Magna Carta he was put in charge of Rochester Castle. When John successfully besieged it, he was captured and imprisoned. To secure his release he agreed to surrender Belvoir castle and his wife and son as hostages for his good behaviour. As soon as Henry III acceded, William transferred his allegiance to the new royal party, regained Belvoir and participated in the royalist siege of Lincoln. Through his mother he was related to the powerful Clare family.

Richard de Clare/Gilbert de Clare

They were one of the richest families in the land. Richard FitzGilbert was a tutor of William the Conqueror and came to England shortly after the invasion. He suppressed a rebellion in East Anglia and was rewarded for his services with a large number of lordships in Kent and East Anglia. These included the lordship of Clare in Suffolk with the right to build a castle there. He was the eighth richest landowner recorded in the Domesday Book. The family subsequently was granted the earldom of Hertford. Richard de Clare was born in 1153 and added the lordship of Glamorgan to the family's possessions. He joined the rebel party and he and his son were both among the 25 guarantors of the Charter. When the King built up a new army he razed Clare Castle. Richard supported Prince Louis, but after the siege of Lincoln rejoined the royal party of Henry III. One of Richard's daughters had married William Mountfichet. His son, Gilbert, was also a guarantor of the Charter.

Richard de Montfichet

Richard de Montfichet was born about 1190. His principal castle was near modern Stansted Mountfichet. His family had also held a castle within the walls of London called Montfichet or Montfiquit Tower. This latter rendering may suggest that the family originated from Montfiquet, a village between Bayeux and St Lo. There is a reference to the London castle in a Charter of 1136.[6] A chronicle of the revolt against Henry II in 1173–74 states that it was strengthened by Gilbert Muntfichet, a cousin of Walter Fitzrobert, who held Baynard Castle.[7] Gilbert sided with Henry II's son Richard in the rebellion against his father and following its failure was deprived of custody of the forests of Essex.[8] Stow, in his Survey of London published in 1598, states that the London castle was razed in 1213. There is no other evidence of this. It is mentioned in a Charter of 1275 in which it is sold to the Archbishop of Canterbury (Baynard's castle was sold at the same time and the land utilised to build the priory of the black friars).[9] Archaeological evidence suggests it stood just to the south of Ludgate Hill, about halfway between Ludgate and St Paul's.[10] Richard's father was an important royal servant to Richard I.[11] He died in 1203 when his son was only about 10 years old. Roger de Lacy paid £1,000 to the Crown for his wardship.[12] The Montfichet family were related to the Clares. Richard junior fought in the Poitou campaign. Thereafter he joined the rebels. The custody of the forests of Essex was restored to Richard a few days after the grant of Magna Carta. Richard remained in the rebel party until he was taken prisoner at Lincoln and his lands forfeited. By October 1217 he had sworn allegiance to Henry III and his lands and his control of the forests were returned. He went on to become a Baron of the Exchequer and to witness the confirmation of the Charter in 1237. In 1244 he was one of the committee established to consider Henry III's demand for a subsidy, which led to the Provisions of Oxford. He died in 1267.

Geoffrey de Mandeville

Another powerful East Anglian family was the Mandevilles, who appear to have been among the Conqueror's wealthiest tenants in chief. They became Constables

---

[6] FM Stenton, *Norman London, An Essay*, Leaflet no 93 (Historical Association) cited in Brooke and Keir (n 1).

[7] *Fantosme's Chronicle* cited in Stenton (n 6).

[8] *Oxford Dictionary of National Biography*.

[9] W Page, *London: Its Origins and Early Development* (London,1923).

[10] Bruce Watson, 'The Excavation of a Norman Fortress on Ludgate Hill' (1992) 6(14) *London Archaeologist*.

[11] *Oxford Dictionary of National Biography*.

[12] ibid.

of the Tower of London and Sheriffs of Essex. Geoffrey de Mandeville was created Earl of Essex in 1139 and both Stephen and Matilda sought to use his power to control the City.[13] The first Earl of Essex died in 1144 and his sons Geoffrey (d 1166) and William (d 1189) succeeded to the title, but were not Constables of the Tower. William was a loyal servant of Henry II and carried the crown at Richard I's coronation. He died without children. The bloodline was broken at that point. William had an aunt called Beatrice de Saye. Her son-in-law was Geoffrey Fitzpeter. He now succeeded to the Mandeville lands in Essex, but not to the title. He adopted the name of Mandeville. He became Chief Justiciar to both Richard and John and the latter, on his coronation, restored the title of Earl of Essex to him. He died in 1213 and his son Geoffrey succeeded him. Geoffrey Fitzgeoffrey de Mandeville was one of the guarantors. The Mandeville family were connected by marriage to other East Anglian nobles and also to the northern baronies – for instance to the de Lacy's – and the Earl of Oxford. Geoffrey was instrumental in subduing East Anglia when Prince Louis invaded.

Geoffrey de Saye

A Norman family with a longer history were the de Sayes. They came from near Caen. One of them was a companion of William the Conqueror before and after his Conquest. The guarantor Geoffrey de Saye was Lord of West Greenwich in Kent, but also held lands at Sawbridgeworth in Essex. He was middle aged in 1215, but had only recently come into possession of his inheritance. He was related to the Mandevilles.

William Forz

William Forz, count of Aumale, was one who joined the rebellion late in the day. Aumale is a small *comte* (county) in north-east Normandy. The Forz family were minor nobles from Poitou, though William's father accompanied Richard I to the Holy Land. His mother was Countess of Aumale and married first William Mandeville, Earl of Essex, and second, William's father. When his father died he came to England to claim the lands that belonged to the Aumales in England. These included the honour of Holderness and Skipton in Yorkshire. Robert de Ros petitioned the King on his behalf and John granted him his inheritance, on the condition that he married the daughter of Richard de Montfichet. He joined the rebel cause

---

[13] On the first Earl of Essex, see JH Round, *Geoffrey Mandeville* (London, 1892); on the family more generally see Brooke and Keir (n 1) and also *Oxford Dictionary of National Biography*.

after the fall of London. When John repudiated the Charter he rejoined the royal party and went on John's punitive expedition to the north. He was granted lands forfeited by rebels. When John died he swore allegiance to Henry III and witnessed the reissues of the Charter in 1216 and 1225. He later rebelled against the new government when they attempted to claim land confiscated from the rebels and claimed by William. He was defeated and his castle at Bytham destroyed. He seems to have regained royal favour, because he went on various embassies for the Crown. In 1241, after the death of his wife, he went on pilgrimage but died before he reached the Holy Land.

Robert de Vere

Another powerful family linked to the Earls of Essex were the de Veres, who came originally from near Caen. Robert de Vere was the son of the first Earl of Oxford and Agnes of Essex. Through his mother he inherited estates in East Anglia, including Castle Hedingham. His father was Master Chamberlain and Robert inherited this office. He had many kinsmen among the rebels. When John repudiated the Charter and marched into Essex in 1216 he took Castle Hedingham and gave it to a loyal baron. This prompted Robert to renew his oath of loyalty to John. When, however, Prince Louis landed he swore allegiance to him. After the accession of Henry III he rejoined the royal party, though he did not recover his lands and office until 1218.

William Huntingfield

William of Huntingfield's family came from Caen. They came to England after the Conquest and were granted fees of baronies in Suffolk and Norfolk. William was for a time custodian of Dover Castle, though he had to surrender his son and daughter as hostages of his good behaviour. Later he became sheriff of Norfolk and Suffolk. He was one who did go on the 1214 Poitou expedition. His mother was the daughter of Saer de Quincy. He joined the rebels at Stamford before their march south to take London. When Prince Louis arrived he helped to subdue East Anglia. William was taken prisoner at Lincoln. He later declared his allegiance to Henry III and by 1218 was a member of the royal council.

William Malet

The Malet family came from near Le Havre in Normandy. Two Malet brothers fought at the Battle of Hastings. Both brothers were named as tenants in chief in the Domesday Book. One held 221 manors in Suffolk alone. Their descendants were royal stewards. William Malet, born in 1175, was a very substantial landowner. He owned estates not only in East Anglia but also in Somerset (hence Shepton Mallet). On his mother's side he was connected to the Anglo Saxon aristocracy. He became heavily in debt to the Crown and to satisfy this went on the Poitou campaign with 10 knights and 70 soldiers. Maybe he thought the overthrow of John would free him of his debts. He joined the rebels at Stamford before the march to London. There is some uncertainty about the date of his death, but he was certainly dead by 1217.

William de Lanvelei

The Lanvelei family came from Lanvallay, near Dinan and just south of St Malo in Brittany. This is not far from the Cotentin peninsula. His grandfather had been brought to England by Henry II and acted as an administrator for him. He married into the St Clair family from whom he inherited estates in various parts of England. The Lanveleis were lords of Standway in the Cotswolds. They also held lands in Great Bromley in Essex, were governors of Colchester Castle and held lands in Walkern in Hertfordshire (in Walkern church there is an unusual effigy of the Magna Carta earl with visor closed). He married Robert Fitzwalter's niece.

Henry de Bohun

The de Bohun family came from the Cotentin peninsula and accompanied William I on the invasion of England. Henry de Bohun was born in 1176. His uncle was William the Lion King of Scotland. At John's accession Henry was made Earl of Hereford and Constable of England. Henry married a daughter of the Earl of Essex. In 1212 the Earl of Salisbury claimed the honour of Trowbridge, which Henry regarded as rightfully his. The King took control of the honour which seems to have vexed Henry. He supported the rebels and Prince Louis, but when Henry III acceded he renewed his loyalty. He died in 1220 on a pilgrimage to the Holy Land.

William Marshal

William Marshal was the son of William Marshal, the King's principal advisor (see chapter 2). He seems to have joined the rebel party not long before the grant at Runnymede and to have rejoined his father in the royal party in the course of 1216. It has been suggested that his espousal of the rebel cause was a tactical move by his family to ensure they had a foot in both camps, but there is no way of confirming this.

The Mayor of London

The Mayor of London was one of the guarantors. There is some doubt as to his exact identity. Some texts name Serlo the Mercer and others William Hardel. The two men appear to have been closely associated. Serlo was named as a sheriff from 1206–07 and it appears Hardel succeeded him for he was named for 1207–08.[14] Serlo is named as Mayor for 1214–15 and Hardel for 1215–17.[15] On 2 June 1216 Hardel as mayor, together with Robert Fitzwalter, rendered homage to Prince Louis of France, when he invaded England at the invitation of the rebels.[16] At about the same time Serlo with four others raised 1,000 marks and supplied them to Louis. At the end of Hardel's period of office as mayor, Serlo succeeded him from 1217 to 1222. All of this suggests that the two men effectively ran the City between them. In these circumstances, which one was the guarantor of the grant may be of little importance. Given that Serlo became mayor in 1214, it is probable he was the guarantor.

---

[14] Brooke and Keir (n 1) 373.
[15] ibid 376.
[16] ibid 56.

Appendix C: Translation of Magna Carta 1215

John, by the grace of God, King of England, Lord of Ireland, Duke of Normandy and Aquitaine, Count of Anjou, to the archbishops, bishops, abbots, earls, barons, justiciars, foresters, sheriffs, stewards, servants and all his officials and faithful subjects greeting. Know that we, from reverence for God and for the salvation of our soul and those of all our ancestors and heirs, for the honour of God and the exaltation of Holy Church and the reform of our realm, on the advice of our reverend father, Stephen, Archbishop of Canterbury, Primate of all England and Cardinal of the Holy Roman Church, Henry, Archbishop of Dublin, William of London, Peter of Winchester, Jocelin of Bath and Glastonbury, Hugh of Lincoln, Walter of Worcester, William of Coventry and Benedict of Rochester, bishops, Master Pandulf, subdeacon and member of the household of the lord pope, brother Aimeric, master of the knighthood of the Temple in England, and the noble men, William Marshal, Earl of Pembroke, William, Earl of Salisbury, William, Earl of Warenne, William, Earl of Arundel, Alan of Galloway, Constable of Scotland, Warin fitz Gerold, Peter fitz Herbert, Hubert de Burgh, seneschal of Poitou, Hugh de Neville, Matthew fitz Herbert, Thomas Basset, Alan Basset, Philip d'Aubigné, Robert of Ropsley, John Marshal, John fitz Hugh and others, our faithful subjects:

1.   In the first place have granted to God and by this our present Charter have confirmed, for us and our heirs in perpetuity, that the English church shall be free, and shall have its rights undiminished and its liberties unimpaired: and we wish it thus observed, which is evident from the fact that of our own free will before the quarrel between us and our barons began, we conceded and confirmed by our charter freedom of elections, which is thought to be of the greatest necessity and importance to the English church, and obtained confirmation of this from the lord pope Innocent III, which we shall observe and wish our heirs to observe in good faith in perpetuity. We have also granted to all the free men of our realm for ourselves and our heirs for ever, all the liberties written below, to have and hold, them and their heirs from us and our heirs.

2.   If any of our earls or barons, or others holding of us in chief by knight service shall die, and at his death his heir be of full age and owe relief, he shall have his inheritance on payment of the ancient relief, namely the heir or heirs of an earl £100 for a whole earl's barony, the heir or heirs of a baron £100 for a whole barony, the heir or heirs of a knight 100s. at most for a whole knight's fee; and anyone who owes less shall give less according to the ancient usages of fiefs.

3.   If, however, the heir of any such person has been under age and in wardship, when he comes of age he shall have his inheritance without relief or fine.

4.   The guardian of the land of such an heir who is under age shall not take from the land more than the reasonable revenues, customary dues and services, and that without destruction and waste of men or goods. And if we entrust the wardship of the land of such a one to a sheriff, or to any other who is answerable to us for its revenues, and he destroys or wastes the land in his charge, we will take amends of him, and the land shall be entrusted to two lawful and prudent men of that fief who will be answerable to us for the revenues or to him to whom we have assigned them. And if we give or sell to anyone the wardship of any such land and he causes destruction or waste, he shall lose the wardship and it shall be transferred to two lawful and prudent men or the fief who shall be answerable to us as is aforesaid.

5.   Moreover so long as the guardian has the wardship of the land, he shall maintain the houses, parks, preserves, fishponds, mills and other things pertaining to the land from its revenues; and he shall restore to the heir when he comes of age all his land stocked with ploughs and wainage such as the agricultural season demands and the revenues of the estate can reasonable bear.

6.   Heirs shall be given in marriage without disparagement, yet so that before a marriage is contracted it shall be made known to the heir's next of kin.

7.   After her husband's death, a widow shall have her marriage portion and her inheritance at once and without any hindrance; nor shall she pay anything for her dower, her marriage portion, or her inheritance which she and her husband held of the day of her husband's death; and she may stay in her husband's house for forty days after his death, within which period her dower shall be assigned to her.

8.   No widow shall be compelled to marry so long as she wishes to live without a husband, provided that she gives security that she will not marry without our consent if she holds of us, or without the consent of the lord of whom she holds, if she holds of another.

9.   Neither we nor our bailiffs will seize any land or rent in payment of a debt so long as the chattels of the debtor are sufficient to repay the debt; nor shall the sureties of the debtor be distrained so long as the debtor himself is capable of paying the debt; and if the principal debtor defaults in the payment of the debt, having nothing wherewith to pay it, the sureties shall be answerable for the debt; and, if they wish, they may have the lands and revenues of the debtor until they have received satisfaction for the debt they paid on his behalf, unless the principal debtor shows us that he has discharged his obligations to the sureties.

10.   If anyone who has borrowed from the Jews any amount, great or small, dies before the debt is repaid, it shall not carry interest as long as the heir is under age, of whomsoever he holds; and if that debt fall into our hands, we will take nothing except the principal sum specified in the bond.

11.   And if a man dies owing a debt to the Jews, his wife may have her dower and pay nothing of that debt; and if he leaves children under age, their needs shall be met in a manner in keeping with the holding of the deceased; and the debt shall be paid

out of the residue, saving the service due to the lords. Debts owing to others than Jews shall be dealt with likewise.

12.   No scutage or aid is to be levied in our realm except by the common counsel of our realm, unless it is for the ransom of our person, the knighting of our eldest son or the first marriage of our eldest daughter; and for these only a reasonable aid is to be levied. Aids from the city of London are to be treated likewise.

13.   And the city of London is to have all its ancient liberties and free customs both by land and water. Furthermore, we will and grant that all other cities, boroughs, towns and ports shall have all their liberties and free customs.

14.   And to obtain the common counsel of the realm for the assessment of an aid (except in the three cases aforesaid) or a scutage, we will have archbishops, bishops, abbots, earls and greater barons summoned individually by our letters, and we shall also have summoned generally through our sheriffs and bailiffs all those who hold of us in chief, for a fixed date, with at least forty days' notice, and at a fixed place; and in all letters of summons we will state the reason for the summons. And when the summons has thus been made, the business shall go forward on the day arranged according to the counsel of those present, even if not all those summoned have come.

15.   Henceforth we will not grant anyone that he may take an aid from his free men except to random his person, to make his eldest son a knight and to marry his eldest daughter once; and for these purposes only a reasonable aid is to be levied.

16.   No man shall be compelled to perform more service for a knight's fee or for any other free tenement than is due therefrom.

17.   Common pleas shall not follow our court but shall be held in some fixed place.

18.   Recognizances of novel desseisin, most d'ancestor, and darrein presentment shall not be held elsewhere than in the court of the county in which they occur, and in this manner: we, or if we are out of the realm our chief justiciar, shall send two justices through each county four times a year who, with four knights of each county chosen by the county, shall hold the said assizes in the county court on the day and in the place of meeting of the county court.

19.   And if the said assizes cannot all be held on the day of the county court, so many knights and freeholders of those present in the county court on that day shall remain behind as will suffice to make judgements, according to the amount of business to be done.

20.   A free man shall not be amerced for a trivial offence, except in accordance with the degree of the offence; and for a serious offence he shall be amerced according to its gravity, saving his livelihood; and a merchant likewise, saving his merchandise; in the same way a villein shall be amerced saving his wainage; if they fall into our mercy. And none of the aforesaid amercements shall be imposed except by the testimony of reputable men of the neighbourhood.

21.   Earls and barons shall not be amerced except by their peers and only in accordance with the nature of the offence.

22.   No clerk shall be amereced on his lay tenement except in the manner of others aforesaid and without reference to the size of his ecclesiastical benefice.

23.   No vill or man shall be forced to build bridges at river banks, except those who ought to do so by custom and law.

24.   No sheriff, constable, coroners or other of our bailiffs may hold pleas of our Crown.

25.   All shires, hundreds, wapentakes and ridings shall be at the ancient farm without any increment, except our demesne manors.

26.   If anyone holding a lay fief of us dies and our sheriff or bailiff shows our letters patent of summons for a debt which the deceased owed to us, it shall be lawful for the sheriff or our bailiff to attach and list the chattels of the deceased found in lay fee to the value of that debt, by the view of lawful men, so that nothing is removed until the evident debt is paid to us, and the residue shall be relinquished to the executors to carry out the will of the deceased. And if he owes us nothing, all the chattels shall be accounted as the deceased's saving their reasonable shares to his wife and children.

27.   If any free man dies intestate, his chattels are to be distributed by the nearest relations and friends, under the supervision of the Church, saving to everyone the debts which the deceased owed him.

28.   No constable or any other of our bailiffs shall take any man's corn or other chattels unless he pays cash for them at once or can delay payment with the agreement of the seller.

29.   No constable is to compel any knight to give him money for castle guard, if he is willing to perform that guard in his own person or by another reliable man, if for some good reason he is unable to do it himself; and if we take or send him on military service, he shall be excused the guard in proportion the period of his service.

30.   No sheriff or bailiff or ours or anyone else is to take horses or carts of any free man for carting without his agreement.

31.   Neither we nor our bailiffs shall take other men's timber for castles or other work of ours, without the agreement of the owner.

32.   We will not hold the lands of the convicted felons for more than a year and a day, when the lands shall be returned to the lords of the fief.

33.   Henceforth all fish-weirs shall be completely removed from the Thames and the Medway and throughout all England, except on the sea cost.

34.   The writ called *praecipe* shall not, in future, be issued to anyone in respect of any holding whereby a free man may lose his court.

35.   Let there be one measure of wine throughout our kingdom and one measure of ale and one measure of corn, namely the London quarter, and one width of cloth whether dyed, russet or halberjet, namely two ells within the selvedges. Let it be the same with weights as with measures.

36.   Henceforth nothing shall be given or taken for the writ of inquisition of life or limb, but it shall be given freely and not refused.

37.   If anyone holds of us by fee-farm, by socage or by burgage, and holds land of someone else by knight service, we will not, by virtue of that fee-farm, socage or burgage, have wardship of his heir or of land of his that belongs to the fief of

another; nor will we have custody of that fee-farm or socage or burgage unless such fee-farm owes knight service. We will not have custody of the heir or land of anyone who holds of another by knight service, by virtue or any petty sergeant which he hold of us by the service of rendering to us knives or arrows of the like.

38.   Henceforth no bailiff shall put anyone on trial by his own unsupported allegation, without bringing credible witness to the charge.

39.   No free man shall be taken or imprisoned or disseised or outlawed or exiled or in any way ruined, nor will we go or send against him, except by the lawful judgement of his peers or by the law of the land.

40.   To no one will we sell, to no one will we deny or delay right or justice.

41.   All merchants are to be safe and secure in leaving and entering England, and in staying and travelling in England, both by land and by water, to buy and sell free from all maletotes by the ancient and rightful customs, except, in time of war, such as come from an enemy country. And if such are found in our land at the outbreak of war they shall be detained without damage to their persons or goods, until we or our chief justiciar know how the merchants or our land are treated in the enemy country; and if ours are safe there, the others shall be safe in our land.

42.   Henceforth anyone, saving his allegiance due to us, may leave our realm and return safe and secure by land and water, save for a short period in time of war on account of the general interest of the realm and excepting those imprisoned and outlawed according to the law of the land, and natives of an enemy country, and merchants, who shall be treated as aforesaid.

43.   If anyone dies who holds of some escheat such as the honours of Wallingford, Nottingham, Boulogne or Lancaster, or of other escheats which are in our hands and are baronies, his heir shall not give any relief or do any service to us other than what he would have done to the baron if that barony had been in a baron's hands; and we shall hold it in the same manner as the baron held it.

44.   Henceforth men who live outside the forest shall not come before our justices of the forest upon a general summons, unless they are impleaded or are sureties for any person or persons who are attached for forest offences.

45.   We will not make justices, constables, sheriffs or bailiffs who do not know the law of the land and mean to observe it well.

46.   All barons who have founded abbeys of which they have charters of the kings of England, or ancient tenure, shall have custody thereof during vacancies, as they ought to have.

47.   All forests which have been afforested in our time shall be disafforested at once; and river banks which we have enclosed in our time shall be treated similarly.

48.   All evil customs of forests and warrens, foresters and warreners, sheriffs and their servants, river banks and their wardens are to be investigated at once in every county by twelve sworn knights of the same county who are to be chosen by worthy men of the county, and within forty days of the inquiry they are to be abolished by them beyond recall, provided that we, or our justiciar, if we are not in England, first know of it.

49.   We will restore at once all hostages and charters delivered to us by Englishmen as securities for peace or faithful service.

50.   We will dismiss completely from their offices the relations of Gerard d'Athée that henceforth they shall have no office in England, Engerlard de Cigogné, Peter and Guy and Andrew in Chanceaux, Guy de Cigogné, Geoffrey de Martigny with his brothers, Philip Mark with his brothers and his nephew, Geoffrey, and all their followers.

51.   Immediately after concluding peace, we will remove from the kingdom all alien knights, crossbowmen, sergeants and mercenary soldiers who have come with the horses and arms to the hurt of the realm.

52.   If anyone has been disseised or deprived by us without lawful judgement of his peers of lands, castles, liberties, or his rights we will restore them to him at once; and if any disagreement arises on this, then let it be settled by the judgement of the Twenty-Five barons referred to below in the security clause. But for all those things of which anyone was disseised or deprived without lawful judgement of his peers by King Henry our father, or by King Richard our brother, which hold in our hand or which are held by others under our warranty, we shall have respite for the usual crusader's term; excepting those cases in which a plea was begun or inquest made on our order before we took the cross; when, however, we return from our pilgrimage, or if perhaps we do not undertake it, we will at once do full justice in these matters.

53.   We shall have the same respite, and in the same manner, in doing justice on disafforesting or retaining those forests which Henry our father or Richard our brother afforested, and concerning custody of lands which are of the fee of another, the which wardships we have had hitherto by virtue of a fee held of us by knight's service, and concerning abbeys founded on fees other than our own, in which the lord of the fee claims to have a right. And as soon as we return, or if we do not undertake our pilgrimage, we will at once do full justice to complainants in these matters.

54.   No one shall be taken or imprisoned upon the appeal of a woman for the death of anyone except her husband.

55.   All fines which were made with us unjustly and contrary to the law of the land, and all amercements imposed unjustly and contrary to the law of the land, shall be completely remitted or else they shall be settled by the judgement of the Twenty-Five barons mentioned below in the security clause, or by the judgement of the majority of the same, along with the aforesaid Stephen, Archbishop of Canterbury, if he can be present, and others whom he wishes to summons with him for this purpose. And if he cannot be present the business shall nevertheless proceed without him, provided that if any one or more of the aforesaid Twenty-Five barons are in such a suit they shall stand down in this particular judgement, and shall be replaced by others chosen and sworn in by the rest of the same Twenty-Five, for this case only.

56.   If we have disseised or deprived Welshman of lands, liberties or other things without lawful judgement of their peers, in England or in Wales, they are to be

returned to them at once; and if a dispute arises over this it shall be settled in the March by the judgement of their peers; for tenements in England according to the law of England, for tenements in Wales according to the law of Wales, for tenements in the March according to the law of the March. The Welsh are to do the same to us and ours.

57.   For all those things, however, of which any Welshman has been disseised or deprived without lawful judgement of his peers by King Henry our father, or King Richard our brother, which we have in our possession or which others hold under our legal warranty, we shall have respite for the usual crusader's term; excepting those cases in which a plea was begun or inquest made on our order before we took the cross. However, when we return, or if perhaps we do not go on our pilgrimage, we will at once give them full justice in accordance with the laws of the Welsh and the aforesaid regions.

58.   We will restore at once the son of Llywelyn and all the hostages from Wales and the charters delivered to us as security for peace.

59.   We will treat Alexander, King of the Scots, concerning the return of his sisters and hostages and his liberties and rights in the same manner in which we will act towards our other barons of England, unless it ought to be otherwise because of the charters which we have from William his father, formerly King of the Scots; and this shall be determined by the judgement of his peers in our court.

60.   All these aforesaid customs and liberties which we have granted to be held in our realm as far as it pertains to us towards our men, shall be observed by all men of our realm, both clerk and lay, as far as it pertains to them, towards their own men.

61.   Since, moreover, we have granted all the aforesaid things for God, for the reform of our realm and the better settling of the quarrel which has arisen between us and our barons, wishing these things to be enjoyed fully and undisturbed in perpetuity, we give and grant them the following security: namely, that the barons shall choose any twenty-five barons of the realm they wish, who with all their might are to observe, maintain and cause to be observed the peace and liberties which we have granted and confirmed to them by this our present charter; so that if we or our justiciar or our bailiffs or any of our servants offend against anyone in any way, or transgress any of the articles of peace or security, and the offence is indicated to four of the aforesaid twenty-five barons, those four barons shall come to us or our justiciar, if we are out of the kingdom, and shall bring it to our notice and ask that we have it redressed without delay. And if we, or our justiciar, should we be out of the kingdom, do not redress the offence within forty days from the time when it was brought to the notice of us or our justiciar, should we be out of the kingdom, the aforesaid four barons shall refer the case to the rest of the twenty-five barons and those twenty-five barons with the commune of all the land shall distrain and distress us in every way they can, namely by seizing castles, lands and possessions, and in such other ways as they can, saving our person and those of our queen and of our children, until, in their judgement, amends have been made; and when it has been redressed they are to obey us as they did before. And anyone in the land who wishes

may take an oath to obey the orders of the said twenty-five barons in the execution of all the aforesaid matters, and to join with them in distressing us to the best of his ability, and we publicly and freely permit anyone who wishes to take the oath, and we will never forbid anyone to take it. Moreover we shall compel and order all those in the land who of themselves and of their own free will are unwilling to take an oath to the twenty-five barons to distrain and distress us with them, to take the oath as aforesaid. And if any of the twenty-five barons dies or leaves the country or is otherwise prevented from discharging these aforesaid duties, the rest of the aforesaid barons shall on their own decision choose another in his place, who shall take the oath in the same way as the others. In all matters the execution of which is committed to those twenty-five barons, if it should happen that the twenty-five are present and disagree among themselves on anything, or if any of them who has been summoned will not or cannot come, whatever the majority of those present shall provide or order is to be taken as fixed and settled as if the whole twenty-five has agreed to it; and the aforesaid twenty-five are to swear that they will faithfully observe all the aforesaid and will do all they can to secure its observance. And we will procure nothing from anyone, either personally or through another, by which any of these concessions and liberties shall be revoked or diminished; and if any such thing is procured, it shall be null and void, and we will never use it either ourselves or through another.

62.　And we have completely remitted and pardoned to all any ill will, grudge and rancour that have arisen between us and our subjects, clerk and lay, from the time of the quarrel. Moreover we have fully forgiven and completely condoned to all, clerk and lay, as far as pertains to us, all offences occasioned by the said quarrel from Easter in the sixteenth year of our reign to the conclusion of peace. And moreover we have caused letters patent of the Lord Stephen, Archbishop of Canterbury, the Lord Henry, Archbishop of Dublin, the aforesaid bishops and Master Pandulf to be made for them on this security and the aforesaid concessions.

63.　Wherefore we wish and firmly command that the English church shall be free, and the men in our realm shall have and hold all the aforesaid liberties, rights and concessions well and peacefully, freely and quietly, fully and completely for them and their heirs of us and our heirs in all things and places for ever, as is aforesaid. Moreover an oath has been sworn, both on our part and on the part of the barons, that all these things aforesaid shall be observed in good faith and without evil intent. Witness the abovementioned and many others. Given under our hand in the meadow which is called Runnymede between Windsor and Staines on the fifteenth day of June in the seventeenth year of our reign.

Appendix D: The Petition of Right 1628

The Petition exhibited to his Majesty by the Lords Spiritual and Temporal, and Commons, in this present Parliament assembled, concerning divers Rights and Liberties of the Subjects, with the King's Majesty's royal answer thereunto in full Parliament.

To the King's Most Excellent Majesty,

Humbly show unto our Sovereign Lord the King, the Lords Spiritual and Temporal, and Commons in Parliament assembled, that whereas it is declared and enacted by a statute made in the time of the reign of King Edward I, commonly called Statutum de Tallagio non Concedendo, that no tallage or aid shall be laid or levied by the king or his heirs in this realm, without the good will and assent of the archbishops, bishops, earls, barons, knights, burgesses, and other the freemen of the commonalty of this realm; and by authority of parliament holden in the five-and-twentieth year of the reign of King Edward III, it is declared and enacted, that from thenceforth no person should be compelled to make any loans to the king against his will, because such loans were against reason and the franchise of the land; and by other laws of this realm it is provided, that none should be charged by any charge or imposition called a benevolence, nor by such like charge; by which statutes before mentioned, and other the good laws and statutes of this realm, your subjects have inherited this freedom, that they should not be compelled to contribute to any tax, tallage, aid, or other like charge not set by common consent, in parliament.

II. Yet nevertheless of late divers commissions directed to sundry commissioners in several counties, with instructions, have issued; by means whereof your people have been in divers places assembled, and required to lend certain sums of money unto your Majesty, and many of them, upon their refusal so to do, have had an oath administered unto them not warrantable by the laws or statutes of this realm, and have been constrained to become bound and make appearance and give utterance before your Privy Council and in other places, and others of them have been therefore imprisoned, confined, and sundry other ways molested and disquieted; and divers other charges have been laid and levied upon your people in several counties by lord lieutenants, deputy lieutenants, commissioners for musters, justices of peace and others, by command or direction from your Majesty, or your Privy Council, against the laws and free custom of the realm.

III. And whereas also by the statute called 'The Great Charter of the Liberties of England,' it is declared and enacted, that no freeman may be taken or imprisoned or be disseized of his freehold or liberties, or his free customs, or be outlawed or exiled, or in any manner destroyed, but by the lawful judgment of his peers, or by the law of the land.

IV. And in the eight-and-twentieth year of the reign of King Edward III, it was declared and enacted by authority of parliament, that no man, of what estate or condition that he be, should be put out of his land or tenements, nor taken, nor imprisoned, nor disinherited nor put to death without being brought to answer by due process of law.

V. Nevertheless, against the tenor of the said statutes, and other the good laws and statutes of your realm to that end provided, divers of your subjects have of late been imprisoned without any cause showed; and when for their deliverance they were brought before your justices by your Majesty's writs of habeas corpus, there to undergo and receive as the court should order, and their keepers commanded to certify the causes of their detainer, no cause was certified, but that they were detained by your Majesty's special command, signified by the lords of your Privy Council, and yet were returned back to several prisons, without being charged with anything to which they might make answer according to the law.

VI. And whereas of late great companies of soldiers and mariners have been dispersed into divers counties of the realm, and the inhabitants against their wills have been compelled to receive them into their houses, and there to suffer them to sojourn against the laws and customs of this realm, and to the great grievance and vexation of the people.

VII. And whereas also by authority of parliament, in the five-and-twentieth year of the reign of King Edward III, it is declared and enacted, that no man shall be forejudged of life or limb against the form of the Great Charter and the law of the land; and by the said Great Charter and other the laws and statutes of this your realm, no man ought to be adjudged to death but by the laws established in this your realm, either by the customs of the same realm, or by acts of parliament: and whereas no offender of what kind soever is exempted from the proceedings to be used, and punishments to be inflicted by the laws and statutes of this your realm; nevertheless of late time divers commissions under your Majesty's great seal have issued forth, by which certain persons have been assigned and appointed commissioners with power and authority to proceed within the land, according to the justice of martial law, against such soldiers or mariners, or other dissolute persons joining with them, as should commit any murder, robbery, felony, mutiny, or other outrage or misdemeanor whatsoever, and by such summary course and order as is agreeable to martial law, and is used in armies in time of war, to proceed to the trial and condemnation of such offenders, and them to cause to be executed and put to death according to the law martial.

VIII. By pretext whereof some of your Majesty's subjects have been by some of the said commissioners put to death, when and where, if by the laws and statutes of the land they had deserved death, by the same laws and statutes also they might, and by no other ought to have been judged and executed.

IX. And also sundry grievous offenders, by color thereof claiming an exemption, have escaped the punishments due to them by the laws and statutes of this your realm, by reason that divers of your officers and ministers of justice have unjustly refused or forborne to proceed against such offenders according to the same laws and statutes, upon pretense that the said offenders were punishable only by martial law, and by authority of such commissions as aforesaid; which commissions, and all other of like nature, are wholly and directly contrary to the said laws and statutes of this your realm.

X. They do therefore humbly pray your most excellent Majesty, that no man hereafter be compelled to make or yield any gift, loan, benevolence, tax, or such like charge, without common consent by act of parliament; and that none be called to make answer, or take such oath, or to give attendance, or be confined, or otherwise molested or disquieted concerning the same or for refusal thereof; and that no freeman, in any such manner as is before mentioned, be imprisoned or detained; and that your Majesty would be pleased to remove the said soldiers and mariners, and that your people may not be so burdened in time to come; and that the aforesaid commissions, for proceeding by martial law, may be revoked and annulled; and that hereafter no commissions of like nature may issue forth to any person or persons whatsoever to be executed as aforesaid, lest by color of them any of your Majesty's subjects be destroyed or put to death contrary to the laws and franchise of the land.

XI. All which they most humbly pray of your most excellent Majesty as their rights and liberties, according to the laws and statutes of this realm; and that your Majesty would also vouchsafe to declare, that the awards, doings, and proceedings, to the prejudice of your people in any of the premises, shall not be drawn hereafter into consequence or example; and that your Majesty would be also graciously pleased, for the further comfort and safety of your people, to declare your royal will and pleasure, that in the things aforesaid all your officers and ministers shall serve you according to the laws and statutes of this realm, as they tender the honor of your Majesty, and the prosperity of this kingdom.

Appendix E: Bill of Rights 1689

An Act Declaring the Rights and Liberties of the Subject and Settling the Succession of the Crown

Whereas the Lords Spiritual and Temporal and Commons assembled at Westminster, lawfully, fully and freely representing all the estates of the people of this realm, did upon the thirteenth day of February in the year of our Lord one thousand six hundred eighty-eight present unto their Majesties, then called and known by the names and style of William and Mary, prince and princess of Orange, being present in their proper persons, a certain declaration in writing made by the said Lords and Commons in the words following, viz.:

Whereas the late King James the Second, by the assistance of divers evil counsellors, judges and ministers employed by him, did endeavour to subvert and extirpate the Protestant religion and the laws and liberties of this kingdom;

By assuming and exercising a power of dispensing with and suspending of laws and the execution of laws without consent of Parliament;

By committing and prosecuting divers worthy prelates for humbly petitioning to be excused from concurring to the said assumed power;

By issuing and causing to be executed a commission under the great seal for erecting a court called the Court of Commissioners for Ecclesiastical Causes;

By levying money for and to the use of the Crown by pretence of prerogative for other time and in other manner than the same was granted by Parliament;

By raising and keeping a standing army within this kingdom in time of peace without consent of Parliament, and quartering soldiers contrary to law;

By causing several good subjects being Protestants to be disarmed at the same time when papists were both armed and employed contrary to law;

By violating the freedom of election of members to serve in Parliament;

By prosecutions in the Court of King's Bench for matters and causes cognizable only in Parliament, and by divers other arbitrary and illegal courses;

And whereas of late years partial corrupt and unqualified persons have been returned and served on juries in trials, and particularly divers jurors in trials for high treason which were not freeholders;

And excessive bail hath been required of persons committed in criminal cases to elude the benefit of the laws made for the liberty of the subjects;

And excessive fines have been imposed;

And illegal and cruel punishments inflicted;

And several grants and promises made of fines and forfeitures before any conviction or judgment against the persons upon whom the same were to be levied;

All which are utterly and directly contrary to the known laws and statutes and freedom of this realm;

And whereas the said late King James the Second having abdicated the government and the throne being thereby vacant, his Highness the prince of Orange (whom it hath pleased Almighty God to make the glorious instrument of delivering this kingdom from popery and arbitrary power) did (by the advice of the Lords Spiritual and Temporal and divers principal persons of the Commons) cause letters to be written to the Lords Spiritual and Temporal being Protestants, and other letters to the several counties, cities, universities, boroughs and cinque ports, for the choosing of such persons to represent them as were of right to be sent to Parliament, to meet and sit at Westminster upon the two and twentieth day of January in this year one thousand six hundred eighty and eight [old style date], in order to such an establishment as that their religion, laws and liberties might not again be in danger of being subverted, upon which letters elections having been accordingly made;

And thereupon the said Lords Spiritual and Temporal and Commons, pursuant to their respective letters and elections, being now assembled in a full and free representative of this nation, taking into their most serious consideration the best means for attaining the ends aforesaid, do in the first place (as their ancestors in like case have usually done) for the vindicating and asserting their ancient rights and liberties declare

That the pretended power of suspending the laws or the execution of laws by regal authority without consent of Parliament is illegal;

That the pretended power of dispensing with laws or the execution of laws by regal authority, as it hath been assumed and exercised of late, is illegal;

That the commission for erecting the late Court of Commissioners for Ecclesiastical Causes, and all other commissions and courts of like nature, are illegal and pernicious;

That levying money for or to the use of the Crown by pretence of prerogative, without grant of Parliament, for longer time, or in other manner than the same is or shall be granted, is illegal;

That it is the right of the subjects to petition the king, and all commitments and prosecutions for such petitioning are illegal;

That the raising or keeping a standing army within the kingdom in time of peace, unless it be with consent of Parliament, is against law;

That the subjects which are Protestants may have arms for their defence suitable to their conditions and as allowed by law;

That election of members of Parliament ought to be free;

That the freedom of speech and debates or proceedings in Parliament ought not to be impeached or questioned in any court or place out of Parliament;

That excessive bail ought not to be required, nor excessive fines imposed, nor cruel and unusual punishments inflicted;

That jurors ought to be duly impanelled and returned, and jurors which pass upon men in trials for high treason ought to be freeholders;

That all grants and promises of fines and forfeitures of particular persons before conviction are illegal and void;

And that for redress of all grievances, and for the amending, strengthening and preserving of the laws, Parliaments ought to be held frequently.

And they do claim, demand and insist upon all and singular the premises as their undoubted rights and liberties, and that no declarations, judgments, doings or proceedings to the prejudice of the people in any of the said premises ought in any wise to be drawn hereafter into consequence or example; to which demand of their rights they are particularly encouraged by the declaration of his Highness the prince of Orange as being the only means for obtaining a full redress and remedy therein. Having therefore an entire confidence that his said Highness the prince of Orange will perfect the deliverance so far advanced by him, and will still preserve them from the violation of their rights which they have here asserted, and from all other attempts upon their religion, rights and liberties, the said Lords Spiritual and Temporal and Commons assembled at Westminster do resolve that William and Mary, prince and princess of Orange, be and be declared king and queen of England, France and Ireland and the dominions thereunto belonging, to hold the crown and royal dignity of the said kingdoms and dominions to them, the said prince and princess, during their lives and the life of the survivor to them, and that the sole and full exercise of the regal power be only in and executed by the said prince of Orange in the names of the said prince and princess during their joint lives, and after their deceases the said crown and royal dignity of the same kingdoms and dominions to be to the heirs of the body of the said princess, and for default of such issue to the Princess Anne of Denmark and the heirs of her body, and for default of such issue to the heirs of the body of the said prince of Orange. And the Lords Spiritual and Temporal and Commons do pray the said prince and princess to accept the same accordingly.

And that the oaths hereafter mentioned be taken by all persons of whom the oaths of allegiance and supremacy might be required by law, instead of them; and that the said oaths of allegiance and supremacy be abrogated.

I, A.B., do sincerely promise and swear that I will be faithful and bear true allegiance to their Majesties King William and Queen Mary. So help me God.

I, A.B., do swear that I do from my heart abhor, detest and abjure as impious and heretical this damnable doctrine and position, that princes excommunicated or deprived by the Pope or any authority of the see of Rome may be deposed or murdered by their subjects or any other whatsoever. And I do declare that no foreign prince, person, prelate, state or potentate hath or ought to have any jurisdiction, power, superiority, pre-eminence or authority, ecclesiastical or spiritual, within this realm. So help me God.

Upon which their said Majesties did accept the crown and royal dignity of the kingdoms of England, France and Ireland, and the dominions thereunto belonging, according to the resolution and desire of the said Lords and Commons contained in the said declaration. And thereupon their Majesties were pleased that the said Lords Spiritual and Temporal and Commons, being the two Houses of Parliament, should continue to sit, and with their Majesties' royal concurrence make effectual provision for the settlement of the religion, laws and liberties of this kingdom, so that the same for the future might not be in danger again of being subverted, to which the said Lords Spiritual and Temporal and Commons did agree, and proceed to act accordingly. Now in pursuance of the premises the said Lords Spiritual and Temporal and Commons in Parliament assembled, for the ratifying, confirming and establishing the said declaration and the articles, clauses, matters and things therein contained by the force of law made in due form by authority of Parliament, do pray that it may be declared and enacted that all and singular the rights and liberties asserted and claimed in the said declaration are the true, ancient and indubitable rights and liberties of the people of this kingdom, and so shall be esteemed, allowed, adjudged, deemed and taken to be; and that all and every the particulars aforesaid shall be firmly and strictly holden and observed as they are expressed in the said declaration, and all officers and ministers whatsoever shall serve their Majesties and their successors according to the same in all time to come. And the said Lords Spiritual and Temporal and Commons, seriously considering how it hath pleased Almighty God in his marvellous providence and merciful goodness to this nation to provide and preserve their said Majesties' royal persons most happily to reign over us upon the throne of their ancestors, for which they render unto him from the bottom of their hearts their humblest thanks and praises, do truly, firmly, assuredly and in the sincerity of their hearts think, and do hereby recognize, acknowledge and declare, that King James the Second having abdicated the government, and their Majesties having accepted the crown and royal dignity as aforesaid, their said Majesties did become, were, are and of right ought to be by the laws of this realm our sovereign liege lord and lady, king and queen of England, France and Ireland and the dominions thereunto belonging, in and to whose princely persons the royal state, crown and dignity of the said realms with all honours, styles, titles, regalities, prerogatives, powers, jurisdictions and authorities to the same belonging and appertaining are most fully, rightfully and entirely invested and incorporated, united and annexed. And for preventing all questions and divisions in this realm by reason of any pretended titles to the crown, and for preserving a certainty in the succession thereof, in and upon which the unity, peace, tranquility and safety of this nation doth under God wholly consist and depend, the said Lords Spiritual and Temporal and Commons do beseech their Majesties that it may be enacted, established and declared, that the crown and regal government of the said kingdoms and dominions, with all and singular the premises thereunto belonging and appertaining, shall be and continue to their said Majesties and the survivor of them during their lives and the life of the survivor of them, and that the entire, perfect and full exercise of the regal power and government be only in and executed by his Majesty in the names of both their Majesties during their joint lives; and after their deceases the said crown and premises shall be and remain to the heirs of the body of her Majesty, and for default of such issue to her Royal Highness the Princess Anne of Denmark and the heirs of the body of his said Majesty; and thereunto the said Lords Spiritual and Temporal and Commons do in the name of all the people aforesaid most humbly and faithfully submit themselves, their heirs and posterities for ever, and do faithfully promise that they will stand to, maintain and defend their said Majesties, and also the limitation and succession of the crown herein specified and contained, to the utmost of their powers with their lives and estates against all persons whatsoever that shall attempt anything to the contrary. And whereas it hath been found by experience that it is inconsistent with the safety and welfare of this Protestant kingdom to be governed by a popish prince, or by any king or queen marrying a papist, the said Lords Spiritual and Temporal and Commons do further pray that it may be enacted, that all and every person and persons that is, are or shall be reconciled to or shall hold communion with the see or Church of Rome, or shall profess the popish religion, or shall marry a papist, shall be excluded and be for ever incapable to inherit, possess or enjoy the crown and government of this realm and Ireland and the dominions thereunto belonging or any part of the same, or to have, use or exercise any regal power, authority or jurisdiction within the same; and in all and every such case or cases the people of these realms shall be and are hereby absolved of their allegiance; and the said crown and government shall from time to time descend to and be enjoyed by such person or persons being Protestants as should have inherited and enjoyed the same in case the said person or persons so reconciled, holding communion or professing or marrying as aforesaid were naturally dead; and that every king and queen of this realm who at any time hereafter shall come to and succeed in the imperial crown of this kingdom shall on the first day of the meeting of the first Parliament next after his or her coming to the crown, sitting in his or her throne in the House of Peers in the presence of the Lords and Commons therein assembled, or at his or her coronation before such person or persons who shall administer the coronation oath to him or her at the time of his or her taking the said oath (which shall first happen), make, subscribe and audibly repeat the declaration mentioned in the statute made in the thirtieth year of the reign of King Charles the Second entitled, 'An Act for the more effectual preserving the king's person and government by disabling papists from sitting in either House of Parliament'. But if it shall happen that such king or queen upon his or her succession to the crown of this realm shall be under the age of twelve years, then every such king or queen shall make, subscribe and audibly repeat the same declaration at his or her coronation or the first day of the meeting of the first Parliament as aforesaid which shall first happen after such king or queen shall have attained the said age of twelve years. All which their Majesties are contented and pleased shall be declared, enacted and established by authority of this present Parliament, and shall stand, remain and be the law of this realm for ever; and the same are by their said Majesties, by and with the advice and consent of the Lords Spiritual and Temporal and Commons in Parliament assembled and by the authority of the same, declared, enacted and established accordingly.

II. And be it further declared and enacted by the authority aforesaid, that from and after this present session of Parliament no dispensation by _non obstante_ of or to any statute or any part thereof shall be allowed, but that the same shall be held void and of no effect, except a dispensation be allowed of in such statute, and except in such cases as shall be specially provided for by one or more bill or bills to be passed during this present session of Parliament.

III. Provided that no charter or grant or pardon granted before the three and twentieth day of October in the year of our Lord one thousand six hundred eighty-nine shall be any ways impeached or invalidated by this Act, but that the same shall be and remain of the same force and effect in law and no other than as if this Act had never been made.

Appendix F: Bill of Rights 1789 (United States)

The Preamble to The Bill of Rights

Congress of the United States
begun and held at the City of New-York, on
Wednesday the fourth of March, one thousand seven hundred and eighty nine.

THE Conventions of a number of the States, having at the time of their adopting the Constitution, expressed a desire, in order to prevent misconstruction or abuse of its powers, that further declaratory and restrictive clauses should be added: And as extending the ground of public confidence in the Government, will best ensure the beneficent ends of its institution.

RESOLVED by the Senate and House of Representatives of the United States of America, in Congress assembled, two thirds of both Houses concurring, that the following Articles be proposed to the Legislatures of the several States, as amendments to the Constitution of the United States, all, or any of which Articles, when ratified by three fourths of the said Legislatures, to be valid to all intents and purposes, as part of the said Constitution; viz.

ARTICLES in addition to, and Amendment of the Constitution of the United States of America, proposed by Congress, and ratified by the Legislatures of the several States, pursuant to the fifth Article of the original Constitution.

Note: The following text is a transcription of the first ten amendments to the Constitution in their original form. These amendments were ratified December 15, 1791, and form what is known as the "Bill of Rights."

Amendment I

Congress shall make no law respecting an establishment of religion, or prohibiting the free exercise thereof; or abridging the freedom of speech, or of the press; or the right of the people peaceably to assemble, and to petition the Government for a redress of grievances.

Amendment II

A well regulated Militia, being necessary to the security of a free State, the right of the people to keep and bear Arms, shall not be infringed.

Amendment III

No Soldier shall, in time of peace be quartered in any house, without the consent of the Owner, nor in time of war, but in a manner to be prescribed by law.

Amendment IV

The right of the people to be secure in their persons, houses, papers, and effects, against unreasonable searches and seizures, shall not be violated, and no Warrants shall issue, but upon probable cause, supported by Oath or affirmation, and particularly describing the place to be searched, and the persons or things to be seized.

Amendment V

No person shall be held to answer for a capital, or otherwise infamous crime, unless on a presentment or indictment of a Grand Jury, except in cases arising in the land or naval forces, or in the Militia, when in actual service in time of War or public danger; nor shall any person be subject for the same offence to be twice put in jeopardy of life or limb; nor shall be compelled in any criminal case to be a witness against himself, nor be deprived of life, liberty, or property, without due process of law; nor shall private property be taken for public use, without just compensation.

Amendment VI

In all criminal prosecutions, the accused shall enjoy the right to a speedy and public trial, by an impartial jury of the State and district wherein the crime shall have been committed, which district shall have been previously ascertained by law, and to be informed of the nature and cause of the accusation; to be confronted with the witnesses against him; to have compulsory process for obtaining witnesses in his favor, and to have the Assistance of Counsel for his defence.

Amendment VII

In Suits at common law, where the value in controversy shall exceed twenty dollars, the right of trial by jury shall be preserved, and no fact tried by a jury, shall be otherwise re-examined in any Court of the United States, than according to the rules of the common law.

Amendment VIII

Excessive bail shall not be required, nor excessive fines imposed, nor cruel and unusual punishments inflicted.

Amendment IX

The enumeration in the Constitution, of certain rights, shall not be construed to deny or disparage others retained by the people.

Amendment X

The powers not delegated to the United States by the Constitution, nor prohibited by it to the States, are reserved to the States respectively, or to the people.

Bibliography

Althoff, G, J Fried and P Geary, *The Medieval Conception of the Past* (German Historical Institute, 2008)

Baker, JH, *Spelman's Reports Vols I and II* (Selden Society, London 1976 and 1977)

—— *An Introduction to English Legal History* (London, 1990)

—— (ed), *Dyer's Notebooks, I and II* (Selden Society, 1993 and 1994)

—— *Oxford History of the Laws of England, vol VI 1483–1558* (Oxford, 2003)

—— *The Common Law Tradition: Lawyers, Books and the Law* (London, 2000)

Baldwin, J, 'Master Stephen Langton, Future Archbishop of Canterbury: The Paris Schools and Magna Carta' (2008) CXXIII(53) *English Historical Review* 811

Barlow, F, *The Feudal Kingdom of England 1042–1261*, The Penguin History of England (London, 1999)

Barber, M, *A New Knighthood: A History of the Order of the Temple* (Cambridge, 1994)

Bartlett, R, *England under the Norman and Angevin Kings – Oxford History of England* (Oxford, 2000)

Berkowitz, D, *John Selden's Formative Years* (Washington, DC, 1989)

Billings, W, *A Little Parliament: The Virginia General Assembly in the 17th Century* (Virginia, 1948)

Bingham, T, *The Rule of Law* (London, 2011)

Birch, W, *The Historical Charters and Constitutional Documents of the City of London* (London, 1887)

Blackstone, W, *Commentaries on the Laws of England*, vols 1–4, 3rd edn (Dublin, 1769)

Blanshei, S, *Politics and Justice in Late Medieval Bologna* (Edinburgh, 2012)

Boyer, AD, *Sir Edward Coke and the Elizabethan Age* (Stanford, CA, 2003)

Bradshaw, RL, *God's Battle Axe: The Life of Lord President John Bradshaw* (Manhattan Beach, CA, 2010)

Brooke, C and G Keir, *London 800–1216: The Shaping of a City* (London, 1975)

——, —— and S Reynolds, 'Henry I's Charter for the City of London' (1973) 4 *Journal of the Society of Archivists* 575

Brown, E, 'The Tyranny of a Construct' (1974) 79(4) *American Historical Review* 1063

Butt, R, *Parliament: the Middle Ages* (London, 1989)

Cam, HM, 'Magna Carta – Event or Document?', the Selden Society Lecture 1965, published in *The Selden Society Lectures 1952–2001* (Buffalo, NY, 2003)

Campbell, J, *The Lives of the Chief Justices of England* (London, 1849)

Cantor, L, *The English Medieval Landscape* (London, 1982)

Carpenter, D, *The Minority of Henry III* (London, 1990)

—— *The Struggle for Mastery of Britain 1066–1284*, The Penguin History of England (London, 2004)

—— 'Archbishop Langton and Magna Carta, His Contribution, His Doubts and His Hypocrisy' (2011) CXXVI(522) *English Historical Review* 1041

—— 'Magna Carta 1253' (2013) 86(232) *Bulletin of the Institute of Historical Research*

Carr, AD, *Medieval Wales* (Basingstoke, 1995)

Cheney, CR and MG Cheney, *The Letters of Pope Innocent III (1198–1216) Concerning England and Wales* (Oxford, 1967)

—— and WH Semple, *Selected Letters of Pope Innocent III (1198–1216) Concerning England* (London, 1963)

Church, SD (ed), *King John: New Interpretations* (Woodbridge, 1999)

Christianson, P, *Discourse on History, Law and Governance in the Public Career of John Selden* (Toronto, 1996)

Coke's Reports (London, 1658)

Collyer, J (ed), *Middle Temple's Associations with America* (London, 1998)

Cressy, D, *Dangerous Talk: Scandalous, Seditious and Treasonable Speech in Pre-Modern England* (Oxford, 2010)

Cross, PR and SD Lloyd, *Thirteenth Century England* (Newcastle, 1993)

Crouch, D, *William Marshal, Court, Career and Chivalry in the Angevin Empire 1147–1219* (London, 1990)

—— 'Hugh de Neville' in *Dictionary of National Biography* (Oxford, 2000)

Darby, HC, *Domesday England* (London, 1977)

Davies, N, *The Isles* (Oxford, 1999)

Davis, HWC (ed), *Essays in History, Presented to R L Poole* (Oxford, 1927)

Davies, R, *Conquest, Coexistence and Change: Wales 1063–1415* (Oxford, 2006)

Davis, RH, *A History of Medieval Europe* (Harlow, 2006)

Douglas, D (ed), *English Historical Documents* (London, 1973)

Drinker Bowen, C, *The Lion and the Throne: The Life and Times of Sir Edward Coke* (London, 1957)

Duncan, AM, *Scotland: The Making of the Kingdom* (Edinburgh, 1975)

—— 'John King of England and the Kings of Scotland' in SD Church (ed), *King John: New Interpretations* (Woodbridge, 1999) 245

Elliot, JH, *Empires of the Atlantic: Britain and Spain in America, 1492 –1830* (New Haven, CT, 2006)

Faith, R, *The English Peasantry and the Growth of Lordship* (Leicester, 1997)

Foss, E, *A Biographical Dictionary of the Judges of England* (London, 1870)

Giles, JA (ed), *Flowers of History* (London, 1849)

Goldsworthy, J, *The Sovereignty of Parliament, History and Philosophy* (Oxford, 2010)

Grant, R, *The Royal Forests of England* (Gloucester, 1991)

Green, JA, 'Unity and Disunity in the Anglo Norman State' (1989) 62(148) *Historical Research* 124

Greenway, D, *Historia Anglorum* (Oxford, 1996)

Gregg, P, *Freeborn John: A Biography of John Lilburne* (London, 2000)

Gregory, S (tr) *History of William the Marshal* (London, 2006)

Guizot, M (ed), *History of the Dukes of Normandy* (Paris, 1826)

Hall, CDG (ed), *The Treatise on the Laws and Customs of England Commonly Called Glanvill* (Oxford, 1993)

Hallam, H, *The Constitutional History of England* (London, 1827)

Harding, *England in the Thirteenth Century* (Cambridge, 1993)

Hargreaves, *State Trials* (London, 1776)

Hargreaves, R, *The First Freedom: A History of Free Speech* (Stroud, 2002)

Harris, T, *Revolution: The Great Crisis of the British Monarchy 1685– 1688* (Oxford, 2006)

Harriss, GL, *King, Parliament and Public Finance in Medieval England* (Oxford, 1975)

Havinghurst, AF, 'James II and the Men in Scarlet' (1953) 69 LQR 524

Hazeltine, HD, 'The Influence of Magna Carta on American Constitutional Development' in HE Malden (ed), *Magna Carta Commemoration Essays* (London, 1917)

Hearne, T (ed), *Textus Roffensis* (Oxford, 1720)

Holdsworth, W, *History of English Law* (London, 1903)

Holt, JC, 'Philip Mark and the Shrievalty of Nottinghamshire and Derbyshire' (1952) 56 *Transactions of the Thoroton Society* 18

—— *Magna Carta and Medieval Government* (London, 1985)

—— *Magna Carta* (Cambridge, 2001)

—— *Robin Hood* (London, 2010)

Home, G, *Old London Bridge* (London, 1931)

Hoppit, J, *A Land of Liberty? England 1689–1727* (Oxford, 2000)

Hulme, H, *The Life of Sir John Eliot* (London, 1957)

Jacobs, J (ed), *The Jews of Angevin England: Documents and Records from Latin and Hebrew Sources, Printed and Manuscript, for the First Time Collected and Translated (1854–1916)* (London, 1893)

James I, *The Works of the Most High and Mighty Prince* (London, 1616)

Johnson, C (ed), *Dialogus de Scarario* (London, 1950)

Jones, JR, *The Revolution of 1688 in England* (London, 1984)

Jordan, WC, *The Great Famine: Northern Europe in the Early Fourteenth Century* (Princeton, NJ, 1996)

Keeney, B, *Judgement by Peers* (Harvard Historical Monographs XX, 1940)

Kern, F, *Kingship and Law in the Middle Ages* (Oxford, 1948)

Kosminsky, EA, *Studies in the Agrarian History of England*, trans R Kisch (London, 1966)

Lambeth Palace Manuscripts, BJRL I 107

McKechnie, WS, *Magna Carta* (London, 1914)

McLynn, F, *1066: The Year of the Three Battles* (London, 1998)

Macassey L and Collyer J Middle Templars' Associations with America (London, 1968)

Maddicott, JR, 'Magna Carta and the Local Community 1215–1259' (1984) 102(1) *Past and Present* 25–65

Origins of the English Parliament 924-1327 (Oxford, 2002)

Maitland, FW, *Select Pleas of the Crown* (London, 1881)

—— *Bracton's Notebook* (Cambridge, 1887)

—— *The Constitutional History of England* (Cambridge, 1948)

Major, K (ed), *Acta Stephani Langton Cantuariensis Archiepiscopi AD 1207–1228* (Oxford, 1950)

Malden, HE (ed), *Magna Carta Commemoration Essays* (London, 1917)

Michel, F (ed), *Histoire des Ducs de Normandie* (Paris, 1840)

Miller, J, *James II: A Study in Kingship* (London, 2000)

Millor, WJ and CN Brooke (eds), *Letters of John of Salisbury* (Oxford, 1977)

Munro, DC, *Urban and the Crusaders* (Philadelphia, PA, 1894)

O'Brien, BR, *God's Peace and King's Peace: The Laws of Edward the Confessor* (Philadelphia, PA, 1979)

Ormrod, M, *Edward III* (Oxford, 2012)

Page, W, *London: Its Origins and Early Development* (London, 1923)

Painter, S, *Studies in the History of the English Feudal Barony* (Baltimore, MD, 1943)

—— *The Reign of King John* (Baltimore, MD, 1949)

—— *William Marshal, Knight Errant, Baron and Regent of England* (Baltimore, MD, 1933)

Pallister, A, *Magna Carta: The Heritage of Liberty* (Oxford, 1971)

Parliament Rolls of Medieval England 1275–1504, Vols I–XII (London, 2005)

Plucknett, T, *A Concise History of the Common Law* (Indianapolis, IN, 2010)

Plummer, C (ed), *Governance of England, John Fortescue* (Oxford, 1885)

Pollock, F and FW Maitland, *The History of English Law to the Time of Edward I* (Cambridge, 1895)

Powicke, FM, *Stephen Langton*, Ford Lectures (Oxford, 1927)

—— and CR Cheney, *Councils and Synods With Other Documents Relating to the English Church* (Oxford, 1964)

Raccagni, G, *The Lombard League* (Oxford, 2010)

Reuter, T in Wilks (ed) *The World of John of Salisbury* (Oxford 1984)

W Reynolds, D, *America: Empire of Liberty* (London, 2009)

Reynolds, S, 'Fiefs and Vassals: The Medieval Evidence Reinterpreted' (1997) 15(2) *Law and History Review*

Richardson, G, 'Magna Carta Hibernia' *Institute of Historical Studies* III 31–3

Robertson, G, *The Tyranicide Brief* (London, 2005)

Roth, C, *A History of the Jews in England* (Oxford, 1978)

Round, JH, *Geoffrey de Mandeville* (London, 1892)

—— 'An Unknown Charter of Liberties' (1893) viii *English Historical Review* 288

—— *The Commune of London and Other Studies* (London, 1899)

—— 'King John and Robert Fitzwalter' (1904) *English Historical Review* 19

Rymer, T, *Foedera* (London, 1704–13)

Salisbury, J, 'Policraticus' in C Webb (ed), *European Political Thought: Traditions and Endurance* I (New York, NY, 1978)

Sayers, J, *Innocent III, Leader of Europe* (London, 1994)

Selden, J, *Notes to Fortescue's De Laudibus Legem Angliae* (London, 1660)

Selden Society, *Centenary Guide to Publications* (London, 1987)

Sharp, A, 'The Levellers and the End of Charles I' in J Peacey (ed), *The Regicides and the Execution of Charles I* (London, 1999)

Smith, JE, *John Marshall, Definer of a Nation* (New York, 1996)

Stenton, D, *After Runnymede, Magna Carta in the Middle Ages, Magna Carta Commemoration Essays 1965* (Charlottesville, VA, 1965)

Stenton, F, *The First Century of English Feudalism 1066–1166* (Oxford, 1961)

—— *Anglo Saxon England* (Oxford, 1962)

Stockdale, E and R Holland, *Middle Temple Lawyers and the American Revolution* (Eagan, MN, 2007)

W Stubbs, *Gesta Henrici* (London, 1867)

—— (ed), *Annals of Walter of Coventry*, 1887–88, Rolls Series

—— *Select Charters* and other Illustrations of English Constitutional History from earliest times to the Reign of Edward I (Oxford, 1913)

Thomas, HM, *The English and the Normans: Ethnic Hostility, Assimilation and Identity* (Oxford, 2003)

Thompson, F, *Magna Carta: Its Role in the Making of the British Constitution* (Minneapolis, MN, 1948)

Thorne, SE (ed), Bracton, *The Laws and Customs of England* (Cambridge, MA, 1977)

Trevelyan, GM, *The English Revolution, 1688–1689* (London, 1939)

Tuchman, B, *March of Folly: From Troy to Vietnam* (London, 1984)

Turner, RV, 'King John and Justice' in SD Church (ed), *King John, New Interpretations* (Woodbridge, 1999) 237

—— *Magna Carta* (Harlow, 2003)

Vincent, N, *Peter de Roches: An Alien in English Politics* (Cambridge, 1996)

—— 'King John's Evil Counsellors' in *Oxford Dictionary of National Biography* (Oxford University Press, 2004–14)

Wallace, JM, 'The Date of Sir Robert Filmer's *Patriarcha*' (1980) 23(1) *The Historical Journal* 155–65

Warren, WL, *King John* (New Haven, CT, 1997)

Watson, B, 'The Excavation of a Norman Fortress on Ludgate Hill' 6(14) *London Archaeologist* (London 1992)

Webb, C (ed), *European Political Thought Tradition and Endurance* (New York, NY, 1978)

Webster, P, 'Military Orders at the Court of King John' in PW Edbury (ed), *The Military Orders. Volume 5: Politics and Power* (Farnham, 2012)

Wedgewood, CV, *The Trial of Charles I* (Harmondsworth, 1983)

Wiener, F, 'The Uses and Abuses of Legal History', The Selden Society Lecture 1962, published in *The Selden Society Lectures 1952–2001* (Buffalo, NY, 2003) 276

Williams, G, *Medieval London: From Commune to Capital* (London, 1970)

Williamson, T, *The Origins of Norfolk* (Manchester, 1992)

Young, CR, *The Royal Forests of Medieval England* (Leicester, 1979)

Index